The Mark of the Bundesbank

The Mark of the Bundesbank

Germany's Role in European Monetary Cooperation

Dorothee Heisenberg

LYNNE
RIENNER
PUBLISHERS

BOULDER
LONDON

To my parents,
Jochen and Irene Heisenberg, with love

100 294 2265

Published in the United States of America in 1999 by
Lynne Rienner Publishers, Inc.
1800 30th Street, Boulder, Colorado 80301

and in the United Kingdom by
Lynne Rienner Publishers, Inc.
3 Henrietta Street, Covent Garden, London WC2E 8LU

Library of Congress Cataloging-in-Publication Data
Heisenberg, Dorothee, 1963–
    The mark of the Bundesbank : Germany's role in European monetary
  cooperation / Dorothee Heisenberg.
    Includes bibliographical references and index.
    ISBN 1-55587-689-7 (hc)
    1. Monetary policy—Germany. 2. Deutsche Bundesbank. 3. European
Monetary System (Organization) 4. European Union—Germany.
I. Title.
HG999.5.H45 1999
332.4'6943—dc21   98-29705
                                                         CIP

British Cataloguing in Publication Data
A Cataloguing in Publication record for this book
is available from the British Library.

Printed and bound in the United States of America

    The paper used in this publication meets the requirements
⊗ of the American National Standard for Permanence of
    Paper for Printed Library Materials Z39.48-1984.

    5 4 3 2 1

CONTENTS

TABLES AND FIGURES

ACKNOWLEDGMENTS

This book owes its existence to the intellectual support of a great many people. The first, and by far the largest debt is to David R. Cameron, a tireless mentor during my years at Yale University. Not only was his encouragement of my ideas always enthusiastic regardless of their merit, but his insights and probing questions about my arguments are responsible for most of what is good in this book. I will always be proud to say that I was a student of David Cameron.

In the process of developing this book, I was aided by the wise and copious comments of Kate McNamara and Joseph LaPalombara. Their astute observations and concrete suggestions were invaluable.

The importance of European monetary integration has encouraged a diverse and skilled group of political scientists to study different aspects of the topic. I am grateful for the discussions I have had with, and comments received from, Randy Henning, Matthias Kaelberer, Karl Kaltenthaler, Andy Moravcsik, Thomas Risse, Wayne Sandholtz, and Jim Walsh about this subject. Although our methodologies and conclusions diverged in significant ways, this was a community that could always be counted on to share my interest in the events as they unfolded in Europe. Moreover, their thoughtful analyses of these same events forced me to articulate my views more precisely, and the book is stronger for having had their input.

I would like to single out Mark Harmon for his willingness to engage me in scholarly debate from the outset of my days at Yale. In addition to Mark, there are several other Yalies who deserve my thanks. These friends and colleagues read drafts of this book and provided encouragement that, in the isolated world of writing at home, was worth a great deal. My thanks go to Terri Bimes, Sean Duffy, Deborah Guber, Manik Hinchey, Soo Yeon Kim, Janet Laible, Katie McDermott, Amy Richmond, Adam Scheingate, and Eric Schickler.

The empirical chapters of the study owe a great deal to international statesmen and central bankers who took the time to speak to me about their recollections of pivotal events in European monetary cooperation. Among others, I would like to thank Giuliano Amato, Andries van Agt, Johnny Akerholm, Kenneth Couzens, Etienne Davignon, Daniel Gros, Jean-Yves Haberer, Dennis Healey, Lars Horngren, Reimut Jochimsen, Daniel Lebegue, Edmond Malinvaud, Helmut Schlesinger, Henri Simonet, Hermod Skanland, Hans Tietmeyer, and Leo Tindemans.

As a former banker, I understand the importance of financial assistance in turning an idea into reality. This work would not have been possible without generous financial assistance from various organizations: a Yale fellowship and stipend, a Foreign Language and Area Studies Fellowship, a Yale Council on West European Studies Grant, an Enders Fellowship, and a Yale dissertation fellowship. A MacArthur research grant at the beginning of the dissertation helped me to develop my project, and a DAAD dissertation research grant permitted me to study in Germany.

My good friend April Lindner deserves heartfelt thanks for editing the empirical chapters of the book to make them comprehensible to a layperson. My thanks also go to Bridget Julian at Lynne Rienner Publishers, who shepherded this novice through the publishing process.

Last, but far from least, I owe a great debt to Greg Hager for emotional, financial, and even editorial support during the life of this project. Maybe the book could have been done without him, but I know that it was written by a much happier person because of him. Finally, the book is dedicated to my parents, without whose love and nurturing I would not be the person I am today.

Dorothee Heisenberg

1

Introduction

Imagine Europe in late 2002: a Europe where one travels across borders without exchanging money; a Europe where French wine, Italian shoes, and German cars are bought in euros and cents;[1] and, more globally, a Europe whose currency rivals the dollar in international trade. This brave new world is the realization of European federalists' dreams and the culmination of thirty years of monetary integration in Europe. Arguably, it is the most significant element of European integration since the signing of the Treaty of Rome. How did this monumental achievement of cooperation occur? How could twelve European Union (EU) member states with disparate economies and differing European visions agree to make this enormous leap toward a single currency?[2]

To understand the December 1991 decision at Maastricht creating the timetable for a single currency in Europe, it is necessary to examine the earlier monetary cooperation among the EU member states. Plans for European Monetary Union (EMU) did not emerge sui generis but evolved from a contentious history of monetary cooperation in Europe following the breakdown of the Bretton Woods regime. Understanding EMU therefore requires knowledge of why the member states cooperated in earlier exchange-rate agreements like the "Snake" and the European Monetary System (EMS) and what the perceived flaws of those arrangements were. By noting the historical continuities, the 1991 EMU plan seems somewhat less radical in its thinking than the first EMU plan in the early 1970s (since it had been proposed in substantially the same form) but more adroit in its execution. The member states had experienced different arrangements of monetary cooperation, and those lessons shaped their preferences for the type of arrangement they wanted and helped them to avoid problems that had previously derailed their plans.

If one follows the chronology of European monetary cooperation closely, however, there is a puzzle that is not immediately apparent to

1

casual observers of the European Union: why would Germany agree to EMU at all? To understand why this is a puzzle requires a background on the status quo before EMU negotiations began, a topic described in considerable detail in Chapters 4 and 5. For this introduction, however, it suffices to say that the then-existing currency regime, the EMS, was structured to give Germany the best of all economic worlds. Germany had stable exchange rates with its primary trading partners (thus not disrupting Germany's ability to export into those markets), and at the same time it had monetary policy autonomy so that it could tailor monetary policy to the demands of its domestic economy. Germany's partners, of course, were not equally advantaged since they had to forsake monetary policy autonomy in order to remain in the EMS.

For Germany's partners, therefore, the agreement to forge a single European currency was a step toward having some small measure of control over their monetary policy. With respect to these countries, it is perhaps more fruitful to ask why they would agree to the EMS, which was so favorable to Germany. This question is also explored in this book. For Germany, however, EMU was a retreat from the optimal currency regime, and herein lies the puzzle of German cooperation.

Why did Germany decide to cooperate in EMU? Why did it give up its monetary policy autonomy and its primacy in European monetary matters in order to enter into a currency union with historically inflation-prone, fiscally irresponsible states like Italy, Spain, and Portugal? Moreover, why were Germany's responses to monetary union proposals so schizophrenic? In any given week during the negotiations, a newspaper reader could find one government representative championing the necessity of EMU and another decrying the risk to Germany and Europe. Did Germany have stable, ordered, and coherent preferences for monetary union? Was the government incapable of representing a German position to its European partners? In addition, why did the German political elite ignore the preferences of the German public and conclude a treaty that would relinquish the deutsche mark (DM)? Finally, if Germany genuinely desired EMU and was negotiating in good faith, why did it present its EU partners with, essentially, take-it-or-leave-it proposals?

These are some of the questions about German cooperation that I seek to answer in this book. Explaining German participation in EMU in light of the success of the EMS is a difficult task. By delving into the empirical details, this book shows which actors and institutions had an impact on the European decision. In so doing, it explains the politics behind the member states' decision to move from a stable, functioning currency regime to an untested and tendentious supranational institution.

One of the problems, as noted above, in understanding Germany's willingness to give up the EMS in favor of monetary union is that German preferences for international monetary cooperation seem incoherent. On the one hand, the chancellor was always interested in exchange-rate cooperation, but on the other, finance ministers and central bankers generally expressed significant reservations about cooperation. Fundamentally, this apparent lack of an ordinal preference structure in Germany can be traced to an institutional conflict between the federal government and the independent central bank—the Bundesbank. Thus, in order to understand the origins of Germany's international preferences and negotiation strategies, it is essential to understand the institutional relationship between the Bundesbank and the federal government.

This book traces the manner in which the relationship between the Bundesbank and the federal government shaped Germany's negotiating preferences at the international level. Over time, as the policy successes of the Bundesbank became admired abroad, the bank became more influential domestically. More important, the bank's modified stature domestically impacted the negotiating dynamics at the international level as well. I examine these changes in Bundesbank policy and document the "coming of age" of the Bundesbank as a major actor in determining international monetary cooperation in Europe. As a consequence of earlier lessons in monetary negotiations, Germany's partners eventually learned to consider the Bundesbank's preferences seriously, rather than relying on the federal government to appease the bank. Describing and explaining the changing role of the Bundesbank is the other goal of this book.

Dividing the analysis of the development of European monetary cooperation into Bundesbank and federal government positions makes it possible to trace the institutional changes in the Bundesbank from 1968 to 1998. It also highlights changes in the federal government's positions toward European monetary cooperation. Although all three of the chancellors (Willy Brandt, Helmut Schmidt, and Helmut Kohl) desired currency coordination in the post–Bretton Woods era, they did so to varying degrees and for different reasons. Examining the circumstances surrounding the chancellors' initiatives in these cases makes it possible to scrutinize the underlying motives for cooperation.

To generate some potential answers for the conundrum of German cooperation, insights from different theoretical literatures in international relations, comparative politics, and European integration are used below. As will become quickly obvious, however, this work primarily uses an inductive framework rather than hypothesis testing. The attention here is to empirical detail rather than theory building. Thus, although there is one approach—historical institutionalism—that features the variables that turn out to be significant in this issue area, this book is not a procrustean attempt to form a theory.

I must also acknowledge explicitly what this book does not do. Because I consider Germany's attitudes toward cooperation to have analytic primacy over other factors in explaining international agreement, I do not attempt to explain many other facets of international monetary cooperation. There are elegant insights from diverse literatures that help to explain, for example, why the other countries largely capitulated to Germany's preferences or how the international system constrained the policy choices of the member states. To analyze these questions thoroughly, however, would require focusing as intensively on the preferences of other member states as on Germany, a task beyond the scope of this study. Nevertheless, on occasion the responses of other member states during negotiations are relevant to the emergence of German preferences, and have therefore been included here. For example, the question of why the other member states agreed to the EMS, a system that worked almost entirely in Germany's favor, is examined in detail in Chapter 3.

WHY IS MONETARY COOPERATION DIFFICULT?

Historically, there have been many attempts to stabilize international monetary relations. When successful, these coordination strategies generally contributed to economic expansion and prosperity for all participating states. However, often sovereign states had difficulty accepting the loss of policy autonomy that was the inevitable result of exchange-rate coordination.[3] Because membership in an exchange-rate regime forces a choice between stable exchange rates and complete monetary policy autonomy, there are incentives and disincentives to cooperate. The choice and rules of exchange-rate regimes are therefore consequential because they determine how the costs of adjustments will be borne and what economic constraints a state faces.[4] Thus disagreements about monetary regimes are fundamentally about the character of the member states' economies, an area in which sovereignty is jealously guarded.

Although central bankers and economists have shared a consensus since the 1970s that Keynesian demand-management policies and the Phillips curve[5] are discredited,[6] that consensus seems to collapse when policymakers decide how much growth they are willing to sacrifice for a small risk of inflation. In other words, the degree to which other EU member states are willing to subjugate all other policy objectives to maintain the German standard of acceptable inflation (2 percent or less) is smaller than the oft-repeated consensus would lead one to believe. In fact, the lack of a fundamental consensus about inflation risks remains one of the primary concerns of Bundesbank officials and German economists in the construction of the European Central Bank (ECB).[7]

The question of monetary coordination is therefore not trivial. The costs and benefits of cooperation are unevenly distributed among participants, and they change, depending on the rules of the regime.[8] Moreover, the choice of rules generally advantages one economic philosophy over others.[9] For these reasons, the process of negotiating the rules of a new monetary system is critical and usually extremely controversial. Because essential elements of a sovereign state's economic policymaking toolkit are at stake, cooperation in this issue area is the exception rather than the rule.

Why, then, would Germany agree to cooperate in EMU when the existing regime, the EMS, was so favorable to Germany? Below, five explanations are sketched, and these explanations are then explored in greater detail with their theoretical underpinnings in the following section.

The first explanation is that German policymakers knew that Germany would dominate EMU, and thus the single currency was the means by which Germany would more effectively exploit the other participants' economies. As a large export economy, Germany depends on stable exchange rates at reasonable, not overvalued, rates. These conditions can only be guaranteed by a single currency in the long run. Germans knew that the way to lock in their comparative advantage was to have a single currency.

A second possibility is that Germans supported EMU because their perceptions of "German interests" had been reconfigured by participation in the EU for many years. Germans immediately preferred a multilateral European solution[10] to the problem of exchange-rate instability because they had socially constructed new interests that do not focus narrowly on material or short-term interests. EMU, by this reasoning, was the natural remedy to the existing EMS, which the Germans reluctantly dominated.

Third, even if a Germany-wide interest reconfiguration was not apparent, perhaps the decision can be traced back to Helmut Kohl or Hans-Dietrich Genscher. As German policymakers who came of political age in the early postwar era, they put a great deal of emphasis on Germany's historical legacy and the necessity of continuing to integrate Germany into Europe as much as possible. Perhaps the binding of Germany to Europe was due primarily to the political preferences of a generation of Germans (and, consequently, may change after they pass).

A fourth explanation follows closely the logic of the third, with Kohl's motivation being not a pro-European vision but rather a political deal that would allow German unification in 1990. This explanation assumes that Kohl was coerced by Germany's partners to accept EMU as the quid pro quo for German unification. Since Kohl did not have control over monetary policy anyway, it was an easy choice for him to make.

The final interpretation of Germany's willingness to cooperate is based on domestic politics. Because the Bundesbank was becoming increasingly influential domestically and internationally, Kohl decided to get rid of the rival institution in the most politically expedient way, by "supranationalizing" its functions. Even though the Bundesbank Law could be changed by a simple majority vote in the parliament, that was too public and too politically dangerous. Kohl's version was far more subtle and effective.

THEORETICAL UNDERPINNINGS OF THE EXPLANATIONS

In this section, these five explanations are discussed in greater detail using insights from the theoretical literature. Each explanation is based on assumptions that are highlighted in order to better assess its fit. Thus, the theories have been arranged into five categories of explanation corresponding roughly with the explanations given above: (1) cooperation works in Germany's favor; (2) cooperation is the result of German interest reconfiguration; (3) cooperation furthers EU integration; (4) cooperation is the result of quid pro quo bargaining; and (5) cooperation emanates from domestic structures.

Cooperation Works in Germany's Favor

Perhaps the most common answer to why Germany participated in EMU and monetary cooperation generally is that Germany has benefited disproportionately from that cooperation. The most dramatic statement of this view was British secretary of state for industry Nicholas Ridley's statement that EMU is "a German racket designed to take over the whole of Europe."[11] Most realist conceptions of monetary cooperation essentially embrace Ridley's sentiment, albeit in considerably more diplomatic and scientific language. The most common variant of realist thought in this context is hegemonic stability theory.[12]

Hegemonic stability theory posits that cooperation among sovereign states can only occur if there is a hegemon that has the economic resources and power to organize the system. According to this theory, Germany, as the largest European economy, had the necessary structural power to organize cooperation. Additionally, the export-oriented trade structure of the German economy provided the incentive to stabilize the value of the DM relative to its European trading partners' currencies. Germany organized EMU in order to advantage these sectors, and thus EMU was in Germany's economic self-interest.

Aside from the obvious question of whether Germany is large and dominant enough to be considered even a European hegemon,[13] applying hegemonic stability theory to Germany also depends on which version of hegemony one accepts. Duncan Snidal correctly identified two distinct branches in hegemonic stability theory, corresponding to benign and coercive interpretations of the hegemon's motivation.[14] The benign version assumes that the hegemon organizes cooperation in order to prevent anarchy, even at the expense of its interests. The other participants take advantage of the hegemon by free riding on the system. Thus, in this scenario, Germany cooperated in EMU because it was amenable to accepting a disproportionate share of costs, and the other countries accepted the system proposed by Germany because their costs would be reduced. Germany's willingness to sacrifice its material self-interest in order to organize cooperation must be explained, however. If one accepts the benign version, German cooperation must be explained using additional variables like German identity and Germany's role in the EU.[15] Given that France and other EMS partners were clamoring to have Germany accept EMU, this is the more likely version of the theory. But if one is going to explain Germany's acceptance of EMU with ideational variables, it is unclear what value the hegemonic stability theory adds.

The coercive version of hegemonic stability theory posits that the hegemon organizes cooperation because it can shift the costs of cooperation to the participants, and the hegemon can free ride. With respect to Germany's cooperation in EMU, additional questions arise if one accepts the coercive version. If Germany organized cooperation because it benefited more than the other countries, how can one explain these countries' acceptance of the regimes? How, in short, *could* Germany coerce the other states into joining EMU? As mentioned above, there is little empirical evidence that Germany was coercing the other member states to join EMU. Perhaps it is fair to say that Germany coerced them into accepting Germany's preferences for the rules of EMU, but again, alternative explanations of Germany's ability to coerce, which do not rely on Germany's hegemonic status in Europe, exist.

A second question arising from the coercive explanation is, how and to what extent Germany's willingness to accept a leadership position in Europe changed? Research on postwar German behavior has consistently shown Germany to be unwilling to act unilaterally and to lead.[16] If this consensus about Germany's unwillingness to cooperate is correct, one must ask what has changed about Germany's propensity to lead, and if this is a permanent change or simply an issue-specific anomaly. As will become clear, the German federal government's dominance in this issue area was the result of an institutional configuration that is not replicated in other issue areas.

There are also questions about the economic assumptions underlying Germany's motivation to cooperate. Because the German economy is heavily export-oriented, the "economic self-interest" explanation assumes that the natural outcome of the domestic political process was that Germany would organize exchange-rate stabilization programs among its major trading partners in order to maintain stable exchange rates and to prevent competitive devaluations or extreme currency appreciation.

Using the issue area of European monetary cooperation, some authors explain the EMS decision in terms of conflict and bargaining between sectoral interests favoring either stable exchange rates or price stability.[17] In his examination of the motivations of the weaker-currency countries, Jeffry Frieden analyzes the distributional consequences, showing how the domestic coalitions in France and Italy changed in order to allow linking to the DM.[18] A more recent analysis of Germany's motivation to join the single currency explicitly posits that the export sector's importance to the German economy was a significant factor in Kohl's decision to accept a single currency.[19] In this view, EMU was an economic win for Germany.

There is, however, no explanation of why German business would be largely favorable and supportive, given that the status quo, the EMS, was functioning well and stabilizing exchange rates:

> Anxiety [about currency volatility] is much less [than in Britain] or even non-existent in countries such as France and Germany, which are full members of the European Monetary System. More than 40 per cent of both these countries' trade is with other EMS members. "When French businessmen talk about currency movements these days, they mean the dollar and the yen. They aren't really troubled by fluctuations within Europe," says Mr. Philippe Combin, financial director of the Patronat, the French employers' federation. The BDI, its German equivalent, says *most of its members are happy with the stability provided by the EMS.*[20]

The idea that EMU was in Germany's economic self-interest is usually proposed in conjunction with a situation of no exchange-rate coordination among Germany's export markets at all. If one considers, however, that the EMS was the status quo, it is difficult to make the claim that EMU was an economic benefit to Germany. Moreover, any EMU design would entail political risks against which businesses could not hedge. Thus there were significant costs that would accompany the single currency. Before and during the intergovernmental conference (IGC, the negotiation conferences of the Maastricht Treaty) German businesses were, at best, uncertain and agnostic and, at worst, extremely skeptical. The BDI (Confederation of German industry) and the DIHT (German Chamber of Commerce) did not take public positions to encourage Kohl in his EMU negotiations. At best, they exhorted him to ensure price stability as the primary consideration. Moreover, the banking lobby was openly skeptical of the planned timetable to Maastricht.[21] Thus, to rely on business interests to provide Kohl's motivation is empirically questionable.

Such a sectoral approach explains monetary cooperation in "bottom-up" terms, an unusual element that sets sectoral explanations apart from most of the other theories in this issue area. For the most part, monetary politics were considered "high" politics that were shielded from interest group participation through undemocratic or secretive institutions like the Monetary Committee or the Bundesbank. Moreover, the uncertainty surrounding the potential outcomes, and the fact that the costs of adjustment were diffused among disparate interest groups made the interest calculation among groups difficult. This is the fundamental question: did the sectors and interest groups recognize their interests as clearly as the theory assumes? With respect to the EMS, one can argue, the interests were reasonably clear because it was essentially based on the same dynamics as the "Snake." With EMU, however, the uncertainties surrounding the rules and their effect made clear interest definition much more difficult. Indeed, it is possible that the opacity of interests was a critical element in achieving a deal on EMU at Maastricht.[22] During the IGC, the interests were immobilized because there was no clear-cut cost-benefit analysis to be made. Only after the Treaty had been signed and interests had a basis on which to explore how the single currency might affect them did they begin to take positions on the desirability of EMU.

An additional problem is that, in order to make the link between interest group pressure and negotiating positions at the elite level, it is necessary to show exactly which groups had access to policymakers, through what channels, and with exactly which preferences. Unless we assume that elite policymakers internalized the interests of certain sectors (in precisely the same way),[23] it is imperative to have empirical evidence to demonstrate the access of the interests and the effect of those communications.

Cooperation Is a Result of German Interest Reconfiguration

The literature on this idea encompasses the role of ideas as intervening variables and the role of regimes in reconstructing interests.[24] The main focus of these arguments is that ideas can be causal variables in and of themselves and are not relegated to epiphenomenal status, as the realists assert. As a consequence, ideas can explain at which of several Pareto optimal points cooperation will be established. In the issue area of monetary cooperation, the power of economic ideas has been demonstrated.[25] By focusing on how the consensus among economists and financial journalists changed during the course of the late 1970s and early 1980s, this literature reveals how the ideas of monetarism gained credibility within the economic policymaking elites in Britain.[26] That consensus eventually affected the French policymaking elites and led to the stability of the EMS regime.

Within the ideas literature, there is a divide between those who credit ideas with informing the choice of regimes[27] and those who insist that ideas not only express which point on the Pareto frontier is chosen but also actually *change* the interest calculations and preferences of the states.[28] It is in this context that the Franco-German relationship can be discussed as a causal force. The long-standing personal relationship between the leaders of both countries and the heightened sensitivity to the interests and preferences of France, for example, could explain Germany's willingness to cooperate in EMU. Constructivist theories emphasize the social construction of identity.[29] Not only are Germany's preferences shaping the EU, but EU preferences (as aggregated by the EU institutions) shape the German identity. Thus, it would be difficult to speak of "German" preferences or interests independent of the institutional context of the EU. Certainly, there have been a few aberrations of German preferences being distinct from EU preferences (the most notorious case being the early German recognition of Croatia[30]), but these cases are notable because of their exceptionalism. Overall, say constructivists, German preferences are shaped by Germany's identity as a "European Germany" embedded in the EU's institutional structure. European monetary cooperation, because of this altered interest configuration, is completely explicable.

The hypotheses arising from the reconstructed interests theory are difficult to operationalize and test. What could be considered signs that Kohl's interest calculations reflect the (EU-reconstructed) interests of Germany rather than personal conviction? How can we know that most German policymakers share a similar conception of Germany's interests in order to make the claim that those interests have been reconfigured in the long term by the constraints of EU membership?[31]

Cooperation Furthers EU Integration

There is another explanation for Germany's acceptance of EMU: Kohl's (and Genscher's) personal belief in the importance of EU integration. Both men belong to a generation of policymakers who believed that Germany's past required certain sacrifices of sovereignty in order to be able to act collectively within an integrated Europe. Thus both men were unabashedly federalist in their European visions, and both recognized the potential for EMU to become not only another area that was successfully integrated but also a stepping-stone to further integration in fiscal policy, taxation, and even political integration. To what extent is Germany's cooperation in EMU due to an interest in deepening European integration?

Neofunctionalist, or "spillover" models of integration stand out as the original theories of EU integration.[32] Functional spillover occurs when a previously integrated issue area or policy intersects with an area still controlled by multiple member states. Because it is easier to interact with an integrated entity than with six or fifteen different member states, the second issue area is also integrated. Integration thus follows a functional path.

Political spillover, by contrast, occurs as the administrators and bureaucrats switch loyalty or identity from the national member state level to the supranational entity. This switch does not necessarily require an identity reformation but could be simply an interest calculation based on the increasing power of the supranational entity as it gains critical mass.[33]

The literature on ideas is also relevant here: it has been shown that the foreign policy preferences of *key political elites* (as opposed to a general Germany-wide interest reconfiguration) can redefine a state's interests.[34] Here one would argue that Genscher and Kohl shifted loyalty to the EU because they belonged to a generation of Germans who had come to see Europe as the only viable option for Germany. Europe was in Germany's long-term interest, and short-term considerations or the failure of all Germans to acknowledge this geopolitical reality were irrelevant. They were statesmen who believed with unwavering confidence in their European vision. Even in the face of electoral disapproval, they pushed EMU through and implemented it, and although plenty of opportunities existed to delay the plan after it had been signed at Maastricht, Kohl maintained his support of the single currency.

Cooperation Is the Result of Quid Pro Quo Bargaining

Another familiar hypothesis in explaining German acceptance of EMU is that Kohl traded EMU for German unification.[35] Because the majority of observers of the EMU negotiations acknowledge that there was no economic or material incentive for Germany to abandon the EMS, a corresponding "benefit" needed to be found to have Kohl's decision make sense. The unique possibility of German unification was the only possible carrot the other EU states could offer Kohl to make him give up the DM. According to this logic, EMU was the price demanded by the French to allow German unification in 1990.

This hypothesis rests on the body of theory often described as bargaining or, in the language of EU theory, intergovernmentalism. EU integration occurs when sovereign nations strike grand bargains that link disparate issue areas and policies and permit side payments.[36] In this view, the EU's institutional purpose is solely to facilitate the negotiation of grand bargains by making linkages apparent, acting as a forum for "cheap talk," and being a side-payment clearinghouse. Although sovereignty does indeed get passed up to be pooled at the EU supranational level, states cede only as much sovereignty as can be rationalized to make more efficient policies possible. Ceding limited sovereignty to a supranational institution is seen as a rational solution to certain problems, inasmuch as cooperation in regimes is considered efficient.[37] European integration occurs as long as there are efficiencies to be captured through cooperation, and one would expect to see the pace of integration falling over time as those efficiencies are used up.

Bargaining theory enters into the discussion of intergovernmentalism insofar as it helps to explain the outcomes of certain EU institutional negotiations. Whereas bargaining theory previously assumed preferences and interests to be clear and exogenously given, the newer research stemming from the two-level games framework and Andrew Moravcsik's liberal intergovernmental approach focuses attention on the domestic rather than international factors that shape the preferences of the negotiators.[38] Moreover, the domestic factors not only partly determine the preferences of the negotiating agents but can themselves be a bargaining advantage or disadvantage.

In this context, then, Kohl's preferences for unification were so strong that bargains that the French had been interested in for ten years suddenly seemed possible. The French linked "binding Germany into Europe"—a convenient euphemism for EMU—to French acceptance of German unification, and thus a grand bargain was born.

The problems with this explanation are several; I will highlight three of them. First, the issue of timing is problematic. The most significant step toward making EMU a reality was Genscher's agreement to put EMU on the agenda at Hannover in early 1988. Bundesbank president Hans Tietmeyer went so far as to say that "fundamentally, Genscher put the whole thing in motion."[39] Moreover, the blueprint for EMU, the Delors Report, was published in April 1989; thus much of the architecture was finished before German unification was even thinkable.

Another timing question involves the fact that the EU member states accepted German unification in April 1990 and thereby lost all explicit leverage over EMU. The Maastricht Treaty did not get signed until December 1991, and many of the most formidable problems were not solved until right before the Maastricht summit. Thus, Kohl might easily have failed to accept some of the compromises and conditions and abandoned EMU if he personally did not want to reach an agreement.

A second problem with the bargaining quid pro quo hypothesis is the assumption that François Mitterrand was more significant to German unification than Margaret Thatcher. It is not immediately obvious why Kohl would need to appease his friend Mitterrand with EMU more than he needed to pacify Thatcher. Britain was also one of the "four" in the two-plus-four arrangement that settled the German unification question, and thus Thatcher would also have to be satisfied. It is a minor point, but it does call into question the idea of a grand bargain, since the last thing Thatcher would have demanded from Kohl would have been EMU.

A third problem is more theoretical: if we accept the notion of a grand bargain, we would not expect Kohl to make other demands in addition to German unification (a rather large request). Even aside from all the technical demands made by the Bundesbank, which the other member states knew they had to take very seriously, Kohl made additional demands that were unrelated to EMU. Kohl used his leverage gained from giving up EMS to try to add a political dimension to the bargain. If there is a grand bargain that created EMU, where do the outlines end? Do they include the political union demands that Kohl made (and their relatively minor impact on the Maastricht Treaty), or do they include side payments made to the periphery states (paid for, to a large extent, by Germany) to compensate for the economic effects of EMU? Many of the elements of the Maastricht Treaty do not neatly fit into this idea that Germany was quasi-coerced into giving up the DM for German unification.

Cooperation Emanates from Domestic Structures

Finally, a last hypothesis about Kohl's decision is that supranationalizing the functions of the Bundesbank was the most politically expedient method to eliminate a domestic institutional rival. The history of relations between the Bundesbank and the federal government is replete with examples of policy conflicts that were arbitrated by the public.[40] As this book will demonstrate, over time the Bundesbank was increasingly becoming the dominant party, partly as a result of its international reputation and partly because of the declining public support for politicians. Thus, even though the bank's policies often constrained the chancellor's domestic and international agenda, changing the 1957 Bundesbank Law was politically out of the question. The same effect could be achieved, however, by accepting the dictates of European integration and supranationalizing the bank. Could institutional rivalry have played a role in Kohl's decision?

If it played any role, it was most likely a minor one. There is no evidence in any memoirs of this motivation. Although independent evidence of this reason would be difficult to find, one would expect to find one interview or news story that would hint that domestic issues were the primary motivation. In the absence of any corroborating evidence, one must admit that this motivation is subordinate to other, more international motives.

The institutional rivalry, however, is significant in the context of the strategy and execution of the plan to achieve a single currency. Thus, although domestic institutional rivalry between the federal government and the Bundesbank probably had little to do with Kohl's motivation to join the single currency, it has everything to do with why EMU was institutionalized the way it was. Understanding Kohl's desire to cooperate in EMU is only half the equation: to understand why the euro and the ECB look so German requires knowledge about the history of the Bundesbank–federal government rivalry.

Explaining the outcome of the EMU negotiations requires an emphasis on both the history of monetary relations in Europe and the institutions in Germany that are responsible for international monetary cooperation. By showing how the institutions had interacted in previous negotiations, I can then focus on the path dependence of subsequent negotiations.[41] By the time the Bundesbank was bargaining with the federal government and Germany's international partners about the parameters of EMU, these same institutions had negotiated two other exchange-rate regimes and had participated in a successful and an unsuccessful regime. Their positions in EMU represented their respective positions based on their experiences in the Snake and the EMS.

As the name implies, historical institutionalism does focus on both the path dependence brought about by learning from history and the importance of institutions in constraining the actors.[42] As much as Kohl might have wanted EMU, his negotiation of the Maastricht Treaty was going to be far tougher than his preferences would indicate because of the Bundesbank's veto right. Thus the institutional relationship between the Bundesbank and the government was an essential constraint that all the other member states had to recognize. To understand actual outcomes, then, requires knowledge about the history and institutional rivalry between the Bundesbank and the federal government.

For that reason, this book examines monetary cooperation in Europe after the end of the Bretton Woods regime to demonstrate what effect the institutional rivalry had on the outcome of EMU. Because I use counterfactuals where appropriate, the focus on the history of monetary cooperation becomes somewhat more rigorous and less inevitable.[43]

THE ACTORS AND INSTITUTIONS

In order to make the sometimes secretive and arcane actors and institutions[44] that are analyzed in this study intelligible to the reader, I introduce them and their function. There are four significant actors or groups of actors in this issue area: (1) the German federal government, (2) the Bundesbank, (3) the other EU member governments, and (4) the EU institutions. The first, the German federal government, is defined as the chancellor and his cabinet. The chancellor, as head of the dominant party in the ruling coalition, speaks for his party (and generally has the support of his coalition partners as well) in a system in which party discipline is high.[45] The chancellor is the policy entrepreneur, and monetary coordination initiatives come from his office. In addition, three German ministries are of particular importance in making international monetary commitments: the finance ministry, the economics ministry, and the foreign affairs ministry. However, the policy initiatives that come from these ministries (for example, Genscher's call for greater monetary cooperation in January 1988) usually have the approval of the chancellor.

The Bundesbank, the second actor, is statutorily independent of the federal government, a structure with significant ramifications for monetary cooperation.[46] The mandate of the Bundesbank in the 1957 Bundesbank Law is ambiguous with respect to international cooperation and has thus been the source of conflict between the Bundesbank and the federal government. On the one hand, the law requires the Bundesbank to "support the general economic policy of the Federal Government," but on the other, it explicitly states that the Bundesbank "shall be independent of instructions from the Federal Government."[47]

The Bundesbank's decisions are made in the Central Bank Council (*Zentralbankrat*) which comprises the presidents of each of the *Land* central banks, the Bundesbank president and vice president, and up to eight members of the Frankfurt Directorate. Members of the directorate are charged with conducting the daily business of the central bank and are appointed by the president on the nomination of the chancellor. Central Bank Council members are appointed for an eight-year term that serves to "decouple the timing of the selection of top officials of the Bundesbank from the calendar of parliamentary elections."[48] All Bundesbank scholars agree that it is impossible to find evidence of political manipulation of monetary policy because of the structure of the relationship between the Bundesbank and the federal government. On scales of true central bank independence, it is consistently ranked among the top two.[49]

The third actor is actually a group—the other EU member states. Specifically, it includes the heads of state; the economics, finance, and foreign ministers; and the heads of the treasury and central banks in the (excluding Germany) fourteen EU member states. Although these actors interact with their German counterparts in a myriad of informal and institutionalized forums, there are several key institutionalized forums that are specifically significant for monetary cooperation: the European Council[50] or EU summits (which bring together heads of state or government twice a year), the EU Monetary Committee, the Committee of Central Bank Governors, the Economic and Financial Affairs Council (ECOFIN), the finance ministers meetings, and the Franco-German bilateral summit. Of these, the Monetary Committee and the Committee of Central Bank Governors are less familiar but extremely important.

The Monetary Committee was established under Article 105(2) of the Treaty of Rome "in order to promote coordination of the policies of Member States to the full extent needed for the functioning of the internal market."[51] It was charged with reviewing the monetary and financial condition of the member states and to delivering opinions at the request of the Council or Commission. Each member state appoints two representatives[52]—in practice, the finance minister and the deputy or vice president of the Central Bank—and two additional nonvoting alternates for a two-year term. During the Bretton Woods era, the role of the Monetary Committee was not as significant as it became during and after the EMS negotiations. The role of the Monetary Committee was further institutionalized in the Maastricht Treaty, which added the duties to contribute to the preparation of the work of the Council in numerous areas[53] and to report to the Commission and the Council on the movement of capital and freedom of payments. Under the terms of the Maastricht Treaty, the Monetary Committee was dissolved at the end of stage 2 (December 31, 1998) and was replaced by the Economic and Financial Committee at the beginning of stage 3 (January 1, 1999).

The Committee of Central Bank Governors was established in 1964 based on a Treaty of Rome provision that encouraged central bank cooperation among the member states. As the name implies, the committee comprises the governors of all the member states' central banks. A link to the Monetary Committee and the Commission was institutionalized by allowing the chairman of the Monetary Committee and a Commission member to attend Committee of Central Bank Governors meetings. The objectives[54] of the Committee of Central Bank Governors are to consult on

> the general principles and broad lines of monetary policy, to exchange information regularly about the most important measures that fall within the competence of central banks, to promote the coordination of national monetary policies with the aim of achieving price stability . . . as a necessary condition for the proper functioning of the European Monetary System, to formulate opinions on the overall orientation of monetary and exchange rate policy, and to express opinions to individual governments and the Council of Minister on policies which might affect . . . in particular the functioning of the European Monetary System.[55]

As with the Monetary Committee, the importance of the Committee of Central Bank Governors grew considerably with the establishment of the EMS. The Committee of Central Bank Governors was dissolved at the start of stage 2 (January 1, 1994) and was replaced with the Council of the European Monetary Institute (EMI; the ECB's precursor).

Finally, although they play less of a role in the issue area of monetary cooperation than one might think, the supranational EU bodies should be considered actors independent of their member states. Specifically, the role of the Commission[56] (especially the president and Directorate General II [Economic and Financial Affairs]) as well as the European Parliament (EP) is occasionally relevant to monetary cooperation. Moreover, in the later years of stage 2, the EMI took on a greater role in making judgments about member states' financial situations. After EMU began on January 1, 1999, the ECB was obviously the most important institution of monetary coordination. It remains to be seen how autonomous the ECB will be from member state direction. The Treaty on European Union (TEU, or Maastricht

Treaty) required EU member states to grant institutional independence to their central banks.[57]

OVERVIEW OF THE BOOK

As suggested in the previous discussion, this study focuses on the interaction of the actors described above to explain German cooperation in the various exchange-rate coordination regimes since the breakup of Bretton Woods. Understanding the chancellor's or the Bundesbank's preferences alone is not enough to explain the outcomes of the various negotiations. The interaction of their preferences and the reaction of the other EU member states to those preferences are critical to understanding the outcomes of negotiations.

The next chapter begins the empirical section of the book. It documents numerous conflicts between the Bundesbank and the federal government about international commitments in the years 1968–1978. Chapter 3 focuses on the conflicts between the federal government and the Bundesbank during the course of the EMS negotiations in 1978. Chapter 4 shows how the Bundesbank–federal government relationship changed as the EMS established itself as a viable exchange-rate coordinating mechanism. The Bundesbank's assertiveness vis-à-vis the federal government and the other EU states is highlighted by analyzing its role in the negotiations of EMU in Chapter 5. In the subsequent chapter, the Bundesbank's refusal to consider monetary policies to help the other EU member states is shown to be a primary cause of the currency crises of 1992–1993. Chapter 7 demonstrates that the Bundesbank's dominance continued after 1993, even though the Maastricht Treaty had been signed and ratified. The book concludes with a presentation of an explanation of Germany's role in European monetary cooperation, based on the dynamics of the history of the Bundesbank-government relationship.

NOTES

1. The name of the single currency, the euro, was affixed by the European Council in December 1995, and the subdivision of the euro into 100 cents was decided in April 1996.

2. For consistency, in this book I use "European Union" or EU to designate the European states participating in the Treaty of Rome, even though the name of the organization may not have been EU at the time. The term EU became the latest name for the collection of states on November 1, 1993.

3. See Mundell (1960). The trade-off between policy autonomy and exchange-rate stability exists for all but one state—the state holding the numeraire currency.

In the Bretton Woods system the numeraire was explicitly the dollar, whereas in the Snake and the EMS, it was de facto the DM.

4. For a study of this point, see Kurzer (1993).

5. The Phillips curve posited an inverse relationship between inflation and unemployment; thus a state could have lower unemployment in exchange for accepting higher inflation.

6. See Hall (1989).

7. See, for example the comments of Bundesbank Central Bank Council member Reimut Jochimsen (1994), pp. 124–127; and point 7 in the critical assessment of the TEU by sixty German economists in the *Frankfurter Allgemeine Zeitung,* reprinted in Hrbek (1992).

8. See Kirshner (1995); Simmons (1994).

9. For a study on how the EMS constrained corporatism, see Kurzer and Allen (1993) and Kurzer (1993).

10. Bulmer and Paterson (1996) call this "reflexive multilateralism."

11. *The Spectator,* July 14, 1990. Ridley resigned the following day.

12. Keohane (1980).

13. For an evaluation of this point, see McNamara (1998); Markovits and Reich (1993); Kaelberer (1995).

14. See Snidal (1985).

15. There is no shortage of work on Germany's behavior in the EU. See, for example, Lankowski (1993); Bulmer (1986); Huelshoff (1993); Bulmer and Paterson (1996); Schwarz (1995).

16. See Markovits and Reich (1997); Schwarz (1994); Bleek and Maull (1989); Baring (1994); Baring and Scholz (1994).

17. See, for example, Walsh (1997); Frieden (1994). For an overview of the sectoral argument, see Rogowski (1989). For a critical discussion of the sectoral thesis, see McNamara (1998).

18. Frieden (1994), p. 25.

19. Moravcsik (1998); Kaltenthaler (1998).

20. *Financial Times*, July 28, 1989, emphasis added.

21. See *Financial Times*, December 12, 1991. This contradicts Hefeker's (1997) thesis that the big banks were behind EMU completely.

22. Iida (1993).

23. See Lindblom (1977).

24. The importance of ideas is discussed in Goldstein and Keohane (1993); Hall (1989); Risse-Kappen (1994). On the idea of regimes reconstituting interests, see Cameron (1993).

25. Hall (1989); Cameron (1993); McNamara (1998).

26. Hall (1992).

27. For example, the authors in Goldstein and Keohane (1993).

28. See, for example, Risse-Kappen (1996); Klotz (1995).

29. See Wendt (1992); (1987).

30. See Crawford (1996).

31. This thesis is the dominant one in scholarship about Germany's foreign policy. See Schwarz (1994); Bleek and Maull (1989).

32. The pioneering work in this area was done by Haas (1958) and (1964); see also Lindberg and Scheingold (1970).

33. On this point, see Risse-Kappen (1996), p. 56.

34. Checkel (1997); Sikkink (1991).

35. See Kaltenthaler (1998); Zelikow and Rice (1997); *Der Spiegel,* October 1998.

36. For more on intergovernmentalism, see Moravcsik (1991) and Milward (1992).

37. For more on regimes, see Krasner (1983) and Rittberger (1993b).

38. Moravcsik (1993a); (1998).

39. *Der Spiegel,* March 9, 1998, p. 26.

40. See Katzenstein (1987); Lohmann (1993); Marsh (1992).

41. Pierson (1997) shows that events early in the creation of an institution have a disproportionately large impact on the makeup of the institution. Later decisions are constrained by those earlier ones, and thus the path of the institution is set on a given trajectory and is thus "dependent" on earlier decisions.

42. See Pierson (1996) and (1997); Steinmo et al. (1992).

43. See Tetlock and Belkin (1996) and King, Keohane, and Verba (1994) for methodological issues about qualitative research.

44. The definition of institutions is "the formal rules, compliance procedures, and customary practices that structure the relationships between individuals in the polity and economy." Hall (1992), p. 96.

45. Article 65 of the Basic Law defines the positions of the chancellor and his ministers as follows: "The Chancellor determines and bears responsibility for the general guidelines of governmental policy. Within this policy, each minister conducts the affairs of his department independently and under his own responsibility. The government decides on differences of opinion between ministers. The Chancellor conducts the business of the government in accordance with the rules of procedures adopted by it and approved by the President." See Conradt (1993), p. 145.

46. For more on the Bundesbank, see Marsh (1992); Goodman (1992); Kennedy (1991); Ehrenberg (1991); Robert (1978); Duwendag (1973).

47. Bundesbank Law, para. 12, reproduced in Franz (1990), p. 375.

48. Sturm (1989), p. 2.

49. On the importance of central bank independence, see Alesina and Summers (1993); Cukierman (1992); Woolley (1994); Hall (1994); Schaling (1995); Maxfield (1994).

50. For more on the European Council, see Bulmer and Wessels (1987).

51. Usher (1994), p. 160. For more on the Monetary Committee, see Russell (1973).

52. One of the two appointments must be proposed by the Central Bank.

53. Areas involved include capital movement, balance-of-payments difficulties, coordination and surveillance of economic policy, resolution of "severe difficulties," and excessive deficits procedure. For more areas, see Usher (1994), p. 161ff.

54. As amended in 1990 by Council Decision 90/142. See Usher (1994), p. 163.

55. Ibid., p. 164.

56. Ross (1995) contradicts the view that the Commission is unimportant in monetary matters.

57. Council of the European Communities/Commission of the European Communities (1992), Article 108.

2

The Bundesbank
Rejects Unilateral Floating

The history of European monetary cooperation is fraught with conflict between the Bundesbank and the federal government over the international dimension of monetary policy. However, the Bundesbank's position toward cooperation among EU member states has not always been skeptical. In fact, the Bundesbank paid greater attention to maintaining Germany's international commitments than the federal government did in several currency crises. Over the course of the years from 1969 to 1978, however, Bundesbank quiescence changed to assertiveness as it began to focus on domestic stabilization. This evolution was the result of several factors: a change in the Bundesbank Central Bank Council's makeup that gradually transformed the institutional culture within the Bundesbank; the growing body of experience in exchange-rate management after the closing of the gold window; and the distrust by several Bundesbank members of Chancellor Helmut Schmidt's inflation-fighting competence. By 1978, the Bundesbank was more willing to challenge the government's position openly than it had been in 1972 or 1973.

HISTORICAL BACKGROUND OF THE HAGUE SUMMIT

The beginning of serious attempts at monetary cooperation in Europe took place at the Conference of Heads of State or Government held in The Hague on December 1–2, 1969. The six EU members—France, Germany, Italy, Belgium, the Netherlands, and Luxembourg—met to change the course of European integration, which had stalled in the previous decade. Several of the causes of that stagnation—among them the anti-integrationist stance of French president Charles de Gaulle and the recessions in the late 1960s in several of the member states—had been removed, and the heads of state brought to the summit a new optimism that the EU could be recharged.

21

The existing monetary arrangements between the Six were the rules of the Bretton Woods regime, organized by the United States and Britain in 1946.[1] Under those rules, members declared a par value of their currency in terms of the U.S. dollar and gold, the currencies could vary against the dollar by ±1 percent, and dollars could be exchanged against gold reserves at U.S.$35 per ounce. The dollar parity of a currency could be changed after consultation with the International Monetary Fund (IMF), a practice that was unusual in the early years of the Bretton Woods system.

In the late 1940s and early 1950s, the European countries had made additional arrangements to deal with Europe-specific problems that arose during the reconstruction of Europe. To finance massive balance-of-payments deficits, Marshall Plan money was channeled through the Organization for European Economic Cooperation (OEEC) beginning in 1948,[2] and the European Payments Union (EPU) was created in 1950 under the auspices of the OEEC to clear the intra-European payments on a multilateral basis.[3] In contrast to later forms of intra-European monetary cooperation, the early European coordination relied heavily on U.S. initiatives, guidance, and assistance.

In 1958, the European Monetary Agreement (EMA) replaced the European Payments Union, and the European states agreed to limit their currencies' fluctuations against the dollar to only ±0.75 percent rather than the ±1 percent allowed under the Bretton Woods articles. The motivation for the constriction of the margin of fluctuation against the dollar was one that was present in later regimes as well and therefore deserves to be explained in greater detail.

When a European currency floats ±1 percent against the dollar, it actually floats a total of four times that amount against another European currency, that is, 4 percent.[4] As the European market became more integrated and self-reliant, these large (by the fixed currency standard of the Bretton Woods era) intra-European currency fluctuations were perceived to be more and more onerous by the European leaders. Limiting their currencies' fluctuation to ±0.75 percent against the dollar lowered the intra-European currency fluctuation margins to a maximum of 3 percent (four times .75 percent).

The political antecedents to the EU members' declaration at The Hague were more important even than the economic rationale for monetary union, however. The 1960s had been a decade of stagnation and loss of purpose for the EU. The obstructionist and antifederalist tendencies of de Gaulle had effectively prevented both European Community enlargement and significant Community deepening. The EU had weathered the so-called empty chair crisis, when France's minister refused to attend the meetings of the Council of Ministers for seven months because de Gaulle opposed proposed changes to the Treaty of Rome that moved toward greater federalism in the EU.[5] De Gaulle had also twice vetoed British entry into the EU, making it certain that further progress on enlargement would not occur during his tenure in office. In short, the early and mid-1960s saw the almost complete arrest of all progress toward further integration among the six EU member states because of divergent views of the Community's ultimate purpose.

There were also changes in the monetary relations between the European countries in the late 1960s. A pivotal event was the refusal of Germany to revalue the DM in the wake of strong capital inflows caused by political turmoil in France in May 1968. For months, capital moved out of France, and into Germany, and in November 1968 the Group of Ten held an emergency meeting to compel Germany to revalue the DM and France to devalue the franc. German Chancellor Kurt Kiesinger rejected the devaluation/revaluation agreement that had been negotiated by the Banque de France and the Bundesbank and refused, against the advice of the Bundesbank president Karl Blessing, to revalue the DM. De Gaulle, incensed by German comments that naturally the franc would have to devalue, opted to strengthen capital controls and impose more deflationary policies instead.[6] The issue resulted in a standoff, but it reinforced the feeling in certain parts of the French state that Germany would no longer be content to follow instructions from France, Britain, and the United States in monetary matters.

The resignation of de Gaulle in April 1969 proved to be instrumental in revitalizing the EU. After his election on June 15, 1969, de Gaulle's successor, Georges Pompidou, immediately called on the other EU heads of state to meet in The Hague to discuss the future of the EU, a meeting described as "the most significant within the Community since its inception."[7] In addition to approving the proposals for financing the Common Agricultural Policy (CAP) and the extension of budgetary powers by the EP, the heads of state formally supported the goal of economic and monetary union. It may seem strange that the heads of state were willing to make such major commitments in the period following the stagnation of the 1960s, but the new French and German heads of state made these steps possible. Not only was Pompidou more pro-integration than de Gaulle, but newly elected German chancellor Willy Brandt was also more willing than his predecessor to handle the monetary problems of Europe in a fashion independent of the IMF or the United States. Other political considerations played a part in decisions to go toward "deepening" the Community: Germany was embarking on the beginnings of *Ostpolitik* and wanted to maintain the stability of the EU.[8] Pompidou feared the dilution of the Franco-German partnership with the British accession to the EU and wanted to begin a new initiative that would tie the two states together as leaders of the effort.[9] Furthermore, Pompidou was well aware of Britain's anti-integration position and was therefore particularly predisposed to encourage new initiatives that would deepen the Community and which Britain would have to acknowledge as part of the *acquis communautaire* before accession.[10]

THE MONETARY UNION DECISION AT THE HAGUE SUMMIT

A memo submitted to the Council in February 1969 by Commission vice president Raymond Barre laid the groundwork for the consensus among the EU member states that monetary cooperation was necessary.[11] The First Barre Plan, which followed a February 1968 Commission memo on the possibilities of action in the monetary field, was intended to clarify the Commission's position on the "need for fuller alignment of economic policies in the Community and for an examination of the scope for intensifying monetary cooperation."[12] The plan recommended "concerting of the medium-term economic policies, fuller concerting of the short-term economic policies, and [establishing] Community machinery for monetary cooperation."[13] Under the latter objective, the plan envisioned short-term monetary support, medium-term financial assistance, and amendment of the Treaty of Rome to consolidate monetary cooperation.

These themes were taken up by The Hague summit participants. In the final communiqué of the conference, monetary union merited only the eighth place on the ambitious agenda, but it was no less radical for its placement. The heads of government reaffirmed their

> readiness to expedite the further action needed to strengthen the Community and promote its development into an economic union. They are of the opinion that the integration process should result in a Community of stability and growth. To this end they agreed that, within the Council, on the basis of the [First Barre Plan], . . . a plan in stages will be worked out during 1970 with a view to the creation of an economic and monetary union. The development of monetary co-operation should be based on the harmonization of economic policies. They agreed to arrange for the investigation of the possibility of setting up a European reserve fund which should be the outcome of a joint economic and monetary policy.[14]

In his statement following the summit, Pompidou framed the decision to proceed with monetary union in political terms. He listed three problems facing the Community—completion, strengthening, and enlargement—and stated that they all depended on the answer to one question: "Are we determined to continue building the European Community?" His reply—"I am answering this question with a clear, distinct, and unequivocal 'Yes'. France does want to maintain the Community and to develop it"[15]—reassured his partners and paved the way for the relaunching of the Community of the 1970s.

Brandt, in his postsummit statement, echoed Pompidou's sentiment with regard to progress in the Community but sounded a more cautious note on monetary union:

> My Government is willing to move along the road to economic and monetary union, soberly and realistically, step by step. Structural differences between our States, and the differences which still persist in our economic targets and behaviour, are facts which can only be changed by perseverance and joint efforts. Converging attitudes on the part of the main social groups will also be needed.[16]

Brandt did, however, concede that "if we succeed in elaborating a common economic policy . . . such a development will call for the creation of a European Reserve Fund. Here too I offer my Government's full co-operation."[17]

The difference between the two approaches of Pompidou and Brandt to monetary union—a political versus an economic approach—was to foreshadow a major debate on monetary cooperation between the monetarists and the economists. Although the heads of government asked the Council to draw up a plan leading to EMU, the apparent unity of opinion on the ultimate desirability of the goal of monetary union masked serious fundamental differences on how best to achieve it. Two mutually exclusive approaches to achieving monetary union were championed by the member states. It is worthwhile discussing each approach in detail here because the same issues arose time and again during discussions of European monetary cooperation and continued even through the negotiations of EMU in the Delors Committee.

MONETARISTS VERSUS ECONOMISTS

The central question debated in the Monetary Committee, the Committee of Central Bank Governors, and the Werner Committee was whether to achieve monetary union first and allow the domestic economies to adjust in response to the new constraints (the so-called monetarist approach), or to converge the economies of the member states first and then establish a unified currency as the crowning achievement of that convergence (the "economist" perspective).

The logic of the monetarist position, held by France, Belgium, Luxembourg, and the Commission, was that locking the exchange rates early would create the discipline necessary to converge the economic performance of the member states. Specifically, the monetarists believed that once recourse to manipulations of the external environment, for example, devaluation, was eliminated, countries would necessarily adjust their internal domestic policies to accommodate the single currency. To help with the adjustment, the monetarists envisioned a European Reserve Fund, a form of balance-of-payments aid in which surplus countries lent to deficit countries, thus smoothing the way toward economic convergence. Lending support to the monetarist position was the fact that in 1969 the currencies were moving within very small margins as stipulated by the Bretton Woods and the EMA system. Fixing the currencies was not seen as much more of a restriction.

By contrast, the economist states (Germany, the Netherlands, and Italy) believed that monetary union would only be feasible if the necessary economic convergence had occurred while the countries still had the ability to change exchange rates. Not only would the convergence show political will to achieve monetary union, but also it would give the EMU a chance at success. To the economist heads of state, merging the currencies without first converging the economies would inevitably lead to the fracture of the union.

At base, of course, the preferences of member states for the monetarist or economist approach to EMU reflected each member's underlying economic position. For balance-of-payments deficit countries like France, monetary union—with its attendant institutions—would provide a means to finance those deficits from the beginning of the union on, rather than forcing France to adjust its policies without outside assistance. Conversely, Germany, with its balance-of-payments surpluses, was loath to enter into a monetary union in which it would possibly have to lend indefinitely large sums to support its monetary allies. Essentially, the argument between the monetarists and economists revolved around which countries would bear the burden of economic adjustment, which made resolution of the problem difficult.[18] At The Hague summit, however, these fundamental arguments remained inchoate, and consensus was achieved through vague declarations of intent. The conflict between the two approaches emerged more visibly as the member states and the Commission began to formulate a strategy for achieving monetary union.

A PLAN IN STAGES

With the Second Barre Plan, made public on March 4, 1970, the Commission intended to create a plan in stages for European economic and monetary union as stipulated in point 8 of The Hague summit communiqué.[19] The first blueprint for achieving monetary union, the plan gave the Werner Committee a mandate to flesh out the stages of monetary union.

The Werner Committee, chaired by Luxembourg's prime (and former finance) minister Pierre Werner, consisted of the chairpersons of the Monetary

Committee, the Committee of Governors of the Central Banks, the Medium-Term Economic Policy Committee, the Short-Term Economic Policy Committee, and the Budget Policy Committee and a representative of the Commission. The Werner Committee was charged with elaborating a plan for EMU and, to some extent, arbitrating between the competing visions of the monetarists and economists.[20] It presented an interim report to the Council on May 20, 1970, and released its final report on October 8, 1970.[21] The Council of Ministers passed most of the recommendations of the Werner Report on February 9, 1971. What exactly had the member states actually agreed to by these acts?

The working premise of the Werner Report was that EMU was impossible to create in a single bureaucratic maneuver, and therefore movement in stages would be the best plan. However, conflicts between the member states made agreement on a concrete plan to achieve EMU impossible. Only loose coordination and consultation in the first stage could be approved by the member states; the committee discovered that agreeing on further developments in other stages was impossible.

The Werner plan defined monetary union as "the total and irreversible convertibility of currencies, the elimination of margins of fluctuation in exchange-rates, the irrevocable fixing of parity rates and the complete liberation of movements of capital."[22] Further, the report asserted that "to ensure the cohesion of economic and monetary union, transfers of responsibility from the national to the Community plane will be essential."[23] The most proactive part of the Werner Report was the agreement by the member states to narrow their margins vis-à-vis the dollar as part of the first stage. This proposal to narrow will be examined below because of its significance as the first "Snake." The other aspects of the first stage were less decisive, consisting mainly of further consultations and studies. The requirements of each phase not only illustrate the laxity of certain deliberately vague steps, but they also allow us to see the similarities to and differences from EMU in 1989, thereby highlighting the lessons the member states had learned from the first EMU.

The first phase (1971–1973) provided for greater consultations in the fields of economic and fiscal policy. In the realm of economic coordination, the Council was to determine the procedures for coordination of short-term and budget policy, to lower tax barriers, and to facilitate the free movement of capital. Greater coordination of monetary policy was to be achieved through harmonizing the instruments of monetary policy under the auspices of the EU Monetary Committee and Committee of the Governors of Central Banks. In its relations to non-EU countries, the Community was to gradually adopt common policies and not make use of any provisions that would permit a relaxation of the international exchange-rate regime.[24] Finally, the report required the Monetary Committee and the

Committee of the Governors of Central Banks to draw up by June 30, 1972, a report on the "organization and functions of a European Fund for monetary cooperation."[25]

Because of fundamental conflicts between the member states about the best way to EMU, the second stage was left characteristically vague. The first phase was designed to give the various Community bodies time to study the issues and to converge the economies. The second stage would flow from the progress the first stage had made. The Commission merely required that

> [the Council will] submit to [the Commission] by 1 May 1973 a memo-
> randum on progress in the achievement of economic and monetary union
> and on the measures to be adopted after the completion of the first stage,
> and to present a draft in accordance with Article 236 of the Treaty for
> those measures which could not be implemented on the basis of the ex-
> isting Treaty provisions.[26]

The lack of specific details was due to conflicts between the German and French ministers, representing, respectively, the economist and monetarist positions. Although the Werner Committee's composition looked like an impartial, technocratic group and although it relied on technical advice from the Committee of Central Bank Governors for some of its recommendations, the group consisted of senior ministers from each of the member states, and the committee members represented national government preferences.[27] The first stage thus represented an uneasy "parallelism" between the monetarists and the economists—not a decision to follow one strategy over the other—and most observers agree that the lack of direction made consensus on EMU possible but was ultimately destined to fail.[28]

As to the role of the Bundesbank during this period, it is important to note that there was limited conflict between the federal government and the Bundesbank during the negotiations of the Werner Report because the government's position was closer to the Bundesbank's views than the French government's.[29] Moreover, although there was no representative of the Bundesbank on the Werner Committee, the Bundesbank's preferences were clearly heard in the Committee of Central Bank Governors, which was asked to present technical recommendations on the matter of economic and monetary policy. The Committee of Central Bank Governors definitively rejected the monetarist position in its response to questions submitted by the Werner Committee members, writing that

> the experts consider that it would be premature to adopt [the establish-
> ment of a single Community currency] and [to link the currencies to one
> another by parities and fixed rates] for the first step in the realization of
> economic and monetary union in the Community; and [these steps] would
> be more appropriate to a later stage or even the final objective.[30]

On the entire enterprise of monetary union, the Bundesbank was skeptical, though not uncooperative. The Bundesbank's position that no monetary union would be feasible without sufficient economic coordination overlapped the views of Economics Minister Karl Schiller and Chancellor Brandt, rather than challenging them as would happen in later episodes of cooperation. In its annual report, the Bundesbank reported positively on the progress towards EMU, but added:

> Obviously the decisions of February 1971 do not necessarily ensure the required parallelism in economic and monetary policy. In the sphere of general economic and fiscal policy, . . . only efforts to intensify coordination were agreed, without any guarantees of their actual effectiveness. . . . In order to ensure that . . . the necessary economic policy base is provided for these monetary arrangements, the parties have agreed to a "safe-guard clause" proposed by Germany and stipulating that the validity of some of these monetary arrangements . . . will be limited to five years from the beginning of the first phase.[31]

The "safeguards" that Germany stipulated were the first in a long history of exemptions and exceptions that Germany required in international monetary agreements.

BUNDESBANK SUPPORT OF A REDUCTION IN THE MARGINS

The Bundesbank's polite skepticism of monetary cooperation did not prevent it from agreeing to further commitments. Although the Bundesbank and the other central bankers on the Committee of Central Bank Governors had rejected the immediate fixing of Community currencies, they proposed a concertation of exchange-rate policies vis-à-vis the dollar to damp the intra-Community exchange-rate variability. Fluctuations against the dollar, which at the time could move ±0.75 percent, would be restricted to ±0.6 percent, thus narrowing the band within which the currencies could move relative to the dollar. Because of the graphical representation of the narrow band within the "tunnel" of the original dollar parities being kept by other non-EU member states, the name "Snake" is sometimes given to this agreement. In point of fact, the arrangement envisaged by the Werner Report never materialized in its intended form because of currency turbulence in the spring of 1971, and therefore the monetary arrangement commonly referred to as the Snake did not hatch until April 1972 under very different circumstances. However, the principles behind intra-Community exchange-rate coordination had their genesis in the Werner Report.

The Bundesbank's reaction to the margin reduction plan was cautiously optimistic. On the one hand, the Bundesbank took pains to stress that this would not lead to monetary union without greater economic convergence: "It would . . . be an illusion to expect that the mere reduction of the margins might actually have a coercive influence in the direction of harmonizing the entire economic and financial development in the EEC countries.[32] On the other hand, the bank gleaned the beginnings of a detachment from the dollar, a policy most welcome after the speculative inflows of the late 1960s.

The Committee of Central Bank Governors passed the necessary resolutions to concert their interventions in April 1971 and prepared to narrow the width of the band beginning on June 15. By the end of April, however, the DM was increasingly under pressure again because of inflows of dollars into Germany following reports that the DM was undervalued. The DM 23 billion that flowed into Germany between January and May 1971 caused the Bundesbank to close the foreign exchange markets from May 5 to 9.[33] On May 10, the foreign exchange markets opened again, but the Bundesbank declared its intention to temporarily suspend its intervention obligations in the markets, thereby floating the DM.

The May 1971 crisis is notable for three reasons: (1) the conflict within the Bundesbank Central Bank Council and between the Bundesbank and the federal government about the appropriate policy to cope with the capital inflows, (2) the lack of coordination between the EU members in dealing with the problem despite the Werner Report's emphasis on consultation and coordination, and (3) the derailment of the band of fluctuation agreement.

The Bundesbank had been alerted to the coming crisis in the foreign exchange markets as early as February 1971, and in the Central Bank Council members discussed the options available to Germany. The capital inflows, only some of which could be sterilized, threatened domestic monetary stability, and Bundesbank members were not united in a course of action. It is a telling point about the extent to which the Bundesbank ethos changed in later years that in March 1971 the Bundesbank deliberately lowered interest rates for the sole purpose of discouraging speculative capital flows. In its May 1971 monthly report, the Bundesbank admitted that "the most recent reduction in the discount rate on March 31, 1971 was motivated solely by external considerations; it was no longer in conformity with domestic conditions."[34] It is important to highlight the priority given to international concerns over domestic considerations, as well as the explicit acknowledgment of that fact in the Bundesbank's official reports, especially in light of its later actions and statements in the 1992 EMS crisis.

Within the Central Bank Council (as well as in the chancellor's cabinet), two divergent opinions existed as to the wisest course to stem the capital inflows in the spring of 1971. On the one hand, Bundesbank president Karl Klasen was against floating the DM, saying that the "Community needs fixed mutual exchange-rate relationships and would do so even if there were no common agricultural market."[35] He feared that floating the DM would revalue the DM to a level unacceptable for the export-oriented economy, and he believed that floating would contravene Germany's international currency agreements, the IMF parity limits, and the new EU bands.[36] His preferred solution to the crisis was imposing capital controls in accordance with paragraph 23 of the German Economic Law.[37] This opinion, although common in the Bundesbank at the time, would lose currency as the bank successfully dealt with the inflationary pressures of the 1970s by focusing on domestic stability.

Led by Bundesbank vice president Otmar Emminger, a second faction in the Central Bank Council supported floating the currency. Believing that only floating would give the Bundesbank the autonomy to concentrate on domestic stability, this group wanted to eliminate the intervention obligations from the currency agreements in order to focus entirely on Germany's inflation problems. The emergence of this group of "Germany first" Central Bank Council members foreshadowed a gradual evolution in the Bundesbank toward policy autonomy rather than international cooperation. In 1971, the group was not yet in the majority, and Klasen's opinions prevailed. International commitments were considered significant enough to warrant a temporary loss of domestic stability. In the next few years, however, this view would change.

On May 5, by a vote of 11 to 7, the Central Bank Council recommended imposing capital controls to stem the capital inflows. Within the chancellor's cabinet, however, opinion was also divided, and Brandt was inclined to institute a policy of floating. Economics Minister Karl Schiller preferred a solution involving an EU-currency joint float against the dollar. Most of the currency speculation into the DM was out of the dollar; decoupling the DM from the dollar intervention obligations was therefore thought to be the optimal solution to the crisis, especially as such an arrangement would maintain exchange-rate parity with the other EU members. Schiller was predisposed to reject capital controls for three reasons: (1) for ideological reasons, interference with the free market was unacceptable, (2) imposition of capital controls would be bureaucratically difficult given the large number of foreign exchange market participants, and (3) even if capital controls worked, they would only work on future inflows, not the existing flows that had already entered the country.[38] Floating was the proper course, and if a joint EU float could not be arranged, Schiller and the cabinet were willing to float the DM alone.

This clash of opinions between the Bundesbank council and the cabinet proved highly divisive. Believing that insufficient weight had been given to the Bundesbank's advice by the federal government, the bank wrote a commentary in its August 1971 monthly report detailing their respective legal roles and obligations.

> The obligation incumbent on the bank under the Bundesbank Act to advise the federal government in monetary policy matters of major importance, unlike the obligation to furnish the federal government with information, does not depend on a request to this effect being made by the federal government. This means that the Bundesbank . . . may approach the federal government on its own initiative, and indeed must so approach it when in its due estimation advice to the federal government is called for. It is not without good reason that such advice by the bank was not made dependent on an explicit request by the federal government, for otherwise it might be possible to prevent the Bundesbank from giving undesired advice by not requesting it.[39]

The Bundesbank statement, although noting that the government must consider its advice, implicitly acknowledged the superior position of the government in international monetary policy. In contrast to later conflicts with the government, the Bundesbank was not yet in the position to demand that its wishes be obeyed.

GERMANY FACES ITS EUROPEAN PARTNERS

On May 8, 1971, Schiller requested a special EU Council meeting to discuss the proposal for a joint EU float against the dollar. The EU Council discussions revolved around whether the EU would allow Germany to float, whether it should be a time-constrained float, and whether the other EU members would allow a parity change in the DM at the end of the floating.[40] In a meeting chaired by French finance minster Valéry Giscard d'Estaing, it became clear very quickly that Schiller's preferred alternative of a joint float vis-à-vis the dollar would be opposed by France and Italy. These countries feared a large revaluation in relation to the dollar if they allowed themselves to be "pulled up" by the DM.

The hostile reaction of the other EU members to both a joint float as well as a unilateral DM float made compromise difficult. In the early hours of May 9, the Council finally issued a statement saying that although under normal conditions a system of flexible interest rates within the EU ran counter to a well-functioning system, *for a limited time* states could increase the currency bands. The lukewarm acceptance of the German position masked other differences of opinion, including how limited the time for floating should be and whether there would indeed be a new parity level of the DM when the return to fixed rates was established. This episode of "consultation" between EU Council members was the minimum of "concertation" and should be seen in retrospect as a failure to compromise. The member states by and large felt that a German fait accompli had been foisted on them, and the communiqué issued after of the meeting was a face-saving device to maintain the fiction of cooperation.

The French were especially concerned with bringing the DM quickly back into the fixed-rate regime. In Giscard d'Estaing's opinion, a "limited time" was at most several weeks, as opposed to the German view that it represented at least half a year.[41] Although the German point of view eventually prevailed, Emminger later recalled that Schiller's successor, Helmut Schmidt, learned from this episode that cooperation with the French was essential. Because of these experiences, Schmidt went out of his way to court Giscard d'Estaing once he became finance minister.

In the early morning of May 10, the German chancellor made the final resolution to end the Bundesbank's intervention obligations when the foreign exchange markets reopened that day. Chancellor Brandt told his European colleagues, "We can't always be the nice boys."[42] The Dutch followed the German example and also floated their currency. The new EU interest rate concertation scheme had been damaged even before its beginning, and Germany had for the first time asserted its priority of domestic stability over international regime arrangements. Interestingly, the new German policy stemmed not from the *Bundesbank's* insistence on domestic priorities over international obligations but from the *federal government,* an indication that in the early 1970s the Bundesbank was not in a position to influence significantly international monetary policy.

NIXON SHOCK AND THE SMITHSONIAN AGREEMENT

The DM continued to float during the remaining months of 1971 and was therefore spared some of the currency market turbulence leading up to, and following, the so-called Nixon shock. On August 15, 1971, U.S. president Richard Nixon canceled the Bretton Woods policy of dollar-gold convertibility, thereby freeing the dollar from pent-up currency speculation and causing a wave of speculative capital into the DM. The EU Council met again on August 19 to determine whether a joint float against the dollar was preferred by the member states after the closing of the gold window, but only Belgium had changed its position in favor of a bloc-float against the dollar. France and Italy still feared a revaluation from being tied too closely to the DM, and France eventually established a two-tiered exchange-rate system. Italy joined the Netherlands and Germany in an individual float, while the Benelux countries agreed to float together because of the strong ties between their economies.[43]

By November, Bundesbank president Klasen, never a friend of floating exchange rates, began to criticize openly the existing arrangements, saying that overshooting of exchange rates made rational economic policies difficult.

> We do not live in an unrestrictedly free market economy. We quite deliberately call the system a . . . "social market economy." The epithet

"social" is intended to indicate that undesirable, mistaken developments such as would beset a completely free market economy are rectified by regulative measures. Precisely this is the case when the total freedom of foreign exchange transactions in Germany is exploited to effect transfers of funds, in order to circumvent the national monetary policies pursued by the Bundesbank in the interest of the national economy.[44]

The Central Bank Council repeatedly called for additional safeguards for the German economy against the inflow of short-term funds from abroad. On the federal government's side, there was also a sea change of opinion against pure floating, based on the six months' experience. The government was willing to contemplate changes, including market interventions such as capital controls, because floating did make economic planning unpredictable and difficult.

In early November, a compromise within the EU became possible because of changes in the German and French positions. The French, despite their two-tiered exchange market, had had unacceptably high levels of capital inflows since August and were prepared to consider revaluing the franc, to some extent, in a bloc-float system. French and German negotiators designed a position to present to the United States at the Group of Ten meeting in Rome on November 30, which included the resumption of fixed exchange rates, a repeal of the U.S. surcharge on imports, and a revaluation of Community currencies in conjunction with a devaluation of the dollar.

The terms of an international monetary agreement between the Community member states and the United States were firmed up during a meeting between French president Pompidou and President Nixon on December 13–14. These accords became the basis for the Smithsonian Agreement, signed by the leaders of the Group of Ten on December 19, 1971. Under the terms of the agreement, the width of the parity bands around the dollar was increased from 1 percent (or 0.75 percent as had been the case for the EU member states) to 2.25 percent to decrease speculative capital flows. Convertibility of the dollar was not renewed, but once again the EU was tied to the United States, and subject to U.S. policies.

The increase in parity bands established by the Smithsonian Agreement prompted the Commission to propose a new regime of intra-Community coordination. The new bands, ±2.25 percent relative to the dollar, allowed EU currencies to diverge relative to each other as much as 9 percent (four times 2.25 percent), a margin of divergence that was unacceptably high, given the constraints of the CAP and export market considerations.

In the first months of 1972, Germany continued to receive significant capital inflows because of the dollar's weakness. In February, the Bundesbank lowered the discount rate for the second time in a month, with the sole objective of stemming speculative capital inflows. "This time the lowering of the discount rate was solely oriented on the external balance," wrote Emminger,[45] and the Bundesbank indicated that "from a purely domestic point of view, there would have been no cause to lower the discount rate so significantly."[46] Funds continued to pour into Germany, and on March 1, the federal government, with the Bundesbank's blessing, imposed a cash deposit requirement on all foreign deposits. Although most speculative capital continued to flow into Germany, the dollar's weakness was also adversely affecting other currencies, and the policy preferences of other European states were beginning to change.

THE SNAKE IN THE TUNNEL

On January 12, 1972, the Commission proposed relaunching the EMU project, recommending that intra-EU exchange rates not diverge more than 2 percent. Moreover, the Commission recommended the establishment of the European Monetary Cooperation Fund (EMCF) to administer the short- and medium-term mutual assistance mechanisms agreed to in 1970. The contentious issues were reserve pooling (to which the Germans were violently opposed) and integrating the short-term mutual assistance system with the multilateral intervention mechanism. In order to achieve agreement, these issues were eliminated from consideration for the time being and were relegated to further study by the relevant EU bodies.

The other issues that arose in the ensuing three months before an agreement was finally signed on April 10, 1972, created conflicts between potential creditor countries like Germany and debtor states like France and Italy. France argued that settlements of obligations created by interventions be made in dollars (which were now not convertible into gold), whereas Germany wanted settlements in gold or special drawing rights (SDRs), which were "harder" stores of value. A compromise was reached in March, with the composition of the debtors' reserves determining the percentage of each countries' settlement component. If necessary, the member states could also draw on the short- and medium-term monetary assistance facilities that the Community had established after the Werner Report. The Bundesbank was adamant, however, that the facilities to settle intervention obligations not become a new system of unlimited financing and that all accounts be settled within a month or two of their origination. There was no agreement on the establishment of the EMCF, which would include pooling of reserves.

The Basel agreement, nicknamed the "Snake in the tunnel," provided that EU currencies could not vary more than ±2.25 percent against each other. Intervention would be in EU currencies, not dollars, and interventions before the margins had been breached (so-called intramarginal interventions) would not be allowed unless there had been prior consultation between the member central banks. The system was administered by the Committee of Central Bank Governors, and April 24 was chosen as the date to begin reducing fluctuations to 2.25 percent. The six original participants in the Snake were eager to encourage the new EU applicants, Britain, Ireland, Norway, and Denmark, to join the Snake as soon as possible. The British (and Irish) pound and the Danish krone joined on May 1, and the Norwegian krone joined on May 23.

The Snake did not in any way minimize capital inflows into European currencies and, if anything, made handling the inflows more difficult for the member states. On June 23, in the face of capital outflows brought about by high inflation and current account deficits, the British government decided unilaterally to float the pound, saying that the currency would return to the Snake "as soon as conditions permit"[47]—a platitude that remained the British government's position throughout the 1970s and 1980s. Denmark also reverted to floating the krone.

THE BUNDESBANK'S PREFERENCES PREVAIL

The currency crisis of June-July 1972 resulted in further casualties. Once again, the Bundesbank Central Bank Council and the federal government's cabinet debated whether it was better to float the DM or to erect further capital controls. Within the Bundesbank Central Bank Council, the opinions converged on Klasen's view that further capital controls should be the recommended remedy. Vice President Emminger's view that "in this new global economic environment relative to the dollar, floating is the only possibility" was the minority opinion; the Council again rejected the policy autonomy that floating would give Germany.[48] Emminger recalled, "In the current situation, we wanted to try to defend the December 1971 parities and European Exchange agreement (Snake) which had only been established since April 1972, as long as possible."[49] As before, the majority of the Bundesbank Central Bank Council considered international foreign exchange coordination agreements as superseding domestic monetary factors or ideological commitments.

In a replay of the Bundesbank-cabinet conflict a year earlier, Schiller was vehemently against the imposition of new capital controls. His preferred alternative was to reach an agreement with the other EU member states to set up a joint-float against the dollar. The discussions within the cabinet continued throughout the night and the early morning of June 29 and resulted in a vote by all cabinet members against Schiller in favor of the Bundesbank's recommendation. As a result, Schiller tendered his resignation on July 7, which was accepted without further negotiation or comment by Brandt.

Attuned to the dynamics of the international environment, Schiller's successor, Helmut Schmidt, made his first official visit to Finance Minister Giscard d'Estaing in Paris, where he determined that there was absolutely no possibility of the French agreeing to a joint-float. Once again, Germany would have to take unilateral action against the capital inflows. This time, however, Germany imposed capital controls rather than floating unilaterally. The Bundesbank's preferences had prevailed.

Until January 1973, the capital controls put in place by the Bundesbank decreased the flow of capital into Germany. The world's currency markets became relatively stable, and the Snake functioned fairly efficiently, despite its variable membership.[50] At the Paris summit on October 19–21, 1972, the member states had reaffirmed their commitment to creating EMU by 1980 and lauded the workings of the Snake. For the first time, there was also movement on the issue of the EMCF, including the contentious aspect of pooling reserves. Germany and France agreed that the institution could be created, but only as an intergovernmental organization with the reserves under the control of the Committee of Central Bank Governors.

THE BEGINNING OF THE SCHMIDT-EMMINGER CONFLICT

The international currency system was disrupted once again in January 1973, first because of Italian inflation and later because of the first oil shock. As in the earlier crises, capital flowed primarily into Germany, despite the existing capital controls. Switzerland, also a safe haven for currency speculators, closed its foreign exchange markets on January 23 and decided to float its currency when the markets reopened, increasing the speculative inflows into Germany in February.

As before, the Bundesbank Central Bank Council and the federal government reopened the discussions on the best way to prevent enormous capital inflows.[51] This time, however, Bundesbank president Klasen was hospitalized, leaving Vice President Emminger chairing the Bundesbank meetings. Klasen's absence is important because Klasen and Emminger had radically different views on exchange-rate stabilization. Whereas Klasen was against revaluation of the DM and in favor of capital controls to protect against capital inflows, Emminger felt a DM revaluation was not out of place and that floating the DM was the best alternative to the endless administration of new and more complicated exchange controls.

During his meeting with the federal government, Emminger pleaded for the temporary suspension of dollar interventions. Finance Minister Schmidt was completely against such a move, and the confrontation between Emminger and Schmidt became the basis for longer enmity between the two men. Because of the importance of this rivalry during the establishment of the EMS in 1978 when Emminger was Bundesbank president and Schmidt the chancellor, the conflict between the two deserves further attention here.

Emminger did not trust Schmidt's inflation-fighting resolve. Not only had (then defense minister) Schmidt been against floating in the May 1971 currency crisis, but in a January 26, 1973, *Times* (London) interview, he had indicated that he preferred inflation to revaluation pressure.[52] For his part, Schmidt doubted the extent to which the vice president's plan represented the general opinion of the Central Bank Council and went as far as to call Klasen in the hospital to confirm this fact. Klasen told Schmidt that he and his subordinate disagreed on the advantages of floating. Schmidt's view, that floating would lead to a significant revaluation of the DM and hence the handicapping of Germany's export sector, is relevant to the discussion of the motivations of Schmidt and Giscard d'Estaing in proposing the EMS in 1978. This earlier history between Emminger and Schmidt also casts light on Emminger's intransigence on the EMS proposals that Schmidt presented. Not only was Emminger, for purely technocratic reasons, against obligations that would hinder the Bundesbank's ability to ensure domestic stability, but for personal reasons he was probably also disinclined to support any potentially successful initiative that Schmidt could propose.

During the February 1973 crisis, the federal government was itself divided over the best course. Schmidt was in favor of continuing to meet the international obligations of the Smithsonian agreement, whereas State Secretary for Foreign Affairs Hans Apel announced that the federal government was prepared to create a two-tiered foreign exchange market. With little knowledge of economics, Chancellor Brandt was uninterested in the details of international finance.

On February 9, the Bundesbank's Central Bank Council sent a long position paper to the federal government detailing its stand on the current crisis.[53] It stated unequivocally that the current dollar parity was indefensible and that the Bundesbank had petitioned the federal government unsuccessfully to release the Bundesbank from its intervention obligations. The paper went on to warn against any false hopes that the Bundesbank would be able to sterilize the capital inflows and stated that if the present course were continued, it could not assume responsibility for the negative domestic consequences. For the third time in a week, the Bundesbank requested that it be released from intervention obligations.

The conflict between the Bundesbank and the federal government was defused by an unexpected U.S. proposal to realign the currencies. The dollar was devalued 10 percent and the DM revalued 1 percent. As Emminger wrote, only "the surprise initiative of Paul Volcker spared the federal government a deep conflict with the Bundesbank and freed Helmut Schmidt from the trap of his own making, at least for the time being."[54] The lines of the Bundesbank-government conflict had now been drawn, and the stable preferences of each institution on the issue of international monetary cooperation had emerged. Moreover, the Bundesbank was becoming more assertive and visible.

THE SNAKE IN THE LAKE

The currency realignments, however, did not serve to restore calm in the foreign exchange markets for long. By early March 1973, currency markets were in disarray once again, and on March 1 the Bundesbank's Central Bank Council met in an emergency session again. With Schmidt in the hospital and Karl Otto Pöhl, the state secretary in charge of currency questions, away on vacation, the only federal government minister the Bundesbank could find to approve the Bundesbank's request that the foreign exchange markets be closed temporarily was Economics Minister Hans Friderichs. This proposal was accepted without much discussion, and the markets remained closed, not only in Germany but in most European countries, until March 19. During these weeks, Emminger lobbied the Bundesbank and the federal government to accept his view that the time had come for the European currencies to bloc-float against the dollar. The dollar was rightly seen as the source of the currency instability, and Emminger was determined to divorce the DM from the dollar, either by unilaterally floating again or by his preferred alternative, a joint-float against the dollar.

At Emminger's urging, a special meeting of the EU Council was planned for March 4 to discuss a bloc-float against the dollar. On the German side, for once the federal government and the Bundesbank were in complete agreement about the preferred course of action. Finance Minister Schmidt's change of heart in favor of floating vis-à-vis the dollar was consistent with his earlier opposition to a unilateral German float since he feared a revaluation of the DM relative to Germany's European partners more than to the United States. At the March 4 meeting, there was widespread agreement that non–EU member states should be included in the discussion, and the meetings of March 9, 11, and 16 to discuss a joint-float against the dollar included several non-EU countries that would join the Snake.

On March 11, the decision to bloc-float was made, and France, Germany, the Netherlands, Belgium, Luxembourg, Denmark, Sweden, and Norway all agreed to float jointly against the dollar. Italy, which had left the Snake on February 11, as well as Britain, whose recent status as a new EU member did not make it more amenable to joint EU actions, decided to float independently.

With the German economy decoupled from the vicissitudes of the dollar, the Bundesbank and the federal government worked in tandem to combat inflation. In the case of the government, this meant severe fiscal austerity measures while the Bundesbank practiced a restrictive monetary policy. This policy became the focus of international attention in July, when Britain denounced the Bundesbank for causing huge capital outflows from the pound into the DM and a 16 percent devaluation of the pound vis-à-vis the DM in two months. The disputes came to a head in the last weekend of July in an "interest rate war" between Britain and Germany, culminating in a letter of complaint from Prime Minister Edward Heath to Brandt.

The monetary crisis of March 1973 marks the beginning of a new awareness within the Bundesbank of its influence in the international arena. As the primary force behind the proposals for a European joint-float against the dollar, the Bundesbank was able to persuade its partners to join in the float despite their reservations. Although the Bundesbank was in favor of floating to decouple the DM and dollar, in 1973 it still supported exchange-rate cooperation with its European partners even if that restricted the Bundesbank's policy autonomy. This position was to change over the course of the next five years.

The Problems with the Snake

The floating arrangement of the European currencies relative to the dollar, sometimes referred to as the "Snake in the lake" to distinguish it from the "Snake in the tunnel" (when the European currencies maintained a parity against the dollar) lasted until the beginning of the EMS on March 13, 1979, albeit with varying membership. There were, however, some technical problems with the arrangement. The major flaw was that the European currencies could float ±2.25 percent against each other, but there were no provisions to stipulate exactly what should happen if a country's currency crossed its band with another currency beyond the statement that "when these [±2.25 percent] limits were reached, the participating central banks will intervene on their exchange markets by purchasing or selling the partner currency as the situation requires."[55] There was no sanction for nonintervention on the part of the deviating currency or currencies, nor did the Snake even require consultations or negotiations among the members in the event of a crossing of parities. Moreover, there was no natural forum for Snake countries to discuss and negotiate, had they wanted to; since the Snake included non–EU member states and did not include all EU members, there were no institutional structures in which the currency problems could be discussed, save the ad hoc—and often bilateral—meetings between European heads of state.

The second problem was that the countries with weaker currencies were at a disadvantage because they had to intervene using their strong-currency reserves, which were finite and easily depleted. The problem was mitigated somewhat by the creation, in April 1974, of the EMCF, which cleared the liabilities arising from interventions. However, at the insistence of the Germans, the fund explicitly did not offer credit options (beyond those that already existed among the EU central banks) for acquiring reserves with which to intervene, and thus the problem remained for the weaker-currency countries.

The third problem with the Snake was that it had no mechanism to indicate which currencies should intervene when currencies crossed the band against each other. Generally, the onus was on the weaker-currency country, and it would intervene in order to remain in the regime. For example, when the French franc dropped below the limit against the DM, the French had to intervene despite the fact that the deviation was due to the DM's *appreciation,* not the franc's depreciation. The French, in particular, were keenly aware of the asymmetries in the Snake and were frustrated by this facet of the regime. In his memoirs, Giscard d'Estaing described the Snake this way:

> To avoid a European currency leaving the skin of the Snake, the central bank of the threatened currency had to intervene to bring it back into the interior of the "band." Unfortunately, this arrangement only applied to weak currencies, those which left the Snake toward the bottom. On the strong currencies, those reputed to be "virtuous" and which pulled the Snake toward the top, nothing was imposed.[56]

The search for greater symmetry of obligations in international monetary regimes was a major factor in explaining France's motivation to create the EMS and the EMU.

Not coincidentally, perhaps, the French were the first to leave the Snake once the joint float against the dollar was terminated. Giscard d'Estaing, as finance minister, recognized the problem of intervening to maintain the parity vis-à-vis the DM and presented President Pompidou with the problem in January 1974. Pompidou made the choice of floating the franc on January 19, saying:

> This, however, is not a good policy because we eventually have to coordinate our monetary policy with that of the Germans. I have seen, at the last summit, that they do not understand our situation. As soon as one speaks of currencies, they are totally egotistical. They love to make their superiority felt. Besides, from their point of view, they are not wrong.[57]

The decision to float the franc was important in two ways: first, it made obvious the fact that the French did not really want to adopt the stringent anti-inflation measures necessary to emulate German policy and remain in the regime. Second, it was tangible proof that there was to be no EMU in the foreseeable future and certainly not by 1980. EMU without France was unthinkable.

After the departure of the French franc, the Snake became a stable DM bloc, consisting of the currencies of members who had instituted austerity measures to deal with the first oil shock in October 1973. Unlike France, which had attempted to expand the economy in order to deal with the oil price shock, Germany and the other Snake countries[58] had foregone growth in order to stabilize domestic inflation, and their rates of inflation over the period were considerably lower than those of countries following an expansionary strategy.[59] The similarity of the economic strategy followed by the Snake countries made the Snake a stable arrangement over the next four years, notwithstanding the reentry (July 10, 1975) and "re-exit" (March 15, 1976) of France. For Germany, the Snake proved useful in maintaining exchange rates with some of its European trading partners, but the Snake countries took only 27 percent of German exports, down from 40 percent when they included France.[60] This fact should be remembered as a catalyst for the EMS, since Schmidt had material incentives to find an exchange-rate regime that would encompass France in addition to his professed ideological preferences for greater European integration.

BUNDESBANK PREFERENCES CONGEAL

During these "mini-Snake" years (1974–1978), the Bundesbank became more vocal about its preferences and began to allow the domestic consequences of exchange-rate policies to override exchange-regime commitments. Of course, the Bundesbank had been important in persuading the other European member states to joint-float against the dollar in the 1973 crisis, but there had been no serious conflict with the federal government on the matter. In fact, the federal government had taken the lead in diplomatic negotiations in several critical EU forums. However, there was evidence of growing splits between the positions of the Bundesbank and the federal government. Perhaps it was the Bundesbank's inflation-fighting battles that caused the Bundesbank to place a clear priority on domestic stability to the exclusion of other policies. The increasing influence of Emminger, who was appointed president of the Bundesbank in 1977, may also have contributed to the institutional rift. It did become obvious, however, that the Bundesbank would be a reluctant party to any international commitments that would risk German domestic stability.

An example of the Bundesbank's increasing autonomy from both the federal government and international agreements was Germany's response to U.S. requests that it expand its economy to pull other countries out of recession at the 1978 Bonn summit. In contrast to the federal government, which agreed to expansionary fiscal policies in the form of a tax cut, the Bundesbank refused to loosen monetary policy.

> References to monetary measures were confined to an undertaking to intervene in foreign exchange markets to "counter disorderly conditions." . . . If the thinking behind the Bonn summit was that Germany and Japan should stimulate their economies to lead a "convoy" of countries to faster growth, the Bundesbank clearly was no longer on board the ship.[61]

Signs of Bundesbank recalcitrance and the growing differences between the federal government and Bundesbank positions in the area of international monetary commitments could also be observed in EU efforts to continue on the road to EMU. The Snake had become divorced from the goal of eventual EMU, and therefore it—unlike the goal of EMU[62]–had the support of the Bundesbank. In its 1974 annual report, the Bundesbank noted with some satisfaction that,

> Contrary to the apprehensions of some skeptics the inflows and outflows resulting from the "currency Snake" were not of such dimensions as to seriously affect or even threaten the stability-oriented monetary policy pursued by the Bundesbank. Probably the main explanation for this is that the other participants in the currency bloc have also been trying to pursue stability-oriented policies. Hence, a group of countries with relatively homogeneous economic policies is involved.[63]

As D. C. Kruse observed: "[The Snake] had been transformed gradually, almost imperceptibly, from an initiative preparing the ground for the introduction of a common currency into a currency bloc providing a limited degree of exchange rate stability among its members."[64]

Despite the 1974 surrender of the plan to achieve EMU by 1980, various reports on coordinating monetary policies continued to be drafted in the EU, and the federal government continued to support these efforts in the Council. Five plans or reports on European monetary integration were issued in the period from 1975 to 1976. The Marjolin Report (March 1975), the Fourcade Plan (May 1975), the All Saints' Day Manifesto (November 1975),[65] the Tindemans Report (December 1975), and the Duisenberg Plan (February 1976) showed that the desire to link European exchange rates was far from dead. The commonality of these plans was that they all agreed that some form of monetary policy coordination among EU member states should be achieved; they were, however, far more conservative than The Hague summit communiqué had been on the feasibility of monetary union and the speed with which it might be achieved. With the exception of the All Saints' Day Manifesto, the plans provided new forms of credit to help weaker-currency countries to remain in the Snake.

Bundesbank reaction to these plans was predictable and swift. In its 1975 report it warned that

> a "softening" of the rules for the Snake, as implied in certain reform proposals (especially through a steep increase in mutual credit lines or even the partial pooling of monetary reserves), would not make it possible to dispense with the above-mentioned basic requirement—that is, uniform stabilization policies. It would merely delay necessary adjustments, either in domestic-economic policy or in exchange rates. But in the meantime the inflationary financing of deficits by central bank assistance would be so much greater. This would increase the danger that the Snake, instead of contributing to joint stability, might degenerate into a community of inflation.[66]

The government, however, was anxious to provide inducements for France to reenter the Snake and to recapture the momentum toward greater European integration. In May 1974 Schmidt replaced Brandt as chancellor and Giscard d'Estaing was elected president. These two former finance ministers forged a closer relationship than the one that had existed between their predecessors. The friendship between Giscard and Schmidt did not prevent the second exit of France from the Snake in March 1976, but it served as the foundation for the innovations to the Snake that became the EMS. The negotiations of the EMS are detailed more closely in Chapter 3, but it should be noted that the impetus for the EMS arose from the failure of the Snake to accommodate weaker-currency countries like France. The second exit of France, seen as a humiliation for French attempts to achieve German levels of economic success, guaranteed that France would not try to reenter the Snake a third time. Giscard d'Estaing explained:

> The same Snake cannot be reborn two times! The experience [of leaving the Snake a second time] had been conclusive: we will not succeed at making a European monetary system function as long as the weakest currencies alone have to support the weight of maintaining the divergence, while the strong currencies continue to prance on ahead, without worrying about whether they are being followed by the rest of the train. We have to invent another formula.[67]

The call to "invent another formula" was echoed by Commission president Roy Jenkins in 1977.[68] More than the earlier EU plans and reports, Jenkins's speech carried some weight because of the prominence he placed on monetary cooperation in his presidency.

CONCLUSION

The history of European monetary cooperation in the years 1968–1977 is a litany of grandiose ideas and backtracking during crises by the national governments. Several conclusions can be drawn from the early history of cooperation attempts. The most significant is that the Bundesbank initially took a positive position on international cooperation and was more likely than the federal government to take its international obligations seriously during a crisis. Moreover, the Bundesbank actually lowered interest rates several times during the early years solely in response to international conditions and in overt contradiction to the requirements of the domestic economy. It is thus fair to say that Bundesbank preferences were not fixed as soon as the breakdown of the Bretton Woods system allowed policy autonomy for individual states. The preferences for domestic autonomy emerged from policy failures and interinstitutional conflicts with the federal government. Essentially, given the Bundesbank Law's mandate, it was easier to make the case that the Bundesbank should be consulted when Germany's stability was threatened than to argue it should be consulted when Germany ignored its international commitments.

The close relationship between Brandt and Klasen, coupled with Brandt's disinterest in monetary issues, explains why the federal government's position on monetary union overlapped significantly with Bundesbank preferences. Fundamental policy differences within the Bundesbank and the cabinet, however, created institutional rivalries for the control of policy during currency crises. With the arrival of Schmidt to the chancellory in 1974, the federal government's policies became more focused on European exchange-rate coordination. Emminger's rise in 1977 to the presidency of the Bundesbank set the stage for a struggle over which institution could make international monetary cooperation agreements that would bind Germany. The conflict between the two men marked the divergent positions that the two institutions had taken in the 1973 crisis: Emminger preferred limited or no international commitments that would impede the Bundesbank from eliminating German inflation, and Schmidt wanted stable exchange rates to ensure the profitability of Germany's vital export sector.

Whereas currency crises and the absence of agreement between Germany and the other European member states about the appropriate path to achieve EMU had prevented real progress toward EMU in the 1970s, it was conflict between the Bundesbank and the German federal government that would profoundly affect the final shape of the next exchange-rate regime, the European Monetary System.

NOTES

1. Bordo (1993), pp. 3–108.
2. Milward (1984).
3. Kaplan and Schleiminger (1989).
4. Currency A could be at the floor of its band against the dollar, while currency B could be at the top of its band—a total of 2 percent fluctuation against each other—and then the following day they could theoretically change position completely, resulting in 4 percent fluctuation against each other. Of course, the fluctuations to the dollar would remain within the allowed ±1 percent.
5. Urwin (1995), p. 112.
6. Pompidou made the inevitable decision to devalue the franc by 11.1 percent on August 8, 1969.
7. Urwin (1995), p. 138.
8. Statler (1981), p. 104.
9. Tsoukalis (1977), p. 83.
10. Ibid., p. 84.
11. Commission of the European Communities (1969), pp. 3–15.
12. Ibid., p. 3.
13. Ibid., p. 9.
14. Commission of the European Communities (1970a), p. 15.
15. Commission of the European Communities (1970b), p. 34.
16. Ibid., p. 39.
17. Ibid.
18. Tsoukalis (1977), p. 93.
19. Commission of the European Communities (1970c), pp. 3–14.
20. As a side note, two of the Werner Committee members would play major roles in monetary cooperation in later years. Bernard Clappier would serve as the chairman of the Monetary Committee in the Werner Group, and would go on to become the French negotiator in the initial stages of EMS. Hans Tietmeyer would represent the deputy to the chairman of the Medium-Term Economic Policy Committee on the Werner Committee and would serve as Bundesbank president from 1993.
21. Commission of the European Communities (1970d).
22. Ibid., p. 9.
23. Ibid., p. 10.
24. Ibid., p. 11.
25. Ibid.
26. Ibid., p. 12.
27. Kruse (1980), p. 59.
28. Kruse (1980), pp. 58–79; Tsoukalis (1977), pp. 82–111.
29. Tsoukalis (1977), pp. 86–93.
30. Commission of the European Communities (1970d), p. 42.
31. Deutsche Bundesbank, *Annual Report,* (1970), p. 42.
32. Ibid.
33. Deutsche Bundesbank *Annual Report,* (1971), p. 53.
34. Deutsche Bundesbank, *Monthly Report*, May 1971, p. 7.
35. Ibid., p. 10.
36. Quoted in Emminger (1986), p. 178.
37. Klasen's allies in the cabinet were Defense Minister Helmut Schmidt and the ministers for education and transportation. As chancellor, Schmidt would become the main sponsor of the EMS in 1978.
38. Kruse (1980), p. 86.

39. Deutsche Bundesbank, *Monthly Report,* August 1971, p. 14.

40. Emminger (1986), p. 180.

41. Ibid., p. 182.

42. *Der Spiegel,* May 10, 1971.

43. Kruse (1980), p. 93. Belgium and Luxembourg had established a common currency (Belgium-Luxembourg Economic Union [BLEU]).

44. Deutsche Bundesbank, *Monthly Report,* November 1971, p. 12.

45. Emminger (1986), p. 216.

46. Deutsche Bundesbank, *Monthly Report,* March 1972, p. 7.

47. Cited in Emminger (1986), p. 218.

48. Ibid., p. 215.

49. Ibid., p. 219.

50. On October 10, the Danes rejoined the Snake, but in November the Norwegians dropped out after their (first) unsuccessful EU membership referendum.

51. From February 1 to 9, the Bundesbank received DM 18.6 billion despite the existing capital controls.

52. Schmidt's quote from the *Times* (London) that caused Emminger's suspicion was as follows: "As far as Germany is concerned, because we do not want to change our parity again, we shall not wish as far as inflation is concerned, to be out of general step with the EEC. We would like to be at the tail end of the convoy, but not completely out of the convoy. If we moved out of the convoy we would be in danger of revaluation pressures."

53. Partially reproduced in Emminger (1986), p. 233.

54. Ibid., p. 235.

55. Deutsche Bundesbank, *Annual Report,* 1972, p. 31.

56. Giscard d'Estaing (1988), p. 138.

57. Ibid., p. 140.

58. Comprising the Benelux countries, Denmark, and Norway and Sweden as associate members.

59. In the fourth quarter of 1973, Germany's cost of living index rose 7.3 percent, compared to 8.3 percent for France, 10.3 percent for the UK, and 11.7 percent for Italy. The real differences in strategies were more evident in the fourth quarter of 1974, when the comparable figures were 6.5 percent, 15.0 percent, 18.2 percent, and 24.7 percent, respectively. See Deutsche Bundesbank, *Annual Report,* 1974, p. 55.

60. Deutsche Bundesbank, *Annual Report,* 1973, p. 51.

61. Holtham, (1989), pp. 144, 150. Robert Putnam and Nicholas Bayne described the Bundesbank's motivation as follows: "[T]he Bundesbank seems to have been the last, most reluctant convert. Eventually, however, the Bank capitulated, having in mind particularly the international situation." Putnam and Bayne (1984), pp. 84–87.

62. The Bundesbank could not be openly hostile to the goal of EMU, but it continued to set politically unlikely or impossible preconditions to the forming of monetary union and to insist that monetary union be on its terms, very much like its demands during later negotiations of EMU in 1989.

63. Deutsche Bundesbank, *Annual Report,* 1974, p. 61.

64. Kruse (1980), p. 169.

65. This document did not originate in the EU but reflected the opinions of nine eminent economists. It was published in *The Economist* on November 1, 1975.

66. Deutsche Bundesbank, *Annual Report,* 1975, p. 53.

67. Giscard d'Estaing (1988), p. 142.

68. Jenkins (1978), pp. 1–14.

3

Renegotiating the
EMS Agreement

When negotiations for the EMS began in 1978, the German position encompassed two diametrically opposite viewpoints: the federal government's, which supported further exchange-rate coordination, and the Bundesbank's, which was opposed to most exchange-rate cooperation but legally compelled to support the federal government's policies. These two positions would become the basis for the German version of the EMS rules, which—in the end—resulted in a regime that imposed few policy restrictions on stronger-currency countries.[1] The burden of policy adjustment fell almost entirely on weaker-currency countries, as it had in the Snake. Why then, had France cosponsored Schmidt's EMS initiative?

The dynamic between the Bundesbank and the federal government proved critical to this question. Had the Bundesbank not been autonomous and willing to fight the chancellor on the rules of the EMS, the system would likely have been considerably more favorable for weaker-currency states. Since the Bundesbank's involvement began later in the negotiations, it is possible to discern what Schmidt was negotiating before the Bundesbank's input. How the Bundesbank changed the system and why the weaker-currency states decided to join the system anyway are the two main questions contemplated in this chapter. Why did the countries come together to form a new system initially, and why were the weaker-currency countries unable to change the system despite its unwanted and detrimental consequences on their policies? The first question will be examined in this chapter, and the second question is discussed in Chapter 4.

In this chapter, I argue that weaker-currency countries like France and Italy joined the EMS in 1978 because (1) they believed concessions to weaker-currency countries made by Chancellor Schmidt would remain in the final document, and by the time the Bundesbank had negotiated them away it was politically difficult for them to back out of an initiative they had originally supported; (2) they received promises of side payments

49

from the German government; or (3) they feared exclusion from a major European initiative. Traditionally, explanations of why weaker-currency countries joined the EMS focus on French policymakers' deliberate strategy to lower domestic inflation by pegging the franc to the DM.[2] However, post hoc accounts of the founding of the EMS tend to rely heavily on rational reasons for joining, rather than examining the decisions in a historical context and admitting the messy side of politics—uncertainty, coercion, misinformation, misperception, and the private agendas and egos of elites.

Fundamental differences between the Bundesbank and the federal government during the EMS negotiations explain why many of the concessions to weaker-currency countries that were initially offered were negotiated away between the Bremen and Brussels summits. Therefore, in order to make sense of Germany's schizophrenic EMS negotiating positions at the international level, it is important to understand how the conflict between the Bundesbank and the government shaped the set of viable agreements. The Bundesbank served as a de facto ratifier in monetary agreements, since all regimes affected the statutory competencies of the Bundesbank. Although the federal government had the power to insist *that* cooperation occur, the *content* of cooperation, that is, the rules of the regime, were determined by the Bundesbank.

The Genesis of the EMS Initiative

In 1977, Commission president Roy Jenkins concluded that European monetary cooperation had stalled completely and that a new initiative for monetary cooperation would be an ideal vehicle to restart European cooperation in a number of fields. Calling European Monetary Union the "single major issue, but one which in its ramifications touches every aspect of European life,"[3] he was but one of many EU functionaries to believe that further European integration had to include monetary union.[4] Jenkins's position and the public nature of his calls for new monetary initiatives had more weight than the earlier recommendations. They were, however, insufficient to really launch a new program—for that, the heads of state had to act. Although Jenkins's efforts coincided with the beginnings of the negotiations that led to the EMS, it would be incorrect to ascribe the success of the initiative to Jenkins. The EMS was born out of an intergovernmental bargain between Germany and France and was not associated with, or grounded in, the EU treaties. As a Bundesbank representative declared, "Even if there had not been an EMU, there would have been an EMS."[5]

At the heart of the bargain was the friendship of French president Valéry Giscard d'Estaing and German chancellor Helmut Schmidt. As former finance ministers, the two statesmen had an interest in and were knowledgeable about their economies. Additionally, both had experience

with the Snake and the monetary turmoil of the early 1970s. It is not surprising that they would choose international exchange rates as a matter of
discussion. In 1977, there was also another basis for their friendship—anti-
U.S. sentiment on the part of both leaders.[6] Historically, France had a
stake in keeping the United States out of Europe, and Giscard d'Estaing,
although not as militant as de Gaulle, continued to be interested in
arrangements that were purely European. The changes in Germany were
more significant but subtle. Throughout the turmoil of the 1970s, Germany
had privately decried the lack of U.S. leadership in dealing with the crises.
By 1978, Schmidt, who had experienced President Jimmy Carter's policy
of "benign neglect" as finance minister, became increasingly frustrated by
the lack of U.S. help in maintaining the stability of the dollar. Throughout
1977 and into 1978, the dollar weakened against the DM, causing restive-
ness in the German industry. This set the stage for Schmidt's proposal for
a new monetary coordination system.

MOTIVATIONS AND PREFERENCES

It is important to discuss in detail the reasons for both leaders' renewed interest in exchange-rate concertation. Their reasons are critical in establishing the fact that *their* preferences (and not those of other actors) guided
their states' negotiating positions. This point is quite simple, yet it is occasionally ignored by scholars: these executives could and did make the
monetary decisions based on their own inclinations, rather than some
amalgamation of preferences. The preferences of Giscard d'Estaing, as
president of the Republic, were the *most* important preferences in France.
Although Prime Minister Barre's preferences and opinions held some sway
with Giscard d'Estaing, it is more important to listen to what the latter
says about exchange-rate cooperation with the Germans in his memoirs
than to assume that Barre's motivations were the dominant preferences of
France because they fit with the final result of the EMS.

In Germany, Schmidt was clearly the leader, advocating a new system
of exchange-rate cooperation and making decisions about trade-offs during
the negotiations. However, the Bundesbank, once involved, became the
more important actor due to its ratifier function.

Here I trace the motivation of each leader to show how his preferences
were formed. Schmidt's interest in renewed progress in monetary matters
stemmed primarily from a desire to link the DM to other European currencies (especially the franc) since Germany's trade with the other European
member states was increasing. In his memoirs, Schmidt described his fears:

> The attempts of individual EC states to steer their currencies auton-
> omously by means of statist interventions in export and currency markets

would, in the long run, provoke massive mutual trade restrictions and would ultimately lead to the ruin of the common market. In particular, under a long-term outlook the free trade between Germany and France also seemed at risk—a possibility that caused me great personal concern.[7]

Nor were Schmidt's concerns about France's importance to Germany misplaced. Table 3.1 shows that in 1975, EU member states combined took more of Germany's exports than Germany's five largest export takers and that France was (and remains) Germany's largest export market. The strength of the DM in 1977 was a result not of DM appreciation so much as dollar depreciation and capital flight into a perceived safe currency. Since neither France nor Italy were in the Snake, Germany's currency appreciated relative to the franc and lira. As a result, Germany's export

Table 3.1   Germany's Exports to Specific Countries, 1970–1996

Year	Total (DM millions)	European Union DM millions	%	Five Largest DM millions	%
1970	125,276	45,177	36.06	55,811	44.55
1975	221,589	96,542	43.57	94,372	42.59
1980	350,328	171,994	49.10	160,223	45.74
1985	537,164	267,265	49.75	253,562	47.20
1990	642,785	350,442	54.52	293,239	45.62
1996	783,059	447,599	57.16	327,799	41.86

Year	France DM millions	%	Netherlands DM millions	%	United States DM millions	%
1970	15,118	12.07	11,522	9.20	10,634	8.49
1975	25,962	11.72	22,192	10.01	13,162	5.94
1980	46,615	13.31	33,273	9.50	—	—
1985	64,001	11.91	46,254	8.61	55,545	10.34
1990	83,835	13.04	—	—	46,874	7.29
1996	88,833	11.34	58,083	7.42	58,921	7.52

Year	Belgium/Luxembourg DM millions	%	Italy DM millions	%	United Kingdom DM millions	%
1970	9,277	7.41	9,260	7.39	—	—
1975	16,866	7.61	16,190	7.31	—	—
1980	27,482	7.84	29,936	8.55	22,917	6.54
1985	—	—	41,795	7.78	45,967	8.56
1990	47,756	7.43	59,980	9.33	54,794	8.52
1996	—	—	58,577	7.48	63,385	8.09

Source: Deutsche Bundesbank, *Statistische Beihefte,* various years.

Note: Missing data from a country indicates that in that year, it was not among the top five export markets.

industries were faced with higher and higher hurdles to export i
icant markets. In 1975, France and Italy took 11.7 percent and 7
respectively, of Germany's exports.[8] Knowing that France would not
the Snake a third time, a new system had to be found, one that would better encompass Germany's large export takers than the Snake. Schmidt
would have been almost indifferent to the rules of the exchange-rate system had they been able to support the membership of France and Italy.

The interest of France in a new currency system was more ambiguous.
Often, the major reason cited for French interest was often Giscard d'Estaing's pro-Europe ideals or Barre's interest in emulating German economic policies.[9] Neither of these explanations is entirely satisfactory,
though both contain elements of truth. Giscard d'Estaing *was* anxious to
become a member of a European currency club that would again demonstrate France's leadership position in Europe and which would help reduce
French inflation to some degree. As Table 3.2 shows, French inflation was
9.5 percent, whereas Germany's was 3.6 percent. Moreover, Barre *did*
want to redirect French economic policies by following the lead of "Modell Deutschland": sound labor relations, responsible management, and
supportive but noninterventionist economic and industrial policies. However, as Giscard d'Estaing's memoirs make clear, it is doubtful that he

Table 3.2   Rates of Inflation, 1977–1997 (percentage)

Year	Germany	France	Italy	UK
1997	1.4	1.2	1.8	1.8
1996	1.2	2.0	3.9	2.5
1995	1.9	1.6	5.2	3.4
1994	2.7	1.8	4.0	2.5
1993	3.6	2.1	4.4	1.6
1992	4.2	2.3	5.1	3.8
1991	3.5	3.2	6.4	5.9
1990	2.7	3.4	6.5	9.4
1989	2.8	3.7	6.3	7.8
1988	1.4	2.7	5.1	4.9
1987	0.2	3.1	4.8	4.2
1986	−0.2	2.7	5.8	3.4
1985	2.2	5.9	9.2	6.1
1984	2.4	7.3	10.8	5.0
1983	3.3	9.6	14.7	4.6
1982	5.3	11.8	16.5	8.6
1981	6.3	13.4	17.8	11.9
1980	5.4	13.6	21.2	17.9
1979	4.2	10.7	14.7	13.5
1978	2.7	9.1	12.2	8.3
1977	3.6	9.5	18.5	15.8

Source: IMF, *International Financial Statistics Yearbook,* various years.

wanted to join a currency system that would force the weaker-currency countries to achieve German levels of inflation (2 percent per year or less). The point is that the *degree* of disinflation wanted by Giscard d'Estaing was far less than that provided by a tie to the DM. The conventional wisdom that France wanted to tie its hands and wanted German-esque policies to dominate overlooks key evidence to the contrary, including Giscard d'Estaing's statement that the new system would have to place some of the onus for maintaining certain exchange rates on the stronger-currency countries, as well as the French negotiators' emphasis on achieving a more symmetrical system.

Why then did France join the EMS, a regime that ultimately was dominated by Germany and forced weaker-currency countries to accept extremely disinflationary policies? The argument made here is that France joined because the originally favorable rules of the new system, which Giscard d'Estaing had accepted, changed radically over the course of the negotiations, in large part because of Bundesbank reservations.

SCHMIDT'S SECRET NEGOTIATIONS

Schmidt is generally regarded as the driving force behind the proposals to use the Copenhagen summit on April 7–8, 1978, to introduce the new monetary system.[10] His proposals included the creation of a European Monetary Fund (EMF), partial pooling of reserves, increased use of the European Unit of Account (EUA), and the use of European currencies rather than the dollar in interventions on the currency markets. Improvements like these that would get the stalled monetary integration moving and make the Snake obligations more symmetrical had been under consideration in the Monetary Committee for years and had always been opposed by the Bundesbank.

Schmidt's use of these proposals in his new initiative therefore raised the question of whether he naively believed that the Bundesbank would not oppose these elements (or believed that he could overcome any Bundesbank opposition), or whether he deliberately promised more compromises to weaker-currency countries than he could deliver as a negotiation strategy. Evidence suggests the latter explanation is more likely: Schmidt, a former finance minister, must have realized the implications of these proposals. Moreover, the fact that some of the same proposals (e.g., more financing facilities for intervention) had been held up in the Monetary Committee should have indicated to him the depth of Bundesbank objections. Moreover, he presented the proposals to Giscard d'Estaing with the caveat that they had not been cleared either by his cabinet or the Bundesbank. Indeed, Schmidt lobbied hard that his proposal not be given any publicity, ostensibly because he did not have the cabinet approval to make his personal plan public. In his memoirs, Schmidt admits that he did not want Bundesbank interference in the negotiations before the plan was more concrete because he knew the bank would be hostile to the plans. Tellingly, the details of the plan were negotiated in secret after the Copenhagen summit by representatives of Schmidt, Giscard d'Estaing, and James Callaghan. The negotiators for Germany, France, and Britain (Horst Schulmann, Bernard Clappier, and Ken Couzens, respectively) met without any official government representatives until the Bremen summit in July.

Official discussions about a new monetary system were also held in the usual venues—the EU Monetary Committee, the Committee of Central Bank Governors, and ECOFIN. A paper presented on June 19, 1978, to the ECOFIN from the Committee of Central Bank Governors reflected strong skepticism by the central bankers that linking of the currencies would be possible in the near future. It was, as Peter Ludlow put it, "an almost undiluted statement of the orthodox 'economist' position."[11] Those who would normally negotiate the outlines of the new system and draft the new rules—the officials in the Monetary Committee, ECOFIN, and the Committee of Central Bank Governors—were completely unaware of the parallel negotiations conducted by Clappier, Schulmann, and Couzens.

The Committee of Central Bank Governors' recommendation to ECOFIN included seven principles on which the new system should be based: (1) the new system should include all EU currencies, regardless of economic fitness, though there might be interim arrangements before they joined; (2) it should be symmetrical in terms of the obligations of strong- and weak-currency countries; (3) it should not be damaging to third currencies; (4) the Snake should continue; (5) membership should include an obligation to intervene and to make necessary domestic policy changes; (6) the system should not be rigid but allow changes in the parities; and (7) there should be modifications to the short-term and very short-term finance support arrangements. According to Ludlow, because many of these ideas had been opposed in the Monetary Committee and the Committee of Central Bank Governors by the strong-currency members before, the finance and economic ministers felt reasonably sure that they would not be accepted this time: "It would perhaps be going too far to suggest that the finance and economic ministers as a body felt that they were sharing in the creation of a new monetary system, since several of them went out of their way after the meeting to declare that they expected no such thing to emerge from the European Council at Bremen."[12]

Schmidt knew that the experts would be skeptical of and even hostile to a new system, and he therefore systematically excluded them from the sensitive negotiations creating the outlines of the system. Indeed, the first indication of the secret committee came in an article in *The Economist* on May 26, and although Emminger reportedly asked Schmidt about it, Schmidt stalled him, saying "we can talk about it later."[13]

Key to the secret phase of the negotiations was a general agreement with France about how the costs of maintaining the system would be divided. To the extent that Schmidt had a conscious *strategy* to manipulate the French, his negotiation style entailed giving concessions on several key points to keep them interested. Having the Bundesbank intervene too early and scuttle the basic agreement would likely have ended the attempts to create a new system, but one could always backtrack once the basic framework was agreed upon. Schmidt realized this[14] and made clear to Giscard d'Estaing how important secrecy was.[15] Schmidt also assumed that in any conflict with the Bundesbank, he would prevail, since that had been the experience of other chancellors before him.

The final touches to the preliminary agreement were negotiated privately by Schmidt, Schulmann, Giscard, Clappier, and French foreign minister François Poncet in Schmidt's Hamburg apartment on June 23, 1978. British skepticism of the plan had caused Couzens to quit the group earlier. Schmidt said fairly little about the plan to the press, but what he did say was sure to raise the hackles of the Bundesbank. It seems clear from an interview given to *Business Week* that Schmidt knew that the EMS plan included elements that would prove unacceptable to the Bundesbank. In describing the plan, he indicated:

> I could imagine additional instruments of monetary assistance, of broadening the existing instruments and extrapolating them into the long range field. . . . of course there are . . . some risks. . . . It might mean for Germany . . . that we have to sacrifice some of our reserves. *It might also mean that we have to expand our money supply somewhat more rapidly than we have done until now.*[16]

From the vantage point of the present, it appears foolish that Schmidt would have antagonized the Bundesbank so deliberately. It is important to consider, however, that the institutional importance of the Bundesbank was not nearly as great as it is today, especially in the issue area of international monetary politics. Although Schmidt realized that the Bundesbank would not like his initiative, he believed that if he presented the bank with a fait accompli, the Bundesbank would be unable to impede his work significantly. His miscalculation on this point reinforces the central argument of this book, that the importance of the Bundesbank has increased dramatically over time and rivals the prominence of the federal government in international monetary matters.

THE BREMEN ANNEX

Evidently, Schmidt had presented the French with significant concessions, including a pledge that Germany would reflate its economy as France disinflated. The preliminary agreement was presented to the other heads of states on the event of the July 6–7 Bremen summit. The summit did not change the preliminary agreement significantly, and the Schulmann-Clappier document was reprinted as the annex to the Bremen communiqué.

Three aspects of the Bremen annex were concessions to weaker-currency countries. The first was the statement that the "European Currency Unit (ECU) will be at the centre of the system; in particular it will be used as a means of settlement between EEC monetary authorities."[17] Because "at the centre of the system" was undefined, the ambiguity was probably deliberate, enabling the weaker-currency countries to have a different interpretation than stronger-currency countries. The French interpreted the phrase as meaning that the ECU would be the currency from which the ±2.25 percent bands were to be calculated, replacing the bilateral parities that existed in the Snake. Calculating the bands on a weighed average of all the Community currencies would decrease the number of times a weak currency was likely to cross the lower band and would increase the number of times the stronger currencies would cross the upper band.

The second concession involved the creation of a pool of European currency units (ECUs), or pooling of reserves. The annex called for each country to pledge to the EMCF a suggested amount of 20 percent of dollars and gold as well as a comparable amount of its currencies. These ECUs could then be borrowed and used to settle intervention obligations. Weaker-currency countries would be advantaged somewhat by this feature because they had fewer "hard" reserves; because a smaller absolute amount of their reserves were in dollars and gold, fewer of their reserves would be used to create ECUs, but they could borrow ECUs (and therefore the stronger-currency countries' hard reserves). Additionally, because part of each ECU created was backed to some extent by weaker currencies rather than hard stores of value like the dollar or gold, using the ECU might have the effect of increasing inflation. Since an overhaul of the credit mechanisms of the system was also under discussion, the entire package of ECU creation and credits was very much a concession.

The third concession involved the creation of the EMF, which the annex pledged would happen no later than two years following the inception of the EMS. Again the text was ambiguous, saying only that the EMF would take the place of the EMCF and not detailing the functions of the EMF. However, to the weaker-currency countries, the EMF was to be a supranational central bank, making European monetary policy. The advantage of this institution relative to the intergovernmental EMCF was that monetary policy would be less likely to be as strict as the Bundesbank's and each of the member states would have a voice in the policymaking.

Needless to say, each of these points was anathema to the Bundesbank and the other strong-currency central banks. The Bundesbank had successfully opposed some of these points in the EU Monetary Committee and the

Committee of Central Bank Governors, and it had not changed its position on these matters. In July after the Bremen summit, the Bundesbank began to fight back.

THE BUNDESBANK RESPONDS

Scarcely a week after the summit, on July 12, 1978, Emminger was invited to a special cabinet meeting to discuss the EMS details. There he gave the ministers a preview of his reservations about the Bremen communiqué. He noted that it would be impossible to return to a fixed exchange-rate system and, therefore, that realignments had to be simple and frequent. Furthermore, increasing international liquidity through overly generous financing arrangements and the EMF in particular had to be avoided at all costs, and the provision allowing for interventions in EU currencies would lead to the Bundesbank losing control over DM creation since most EU countries would likely intervene in the DM. Emminger left the meeting with the guarantee that the Bundesbank would be involved in the technical negotiations from that point on.

It was predictable that Emminger would be averse to the EMS initiative on the basis of his dislike and distrust of Schmidt and Emminger's predilection for floating regimes. However, the reservations about the EMS expressed by his former boss, Karl Klasen, showed that the Bundesbank was united in its aversion to the new proposals. Unlike the crises in the early 1970s, when the Bundesbank Central Bank Council had been split between those who wanted to isolate the German economy by floating (Emminger and a minority of other members) and those who wanted to maintain some form of exchange-rate commitments (Klasen), the new proposal struck most members of the Bundesbank as dangerous. Former president Klasen went on record with his reservations on July 14, saying: "I must admit that the Council decision that pleased me most was the agreement not to take a final decision, but to work out details in peace. I only hope that those concerned will approach their task with the utmost caution."[18] The new unity in the Bundesbank may have been due to the difficulties of the Snake. The Snake had made obvious what a system of "helping" weaker-currency states remain in an exchange-rate system would involve, and all of the Central Bank Council now knew it would involve significant market interventions on their part. This unity in the Bundesbank consolidated the institution's power and made it a force to be reckoned with.

Formulating the technical details of the Bremen annex was left to the EU Monetary Committee and the Committee of Central Bank Governors, both of which had Bundesbank representatives. For the technicians, the discussions could be divided into two categories: ECU-related problems and EMF-related problems. At the heart of the ECU discussion was what it would mean operationally to keep the ECU "at the centre of the system." The problem that Giscard d'Estaing and Schmidt had neatly sidestepped by this ambiguous phrase revolved around which currency should be the one to intervene when a currency crossed a band.

DEBATES OVER THE ECU-BASED SYSTEM

The Issue of Parities

The French and the Italian Committee members were adamant that the bands of the EMS be defined using the ECU rather than bilateral parities. The importance of that change was that two currencies would be unlikely to simultaneously cross bands, forcing both countries to intervene. Rather, the ECU-based system would allow one currency to diverge. Since the Snake had been subject to strains caused by the DM's upward movement, the ECU-based system was seen as more equitable in distributing the burdens of disequilibria.[19]

In addition, the central bankers in the two committees were all agreed that the system be made as flexible as possible with respect to parity changes. The French argued that making parity changes in relation to the ECU would be far less publicly visible, and hence politically charged, than making bilateral changes. For this reason, the use of the ECU would facilitate timely realignments.

The Bundesbank was completely opposed to an ECU-based parity system, saying that the bilateral parity system was more symmetrical (since two currencies reached their intervention bands simultaneously), and symmetry of obligations was one of the fundamental tenets of the proposed EMS. To some extent this complaint was disingenuous, since the obligation of the strong-currency countries was to sell strong currencies, whereas the weak-currency member states had to buy depreciating currencies with reserves, thereby decreasing their official reserves. This point was not lost on the negotiators, since the Snake had been based on the bilateral parity system. The French cited statistics indicating that three times out of four, disequilibria in the Snake had arisen because strong currencies had appreciated, not because weak currencies had depreciated.[20] The French negotiators were clearly well aware of the consequences of using the bilateral rather than ECU-based parity system.

The Bundesbank was also concerned that an ECU-based EMS would lead to an "inflation-community." Because the cumulative weights of the weaker-currency countries in the basket outweighed those with strong currencies, the bank was afraid that it would be called upon to support higher levels of domestic inflation by intervening to lessen the strength of the DM. The Bundesbank stated explicitly in its monthly report that "the harmonisation of inflation rates at a 'midway level' would be quite unacceptable to the Federal Republic of Germany."[21]

The conflict between the French and the Bundesbank's vision of the new system reinforces the argument that the original intentions of the French were not to achieve German levels of inflation. The fact that the French were quite insistent on the ECU-based EMS—a system that would have forced the EU member states to converge their inflation on a weighted average EU inflation rate rather than the lowest—confirms that the French government knew what effect the bilateral parity system would have and did *not* want to repeat the Snake experience. Therefore, although it is true that Prime Minister Barre wanted to reduce inflation and follow "Modell Deutschland" to some degree, the pivotal conflict about the bilateral versus the ECU-based system highlights the fact that France did not want to commit itself to achieving German inflation levels.

The issue of which system to use was resolved in the so-called Belgian compromise, which—as history would show—was less a compromise than a capitulation to the Bundesbank. The system would formally rely on the bilateral parities as the Snake had, but it would include the innovation of the "threshold of divergence," which was based on the ECU parities. When one country crossed the threshold of divergence, there was a "presumption" that the country would take appropriate action. There was, however, no *obligation* to intervene before the bilateral parities were reached. The Bundesbank took issue with the formulation of the problem, stating:

> Special importance is attached to the question of whether the Community countries will regard the triggering of the indicator as a reason to take action irrespective of the differential between their currencies in terms of stability or whether, during the envisioned consultations when the need actually arises, they will seek to distribute the burden of adjustment in such a way that the common objective of stability is taken into account. The Bundesbank has resisted all efforts to link the indicator of divergence to an obligation to take action regardless of the cause of the disequilibrium underlying the divergence and regardless of the requirements of stabilisation policy.[22]

The comments of the Bundesbank are further evidence of a trend in the history of monetary cooperation: the federal government would accept an international obligation only to be overruled by the Bundesbank's indications that it would not be bound by the commitment if domestic stability were compromised. Although there were technical problems with the

French proposal to base the system on the ECU, the Belgian compromise was a solution that kept the EMS negotiations from breaking down completely. From the Bundesbank's statements, it is clear that Germany would not have been able to accede to the French proposals,[23] and it is unlikely that France would have continued negotiating a system that so closely resembled the Snake without face-saving changes to aid weaker-currency countries.[24]

The European Monetary Fund

The second issue that threatened the negotiations was that of the EMF's role and the funds available to it. Here the Bundesbank had more leverage to enforce its position, since what was at stake was the very independence of the Bundesbank. Bundesbank resistance forced major modifications in the plans for the role and functions of the EMF. At the Copenhagen and Bremen summits, both Schmidt and Giscard d'Estaing had fully supported a supranational EMF, and French deputy negotiator Clappier suggested that the foundations for the EMF be created immediately after the inception of the EMS: "The transitional period, [Clappier] argued, was a time for 'running in' a system, the essential component of which had already been put into place, rather than for leisurely studies related to an indefinite future."[25] However, a plan to create a supranational structure that would be phased in during the transitional period would have been incompatible with the Bundesbank's intentions. Over half of an internal Bundesbank paper dated September 7, 1978, and summarizing the attitude of the Central Bank Council toward the EMS was related to issues of the EMF:

> No German reserves could be transferred to [the EMF] without special legislation and even if they were . . . the creation of such a fund should in no circumstances limit the autonomy of the Bundesbank in the sphere of monetary policy. [The Bundesbank Central Bank Council's] determination to contemplate no loss of sovereignty in the future was matched by their insistence on the greatest possible caution in devising transitional arrangements. . . . *The fundamental character of the Bundesbank's reservations on the proposals for an EMF and other related issues placed a severe constraint on the discussions of these problems.*[26]

Schmidt's memoirs corroborate that it was the Bundesbank that prevented the creation of a supranational EMF:

> France, under Giscard, was prepared to accept the loss of sovereignty [because of the EMF], which stood at the end of the road; the Bundesbank and many of the German economic professors who considered themselves knowledgeable on this topic were not prepared to accept this (and are still not prepared).[27]

The Bundesbank couched its opposition to the EMF in a legal argument over how the EMS could be created. If the EMS included the EMF, the EMS would, in the Bundesbank's opinion, require ratification according to Article 236 of the Treaty of Rome. By provoking the debate about the legal basis of the EMS, the Bundesbank and others interested in retarding the move to greater monetary cooperation convinced the French and the Italians, who had been pushing hard for immediate establishment of the EMF, to postpone its creation. At stake in the legal argument was whether the EMS should be incorporated into the Treaty of Rome under Article 235 or 236, the principal difference being that Article 236 required ratification of the agreed amendment "by all the member states in accordance with their respective constitutional arrangements," whereas Article 235 required only the approval of Council, acting unanimously on the basis of a proposal from the Commission.

The fate of the EMF was sealed when a majority of the Council's members opined that, legally, even if Article 235 were used for the founding of the EMS, the second phase of the EMS as set out in the agreement—in particular, the provisions for the EMF—would require ratification by all the national governments. Despite their acceptance of the fact that the EMF could not be established immediately, the French and Italians wanted concrete proposals for the creation of the EMF to be included in the treaty. A compromise of sorts was worked out to the effect that institutional questions would be put off, but the language in the December 5, 1978, Brussels European Council resolution was unambiguous in its intention to create the EMF soon:

> We remain firmly resolved to consolidate, not later than two years after the start of the scheme [EMS], into a final system the provisions and procedures thus created. This system will entail the creation of the European Monetary Fund as announced in the conclusions of the European Council meeting at Bremen on 6 and 7 July 1978 as well as the full utilization of the ECU as a reserve asset and a means of settlement. It will be based on adequate legislation at the Community as well as the national level.[28]

Implicit in this statement was the knowledge that creation of the EMF concurrently with the EMS would have been politically impossible due to resistance from the Bundesbank and other member states. Despite France and Italy's efforts to have a thorough discussion on the EMF at that time, other countries—including the Netherlands and Denmark—balked, and the matter was put off. A further concession to the Bundesbank was the concluding sentence in the European Council resolution, which acknowledged that the second phase would be accomplished in accordance with Article 236, as the Bundesbank had demanded.

With the role of the EMF settled for the moment, the issue of funds for the new institution was discussed. Again, the Bundesbank exercised its newfound clout to prevent the EMF from having any reserves at its disposal. The creation of ECUs became a major discussion point, and once again the member states split into their habitual subgroups in advocating one or another proposal. The EU Monetary Committee had prepared five interpretations of what the phrase in the Bremen annex, "created against deposits," could mean: deposits, swaps, collateral, trust contracts, or definitive transfers. At issue was which organization would control the hard reserves against which the ECUs were created. The Bundesbank and the Dutch central bank were adamant that only a deposit or a swap would be accepted, thus allowing control to remain with the member state central banks.

> Even if [a definitive transfer] had been the intention of those who drafted the Annex, it was quickly apparent that neither the Bundesbank nor several other central banks were prepared to contemplate more than either the first or the second interpretations, and by the beginning of September if not earlier even M. Clappier was ready to concede that for the time being at least it would probably be necessary to equate the ECU with "swaps."[29]

The results of the discussions about the ECU made the EMF little more than a renamed EMCF and should be viewed as one of the major examples of how the Bundesbank changed the Bremen annex in a substantive way to the detriment of the weaker-currency countries.

THE EMMINGER LETTER

The most telling fact about the relationship between the Bundesbank and the federal government was the November 1978 letter that Bundesbank president Emminger sent to Schmidt just before the final negotiations of the EMS at the Brussels summit. Despite the myriad of concessions and reinterpretations that the weaker-currency countries had made to stronger-currency members, principally Germany, the Bundesbank was still unwilling to commit the DM to the system. Bundesbank support of the EMS was essential because the Bundesbank had to sign the documents establishing the operating procedures for the system. In fact, Bundesbank law required two signatures. To obtain the necessary approval of the Bundesbank, Schmidt agreed to an intervention "opt-out" proposed in a letter sent by Emminger. Explicitly, the letter confirmed that in an extreme case, the Bundesbank would suspend intervention in the currency markets if domestic monetary stability was threatened by EMS intervention obligations.[30] This explicitly contravened Article 2.2 of the operating procedures, which stated that "interventions shall be unlimited at the compulsory intervention rates." The letter also confirmed the Bundesbank's resistance to the EMF by reiterating its call that any movement toward the second phase of the EMS (the establishment of the EMF) would be done under Article 236 and require the appropriate ratification, meaning, in Germany's case, the agreement of the Bundestag. The Emminger letter has never been released publicly. However, Emminger's memoirs describe the letter in detail (see Figure 3.1). The Emminger letter confirms the existence of a significant difference of opinion between the government and the Bundesbank despite all the changes that had been made.[31] The letter also shows that the Bundesbank, although it could not impede the multilateral monetary cooperation proposed by the government, could set the terms of those agreements.

NEGOTIATIONS WITH THE FRENCH

The semiannual meeting between Chancellor Schmidt and President Giscard d'Estaing on September 14–15, 1978, at Aachen was regarded by the weaker-currency countries, Italy and Britain, as the point at which the French capitulated to the Germans on the technical details of the system. The French were probably responding more to the demands of the Bundesbank than to those of the federal government because Schmidt had received the Bundesbank's reservations a day before the meeting. Among the points that President Emminger stressed in his preliminary September letter to Schmidt was his insistence that the new system "could not be established through the harmonization of inflation rates at an average rate, but must be underpinned with a strict currency, political and economic discipline."[32] Emminger explicitly communicated the Bundesbank's reservations, recommending that credit facilities be restricted, intervention obligations of the Bundesbank be limited, and the system be based on the bilateral parity grid. The chancellor's room for maneuver was thus greatly reduced.

At the Aachen summit, the French and German negotiators agreed that the system should be based on bilateral parities but that the ECU would serve as an indicator of divergence. The durability of the new system would be "ensured above all by the commitment of all concerned to anti-inflationary policies."[33] Ludlow cited evidence to suggest that "French officials . . . would have liked certain parts of the text and in particular the phrases referring to the possible use of the ECU as an indicator of divergence to have been more definite."[34] Further, Clappier argued in the Committee of Central Bank Governors for a "rigorous interpretation of the obligations that would arise if the divergence indicator showed that a currency was out of line."[35] However, although the French had been forced to compromise some of their deeply held tenets for the new system, they

Figure 3.1 The Emminger Letter

Of special importance for us were the agreements between the federal government and the Bundesbank that related specifically to the guarantee of autonomy and its monetary policies. They are summarized in a letter that I wrote in November 1978 to the federal government. The basic contents were:

a. There is agreement between the Bundesbank and the federal government that a final arrangement for EMS, that is, the proposed second phase, can only be considered under Article 236 of the EMS-Agreement (that is, through an international agreement to be ratified by all participants). This also pertains particularly to the creation of a European Monetary Fund and the potentially final step of giving reserves to it.

b. The Bundesbank has received the assurances of the federal government that it will only agree to those arrangements under Article 235 of the EC Agreement, which will safeguard the autonomy of the Bundesbank.

c. The monetary autonomy of the Bundesbank would be particularly in danger if the Bundesbank had excessive responsibility to intervene when there are strong imbalances in the future EMS that would threaten the monetary stability. This would make fulfilling the legal responsibility of the Bundesbank impossible. The Bundesbank assumes, on the basis of multiple reassurances of the chancellor and finance minister, that the federal government will guard the Bundesbank from such an exigency either by a correction in the central rate in EMS or even through a temporary suspension of the intervention requirement.

The decisive point for the policy of stability was certainly the Bundesbank's *limitation on the duty to intervene* [emphasis in original] to an acceptable degree. In the debate in the Bundestag about the newly established EMS on December 6, 1978, Economics Minister [Otto] Lambsdorff supported the commitment of the federal government by elaborating: "the adjustments of exchange rates have always been the purview of the federal government, not the Bundesbank. In the responsibility of the Bundesbank are the duties to intervene and the opportunity not to carry out interventions if it believes, with respect to the money supply and other means, that it cannot do so." Moreover, already in October 1978 Finance Minister [Hans] Matthöfer explained in response to a question about EMS: "It is essential that the Bundesbank keep control over the German money supply." An affirmative majority vote in the Central Bank Council could be obtained only after we were sufficiently protected through our negotiations with Bonn with respect to the intervention obligations.

Source: Emminger (1986), pp. 361–362. Translated by Dorothee Heisenberg.

clearly continued to try to interpret those aspects that were emerging in the new system in the most favorable light. A November 22, 1978, article in *Le Monde* proclaimed that "the concessions of Bonn facilitate the setting up of the monetary system" and enumerated the concessions of the federal government: the usage of the ECU as divergence indicator and the credits attached to the defense of the EMS. The same article noted:

In effect, the countries with economies and currencies that are on the whole weaker wanted to obtain the assurance that the EMS would be . . . more symmetrical than the Snake and that Germany was devoted to the idea of actively playing the game. . . . [The Germans] came sufficiently far to reassure [the weaker countries] and to show that this time their intention was truly to commit to the operation with the constraints which it implies.[36]

It is likely that if the French had known at that time that the indicator of divergence would be unused and that the EMF would never come into being, Giscard d'Estaing might not have joined the EMS or lobbied Italy and Britain to join.

It is of great importance that France maintained its support for the EMS initiative even after the Aachen summit had stripped away several of France's conditions. France had represented the interests of the weaker-currency countries in the beginning of the negotiations, and to some extent, Italy and Britain continued to rely on France to negotiate their position vis-à-vis the stronger-currency countries like Germany and the Netherlands. Moreover, if France and Germany united to create a new system, it was likely to succeed, whereas if either of them was not involved, the system's survival chances were minimal. French support, therefore, was essential to the creation of the EMS, and it behooved the German government to keep France interested.

By the end of September, the French government was in the position of defending a proposal and lobbying the other countries for an agreement that bore considerably less resemblance to the Bremen annex than to the Snake. All along, the members of the Trésor who had been negotiating France's position had privately felt that French support for the initiative was misguided.[37] However, lacking the autonomy of the Bundesbank, they continued to work toward achievement of their superior's wishes. At the higher levels of the French government, it would have been difficult, if not politically impossible, to back out of the agreement that Giscard d'Estaing had so publicly endorsed at the summits and for which he hoped to get credit for reasserting France's place in the EU.

British Fears of Exclusion

October and November 1978 were taken up primarily by finalizing the technical details and lobbying the other EU member states to join. The efforts were concentrated primarily on Italy and Britain, although by early November it was evident that Britain was unlikely to join.[38] There were encouraging signs that Ireland was willing to break its currency union with Britain to join, and Germany concentrated its efforts on persuading Ireland that it would be compensated for such a decision.

The British Treasury had been suspicious of the EMS since the Bremen summit, but it nominally kept the door open to participation right up until December, when it officially declined to enter the exchange-rate mechanism (ERM) but agreed to participate in the EMS. One participant cited the decision at the Aachen summit to use the bilateral parities rather than the ECU as the watershed in Britain's decision. Arguing that the ECU-parity grid would have been less disinflationary, the Treasury considered the issue the "litmus test of the workability of the system," and when it was compromised because "the Germans were having none of it," declined to participate.[39]

The British Government published its reservations about the EMS in a green paper that stressed the importance of symmetry of intervention obligations, greater credit supports for intervention, and means for improved growth and employment.[40] Despite the government's professed desire to lower inflation, linking to the DM was considered far too disinflationary by the chancellor of the exchequer, Denis Healey. A link to a basket of currencies in which the pound would make up 13.3 percent, the French franc 19.8 percent, and the Italian lira 9.5 percent would be sufficiently inflationary to make membership palatable for a Labour government.[41] The green paper explicitly stated that an EMS that the government could join should "provide a basis for improved economic growth and higher employment in the Community, rather than impose further constraints on growth and employment . . . [and] for this reason, the system should impose obligations on its stronger members symmetrical with those falling on its weaker members."[42] Essentially, the British government made its membership in the EMS contingent on the very factors that France had compromised away in September.

Facing an election in the coming months, the Callaghan government was not sanguine about being excluded from the EMS. For this reason, it continued to negotiate and to profess its desire in principle to join. "The Government cannot yet reach their own conclusion on whether it would be in the best interests of the UK to join the exchange-rate regime of the EMS as it finally emerges from the negotiations," it stated as late as November 24, 1978.[43] By that time, it was clear that the EMS would be created even if Britain did not join, and the government was keenly aware of what abstaining from the regime could mean. The government could envision the EMS without Britain strengthening the Franco-German alliance, diminishing Britain's influence over decisions such as CAP reform, and weakening Britain's position in the EU budget dispute—thus repeating much of the history of Britain's relationship with the Community.

In an article based on an exclusive briefing from Callaghan three days before the Brussels summit, *The Guardian* explained the prime minister's motivation:

Mr Callaghan, increasingly fearful of the consequences of British isolation through exclusion from the proposed European monetary system was given the widest possible negotiating brief yesterday by the Cabinet. At the EEC summit . . . he will be free to embrace any solution save complete and immediate membership of the system.[44]

Although Callaghan remained critical of the system, fear of a Franco-German axis and increasing exclusion from European initiatives finally drove him to accept membership in the EMS, but not the ERM. This so-called halfway house was invented by Callaghan and meant that the pound would be part of the ECU but not subject to the ERM bands. Nor was Callaghan's fear unreasonable: once Britain had declined entry into the system, Germany, in the side-payment discussions with Italy and Ireland, refused to make any deals that could potentially benefit Britain as well. These deals included grants through the EU Regional Fund and modifications to the CAP, both of which were of interest to Italy.

SIDE PAYMENTS FOR ITALY

Unlike Britain, Italy and Ireland were motivated to join the EMS less by the fear of exclusion from the initiative than by side payments that accrued to each. Ireland was too small to have pretensions of changing the procedures and rules during the negotiation process and therefore insisted on side payments to join. Nominally, the side payments were to compensate Ireland for the costs of the break with the British pound and the dislocation costs caused by the EMS. Within the Community, there was agreement that the Irish were "the deserving poor" and that the amounts needed to buy off Ireland's entry were small enough to be uncontroversial.[45]

In Italy, the situation was more complicated. The foreign ministry was more inclined to see benefits in joining ("If we did not participate in the EMS, this would show that we are unwilling to accept the challenge . . . of being a fully European country"[46]), whereas the Banca d'Italia had more reservations about the suitability of the system for Italy. The Banca d'Italia required certain conditions in terms of the flexibility of the system, and it "attributed the utmost importance to the presence of Britain in the system, both because with Sterling in, the forces of speculation would not concentrate on the lira in times of crisis, and for more general economic and political reasons."[47] Overall, the Italians wanted the EMS to be looser in its general characteristics than the system that had emerged from the Bremen summit, and the negotiators emphasized the symmetry of obligations, the size of credit facilities, the aversion to a parity-grid system, and the importance of "parallel measures" to compensate for the economic costs that Italy would incur by joining the system. In September the Banca d'Italia laid out its criteria for the new system for the EU Monetary Committee and Committee of Central Bank Governors, which included as its key element a wider bilateral band in combinations with the narrower ECU band. This latter element of the system was designed to make the EMS more flexible without making it less disinflationary (if the intervention obligations from the divergence indicator were taken seriously). This proposal, like most of the British and Italian demands, was ignored by the German and French negotiators. Essentially, the October-November negotiations systematically excluded most, if not all, of Italy's demands on the structure of the system, despite the tough language of Treasury Minister Filippo Pandolfi:

> One thing is certain as far as the position of the Italian Government is concerned: we cannot and will not be satisfied by formal changes hardly sufficient to conceal a reality which would be that of the Snake. It is essential for us to achieve a symmetry of intervention obligations between strong and weak currencies; it is further essential that the system fits all Community currencies and is therefore endowed with adequate elements of flexibility, of which one is certainly the width of the margin.[48]

It should be noted that the demand for an adequate width of the margin was not opposed by the Bundesbank, which had been against Italian participation until Italy's economy converged with the other economies anyway.

In a bilateral meeting between the Bundesbank and the Italian ministers and Banca d'Italia officials on September 16, 1978, the Italian delegation attempted to win some concessions, including a generalized wider bilateral band and compulsory intervention after the divergence indicator had been tripped. Emminger laid down the law for the Italian visitors:

> [He had] no objections to the wider band for those who wanted it, but, as far as he knew neither the British . . . nor the French were in the least interested; a flat no to any obligation of intra-marginal interventions arising from early warning, with a reminder that his Chancellor and the French President had already reached an agreement on this point at the Aachen meeting; and, in an aside, some surprise for Italy's decision to join and a great deal of skepticism on the workability of the system.[49]

Nevertheless, on October 10, Treasury Minister Pandolfi repeated Italy's minimum requirements for joining in a speech before parliament, which included the exchange-rate agreements, the EMF, and "parallel measures"—measures designed to compensate Italy for the costs of joining the EMS. He stated explicitly that all three elements had to be met before Italy would join and that concessions in one could not be compensated by the other two.[50] By November, it was clear to the Italians that none of their proposals would be incorporated into the new exchange-rate system and that the EMF would be postponed for two years. The government was faced with the choice of whether to join or not, given that the new system was no kinder to the weaker-currency countries than the Snake had been.

To make the decision to join more palatable to the Italians, Germany inquired what monetary inducements Italy would consider sufficient to induce Prime Minister Giulio Andreotti to join. Commission president Roy Jenkins even went so far as to press Andreotti to "name a figure" in order to get Italy into the EMS. Italy was primarily interested in grants through the Regional Fund or reform of the CAP, both of which, though they benefited Italy, would also benefit Britain. German government representatives were adamant that the British should not benefit from any EMS-related reforms unless they became full members of the system. That left only loans to be used as inducements to Italy.

The final negotiations for the side payments were made during the Brussels summit. Here again it was evident exactly what was transpiring: the Germans were trying to buy Italy's accession, but the French had decided that the price was becoming too high. "France cannot upset her own financial arrangements in order to ensure the adhesion of those for whom membership ought to be an act of political will rather than a question of cash," Giscard d'Estaing is reported to have told his colleagues.[51] After the original German proposals had been whittled down, a grudging acceptance from France was reached for a package containing loans of up to 1 billion EUAs per year for five years with an interest subsidy of 3 percent. Two-thirds of the loan went to Italy and the remainder to Ireland. This was not as much as Ireland or Italy had hoped for, and both came away from the summit without making commitments. Germany, knowing that Ireland was a special case, secretly negotiated a "sweetener"—a £50 million grant funded by Germany, Belgium, Denmark, the Netherlands, and France, whereupon Prime Minister Jack Lynch formally announced that Ireland would join the EMS. The Italians formally announced their entry into the system on December 12 without receiving any additional funds after their negotiating in Brussels.

CONCLUSION

The negotiation of the EMS demonstrates that Schmidt and Giscard d'Estaing had very different motivations to cooperate. Schmidt was concerned that Germany's ties with the dollar were appreciating its currency vis-à-vis its European trading partners to the detriment of its export sector. Giscard d'Estaing wanted to reclaim the French leadership role in the EU. Although he and Barre concurred that French inflation levels must be brought down, Giscard d'Estaing did not want to achieve German levels of inflation but rather wanted the EU member states to converge on a weighted average inflation rate.

Contrary to their initial, stated objectives, France and the other weaker-currency countries eventually joined a system that closely resembled the Snake in fundamental aspects and thus continued to impose the costs of economic adjustment on the weaker-currency countries. One should ask, therefore, why these countries voluntarily joined a system that was structured contrary to their stated objectives. To understand this apparent contradiction, it is essential to focus on Germany's role in the negotiations. In fact, the German government essentially used a bait-and-switch tactic to get the commitment of France to the system, and side-payments and threats of exclusion to motivate the other weaker-currency countries to join.

Initially, Schmidt promised many concessions for weaker-currency countries, thus tempting Giscard d'Estaing to cosponsor the initiative. Once the French were engaged, the initiative took on a legitimacy greater than the stalled talks on monetary integration had. It became increasingly difficult for Giscard d'Estaing to back out of the system when the rules and procedures were changed by the Bundesbank. It would have been difficult to maintain the fiction of EU economic leadership if France was unwilling to participate in the EMS (which it had cosponsored) just because a couple of the technical points had gone against French preferences.

The institutional conflict between the Bundesbank and the federal government is essential in explaining how the federal government was able to change the terms of cooperation so dramatically between the Bremen and Brussels summits. The statutory independence of the Bundesbank made all the difference. For example, officials within the Trésor thought the EMS initiative a strange idea, but as civil servants, they had to carry out their superior's wishes. In contrast, the Bundesbank had the institutional ability to insist that changes be made.

The major effect of the Bundesbank on the federal government's negotiating position was to dramatically decrease the number of acceptable agreements. Although the federal government was able to enter into agreements—that is, commit the federal republic to cooperate—the content of that cooperation was largely determined by the Bundesbank. Thus it was largely Bundesbank criticisms that forced the changes in the agreement between the Bremen and Brussels summits.

It is unclear how deliberately Schmidt used a bait-and-switch ruse to get his friend Giscard d'Estaing to cosponsor the EMS. The bulk of the evidence suggests that Schmidt indeed knew that many aspects of his original proposals would be rejected by the Bundesbank, and hence he negotiated in secret for as long as possible. It appears, however, that he misjudged both the strength of opposition within the Bundesbank and his government's ability to withstand opposition from the bank. In earlier policy conflicts between the government and the Bundesbank, the government was able to exploit divisions within the Bundesbank and to prevail. Moreover, the Bundesbank had taken the position of supporting international agreements in these earlier conflicts, a position clearly not within the mandate of the Bundesbank and thus easy for the government to override.

Once the Bundesbank became united on a position that would always privilege domestic stability over international commitments, the Bundesbank's institutional mandate made it more difficult for the government to ignore its "recommendations." Schmidt thus became the first chancellor to have to make accommodations to his own policies in light of Bundesbank opposition to them.

Over the next ten years, the EMS would overcome several challenges to become a stable regime, but it remained inhospitable to weaker-currency countries. Why these countries were unable to change the regime despite its unwanted and detrimental consequences to their economic policies will be explored in the following chapter.

NOTES

1. In this chapter, the word "system" is used to distinguish the original rules of the new form of monetary cooperation from the EMS "regime" that gradually evolved over time to have its own workings and norms.

2. See, for example, Goodman (1992); Loriaux (1991), pp. 252–255; Walsh (1994), p. 243; Barrell (1990), pp. 64–72; Giavazzi and Pagano (1988), pp. 1055–1082.

3. Jenkins (1978).

4. See also the Duisenberg Plan, the Tindemans Report, the Marjolin Report, and the Fourcade Plan.

5. Author's interview, March 1994.

6. For Schmidt, the sentiment was anti-Carter rather than anti–United States, but it served the purpose of bringing the two leaders together.

7. Schmidt (1990), p. 249.

8. The second-largest buyer of German exports was the Netherlands in 1975, taking 10 percent of Germany's exports. Belgium and Luxembourg combined were third, with 7.6 percent. Over time, the importance of Italy's market has grown for Germany, while that of the Netherlands has declined, and the Belgium/Luxembourg market is stable. As Table 3.1 makes clear, weaker-currency markets have become more important over time to Germany, and the EU as a whole takes a greater percentage of German exports than Germany's five largest markets.

9. Story (1981); Loriaux (1991).

10. Ludlow (1982), p. 88; Schmidt disputed that he was the originator of the idea (see Schmidt 1990, p. 249). Giscard d'Estaing actually took credit for the initiative by saying, "We spoke [about a new system] with Chancellor Schmidt. I felt he was reticent. He didn't believe in the possibility of success." Giscard d'Estaing (1988), p. 142.

11. Ludlow (1982), p. 96.

12. Ibid., p. 104.

13. Ibid., p. 95.

14. In his memoirs, Schmidt listed the ministries from which he expected support of his plan and wrote, "from the Bundesbank, however, one could expect not only criticism, but also carefully orchestrated resistance." See Schmidt (1990), p. 251.

15. Giscard d'Estaing wrote, "Emminger, is hostile to the project. . . . His point of view is shared by the quasi-totality of German bankers." See Giscard d'Estaing (1988), p. 143.

16. *Business Week*, June 28, 1978, emphasis added.

17. The Bremen annex is reproduced in van Ypersele and Koeune (1985), p. 121.

18. *Die Zeit*, July 14, 1978.

19. For greater detail on the technical aspects of this point, see Ludlow (1982), pp. 158ff.

20. Ibid., p. 153.

21. Deutsche Bundesbank, *Monthly Report*, March 1979, p. 18.

22. Deutsche Bundesbank, *Annual Report*, 1978, p. 55.

23. "The harmonization of inflation rates at a 'midway level' would be quite unacceptable to the Federal Republic of Germany." See Deutsche Bundesbank *Monthly Report,* March 1979, p. 18.

24. "We will not succeed at making a European monetary system function as long as the weakest currencies alone have to support the weight of maintaining the divergence." See Giscard d'Estaing (1988), p. 142.

25. Ludlow (1982), p. 166.

26. Ibid., emphasis added.

27. Schmidt (1990), p. 261.

28. Van Ypersele and Koeune (1985), p. 122.

29. Ibid., p. 169.

30. Although the Bundesbank didn't make public reference to the Emminger letter during the 1992 EMS crisis, the reports of a secret meeting between Kohl and Schlesinger contained references that Helmut Schlesinger explicitly referred to the letter during that meeting. See Eichengreen and Wyplosz (1993).

31. Ellen Kennedy (1991) indicated that the negotiations between the Bundesbank and the federal government over EMS became so ugly that Schmidt threatened to change the Bundesbank Law. The Bundesbank, however, denied that this threat had ever been made.

32. *Der Spiegel*, November 6, 1978, p. 23.

33. Ludlow (1982), p. 184.

34. Ibid.

35. Ibid., p. 185.

36. *Le Monde*, November 22, 1978, p. 1.

37. Author's interview with French official, March 1994.

38. *Times* (London), November 4, 1978, p. 1.

39. Author's interview, March 1994.

40. The European Monetary System, Cmnd. 7405, November 24, 1978, cited in *Keesing's Contemporary Archives*, March 23, 1979, p. 29512.

41. The original weights on March 13, 1979, were DM, 33 percent; Dutch florin, 10.5 percent; Belgian franc, 9.2 percent; Danish krona, 3.1 percent; and Irish punt, 1.2 percent. See van Ypersele and Koeune (1985), p. 58.

42. *Keesing's Contemporary Archives*, March 23, 1979, p. 29512.

43. Ibid., p. 29514.
44. *The Guardian*, December 1, 1978.
45. The Irish initially asked for a £650 million grant over five years and eventually received a grant of £275 million over five years.
46. Foreign Minister Renato Ruggiero, cited in Spaventa (1980), p. 69.
47. Ibid., p. 70.
48. Quoted in ibid., p. 76.
49. Ibid., p. 78.
50. Ibid., p. 76.
51. Ludlow (1982), p. 265.

4

The Bundesbank
Prevents Change

As we have seen, Germany and France created a new exchange-rate system that was quite advantageous to Germany, largely as a result of the Bundesbank's involvement in the later stages of the negotiations. Time and again, critical technical points about the system's functioning were decided on Germany's terms. Once the system was instituted, the Bundesbank continued to dominate the agenda and to prevent changes in the system that would have rectified the asymmetry between weak and strong currencies. In examining why France and Italy did not leave the EMS once it became obvious that further institutional change was unlikely, it is useful to explore the transformation of the EMS from a system to a regime with its own norms.

The transformation and increasing credibility of the system is important for understanding the heightened domestic stature and international importance of the Bundesbank. The EMS's character changed during these years; not only did the system become more stable, with fewer realignments and greater economic convergence of the participants, but it also became a serious force in the monetary relations between European countries. Whereas scholars writing in 1980 and 1981 were cautious in their assessments of the EMS's usefulness, by 1987 the economists and politicians tended to view the EMS as a viable institution that had proved to be a stabilizing influence in turbulent economic times. Moreover, by 1990 some considered it stable enough to build on as a stepping-stone to monetary union. The acceptance by the weaker-currency states of the constraints of the EMS caused the transformation from a system to a regime. More important, the resulting convergence and the new norms of the EMS had the unexpected consequences of institutionalizing the status of the Bundesbank as primus inter pares and legitimizing the Bundesbank's policies. By giving the Bundesbank greater institutional credibility and stature, the other member states elevated the Bundesbank's *domestic* stature to the same level as the federal government. Interinstitutional conflicts thereby grew more frequent, and the Bundesbank became more skeptical of international cooperation.

EMS STABILITY AFTER A SLOW START

The EMS had been scheduled to begin January 1, 1979. However, the French government prevented the inauguration of the system on that date in order to press its demands for reform of the CAP. The issue was arcane and only tangentially related to the EMS. It is unclear why the French picked December 1978 to make an issue of their CAP grievances. Perhaps Giscard d'Estaing, having realized that he had, in essence, cosponsored the Snake II, thought he could at least gain some ground on the intractable conflict over the CAP. Or perhaps he thought he could hold the EMS hostage for domestic political gain. For whatever reason, he did not intercede in the squabbles of the EU agricultural ministers. Why the issue was resolved a few months later when the French finance minister withdrew the "reserve" he had put on the EMS without having achieved any of his CAP demands also remains mysterious. Nevertheless, with little fanfare the system commenced operation on March 13, 1979.

Notwithstanding this inauspicious beginning, the EMS proved relatively stable in the first two years. This stability is all the more remarkable because in 1979 the Bundesbank increased interest rates five times to deal with the effects of the second oil shock, a policy that received criticism from the EMS member states. The Belgians, in particular, accused the Bundesbank of trying to destabilize the EMS, and they and others took their protests to the European Council. The policy of the Bundesbank was criticized by various domestic and international actors as too restrictive for the given circumstances. In turn, the Bundesbank blamed the federal government for the need to maintain high interest rates, citing the budget deficit and the lax fiscal policy government had adopted to deal with the oil shock.[1]

Only two realignments occurred in 1979 (see Table 4.1) and they involved just one currency, the Danish krone, which devalued 9.7 percent against the DM and 7.7 percent against the other currencies. The other member states were able to stem currency outflows through the use of capital controls and market intervention, and no further realignments of other parities took place until March 22, 1981. The stability of the EMS in the first two years was not due, however, to inherent mechanisms that made the EMS more stable than the Snake had been. Indeed, the divergence indicator rarely went off, and contrary to the expectations of the weaker-currency countries, the upper divergence threshold was crossed only once

Table 4.1 EMS Realignments

Date	Currency Realignment	Date	Currency Realignment
September 24, 1979	DM +2.0%	January 12, 1987	DM +3.0%
	DK −2.9%		NG +3.0%
November 30, 1979	DK −4.8%		BB +2.0%
March 23, 1981	IL −6.0%	June 19, 1989	SP enters (±6%)
October 5, 1981	DM +5.5%	January 8, 1990	IL −3.67%
	NG +5.5%		Enters narrow
	FF −3.0%		bands
	IL −3.0%	October 5, 1990	BP enters (±6%)
February 22, 1982	BF −8.5%	April 6, 1992	PE enters (±6%)
	DK −3.0%	September 13, 1992	IL −3.5%
June 14, 1982	DM +4.25%		All others +3.5%
	NG +4.25%	September 16, 1992	BP leaves
	IL −2.75%		IL leaves
	FF −5.75%		SP −5.0%
March 21, 1983	DM +5.5%	November 22, 1992	SP −6.0%
	NG +3.5%		PE −6.0%
	DK +2.5%	January 30, 1993	IP −10.0%
	BF +1.5%	May 14, 1993	SP −8.0%
	FF −2.5%		PE −6.5%
	IL −2.5%	August 2, 1993	ERM bands
	IP −3.5%		widened to ±15%
July 20, 1985	IL −6.0%		DM-NG bands
	All others +2.0%		remain ±2.25%
April 7, 1986	DM +3.0%	January 7, 1995	AS enters
	NG +3.0%	March 6, 1995	SP −7.0%
	DK +1.0%		PE −3.5%
	BF +1.0%	October 12, 1996	FM enters
	FF −3.0%	November 24, 1996	IL reenters
August 4, 1986	IP −8.0%	March 14, 1998	IP +3.0%
			GD enters

Source: Horst Ungerer et al. "European Monetary System: Developments and Perspective" (Washington, D.C.: International Monetary Fund, 1990), Table 3, p. 54; and *Financial Times,* various years.

Note: Currency abbreviations: AS–Austrian schilling; BF–Belgian franc; BP–British pound; DK–Danish krone; DM–deutsche mark; FM–Finnish markka; FF–French franc; GD–Greek drachma; IL–Italian lira; IP–Irish pound; NG–Dutch guilder; PE–Portugese escudo; SP–Spanish peseta.

(by the Danish krone).[2] The primary reason for this stability, according to the Bank for International Settlements, was the weakness of the DM. This situation was not likely to continue indefinitely.

The Bundesbank, which had been fearful of the EMS's obligations generally, took note of the first realignments, commenting that "these adjustments in central rates at least reduced the danger inherent in every fixed rate system of transmitting inflationary stimuli to other countries."[3] It warned, however, that "up to the present no progress has been made towards the harmonization of economic developments on the basis of a high level of monetary stability, such as is necessary if the EMS is to prove durable."[4] And it maintained its critique of the plan for the EMF:

> The "qualitative jump" to the final stage of the EMS requires a new legal basis, both at Community and at national level, and this in turn means that it will be essential for national parliaments to deal with this question. From the point of view of the Bundesbank, when designing the institutional framework of the Fund and further developing the ECU only structures that are compatible in every respect with the creation of a zone of stability in Europe should be chosen.[5]

ATTEMPTS AT INSTITUTIONAL PROGRESS

The potential establishment of the EMF was the Bundesbank's greatest fear once the EMS had functioned for a year. In its 1980 annual report, the Bundesbank grudgingly admitted that its fears about the intervention obligations of the EMS might have been overblown:

> Owing to the restrictive monetary policy being pursued elsewhere, the EMS has not become a source of monetary inflation within the Community, as had to be feared originally in view of the intervention obligations and the greatly enlarged credit facilities in the system.[6]

The bank remained, however, resolutely opposed to the EMF and was able to prevent progress on this issue because it was directly involved in all proposals through its membership in the Monetary Committee and the Committee of Central Bank Governors. It was successful in stalling the EMF, thus removing the immediate threat to its autonomy. In December 1980, the European Council, following the recommendations of the Committee of Central Bank Governors, extended by two years the period of the initial, noninstitutional phase of the EMS. This had the (perhaps) unanticipated consequence of fixing the EMS rules in their transitional structures and giving Germany and others a reason to reject any proposal to improve functioning of the EMS on the grounds that it belonged to the institutional phase that had been postponed by common agreement.[7]

STALLING THE EUROPEAN MONETARY FUND

Evidence suggests that the Bundesbank was the major obstacle to the further institutionalization of the EMS. Former EU Monetary Committee chairman Jean-Yves Haberer indicates that the Bonn government was in favor of the EMF, but that the Bundesbank was against it.[8] Further evidence comes from a French memorandum on the revitalization of the Community presented by the minister for European affairs.

The French Government recommends . . . making greater borrowing facilities available. . . . An attempt should also be made to lessen the deflationary effect in Europe of the third major oil price rise which resulted from the recent trend of the dollar. . . . In the monetary field, where the EMS has been proving its usefulness over the past two years, the French Government is anxious that work now under way in the Community should very soon lead to new plans to facilitate transition to a further stage. It would confine itself to stating one obvious fact: while it is true that the EMS will function more effectively if member states' economies follow a similar pattern, it is also true that the discipline imposed by participation in the system is a powerful incentive to convergence of economic policies and therefore paves the way for future progress.[9]

As this memo makes clear, the French were interested in progress toward the EMF and maintained their traditional monetarist position. The Bundesbank, however, prevented any proposals from being agreed upon in the Monetary Committee. Indeed, two months later, the Economic and Financial Affairs Council (ECOFIN) concluded on December 14, 1981, that "it was not possible as yet to set a date on the transition to the institutional phase and in particular the creation of a European Monetary Fund as well as the permanent transfer of reserves to that Fund." It became clear that a compromise on the EMF was unlikely to be found in the Monetary Committee. On February 15, 1982, ECOFIN witnessed "the usual split between those for whom the attainment of better convergence must precede any significant reinforcement of the EMS [Germany], and those who hope that strengthening the EMS will facilitate the efforts toward more convergence."[10]

In March 1982, the Commission, seeing that progress toward institutionalizing the EMS was lagging, proposed four areas of technical progress: (1) the creation and use of ECUs in the system, including the removal of the constraint that only 50 percent of the amount of a credit could be repaid in ECUs; (2) the private use of ECUs; (3) the strengthening of convergence; and (4) the external relations of the system, including the coordination of Community central banks' intervention in third currencies. These proposals had strong support from France, Belgium, and Italy. However, they were countered by the Bundesbank, which devoted several paragraphs in its annual report outlining its position against the proposals:

The elimination of this acceptance limit should only be considered if, within the context of institutional arrangements for the future European Monetary Fund, the unrestricted use of accumulated ECU balances, i.e. their convertibility into other reserve assets, is assured. . . . Considerable caution is also warranted with respect to demands that one supply one's currency for interventions within the agreed-upon bands in addition to the existing intervention obligations. Intramarginal intervention can have a justification, but must continue to have the agreement of the issuer central bank.[11]

The Bundesbank's position prevailed, and the Commission's proposal languished, since approval of the Commission's draft proposal would have required unanimous approval by all member states. According to one French participant, EMF was not pursued simply "because the Bundesbank was against it."[12] The chairman of the Monetary Committee could only report:

> With regard to the propositions covering the technical aspects of the system . . . the Committee continues to find that no general agreement proves possible at present, either on the proposals as they stand in the draft resolution, or on an alternative group of proposals as set out, for example, in my previous statement to the Council of 15 March 1982.[13]

WHY FRANCE AND ITALY STAYED IN THE EMS

Given the ability of Germany, and especially of the Bundesbank, to prevent changes to the system, it is surprising that France and Italy chose to remain in it. Why did France and Italy not leave the EMS in the face of their evident inability to implement the reforms they desired and to which Germany had initially agreed? Two hypotheses are complementary rather than mutually exclusive: (1) the regime was not unreasonably disinflationary in the first two years of operation, and (2) there began to be a consensus among members about the anti-inflationary policies needed in their respective economies. The first reason has already been explained: with the DM weak during 1979 and 1980, there were fewer strains within the EMS. Coupled with the weakened DM was an emerging consensus among the member states that the second oil shock required a disinflationary response rather than the expansionary policies following by the first oil shock. With the exception of France after June 1981, conservative parties or coalitions ruled the larger member states, and all implemented disinflationary policies. France's socialist government also eventually opted for disinflationary policies.

It is important to examine the second hypothesis more closely. How much disinflation did the weaker-currency states really want? The important analytical difference is between the achievement of the inflation standard set by the Bundesbank (price increases of less than 2 percent annually) and a *convergence* of inflation standards, meaning that the weaker-currency countries would reduce their inflation and the stronger-currency countries would increase their growth and thereby their inflation risk. The EMS functioned on the former model, although the basic premise of the system was inherently implausible, as the *Financial Times* highlighted:

West German monetary officials agree that progress has been made on the economic front by the member states in the past year or two, but they insist this has not gone far enough. If asked bluntly whether they are waiting for the Italian or French inflation levels to join the West German figure at less than 2 per cent, they tend to smile wanly and disclaim any such expectation. The "convergence" argument thus lacks an element of clarity.[14]

Conversely, it was almost delusional to believe that the "convergence" would occur at a price level increase higher than that which the Bundesbank would find acceptable, given the Bundesbank's autonomy. Yet this seemed to be the hope of the weaker-currency countries throughout the first four years of the EMS. In a November 1982 interview, Mitterrand stated directly:

> I believe in the importance of mutual discipline. Does this mean, however, that France, just because it is a member of the EMS, should align its monetary policy on that of its principal partners? No, it means that the members of the EMS should look for fair compromises. If they don't, the internal tensions will break the system itself. You are right to underline the difficulty that flows from the different rates of growth of inflation and of the trade balance between France and Germany. But one could think that the first results that we have obtained at home against inflation as well as *the fight from now on against the rise of unemployment in Germany will lead to our countries converging their points of view.*[15]

As late as November 1982, Mitterrand apparently believed that Germany would expand its economy in order to quell the rise in unemployment, a fundamental misunderstanding of the institutional structures in the German economy. Evidently, although the weaker-currency countries wanted a regime that would help get inflation under control, they continued to expect that Germany would make some of the sacrifices for the regime by allowing its unemployment problem to take precedence over inflation concerns. Obviously such expectations were wrong, and this mistake demonstrates again that, like Chancellor Schmidt, the rest of the world had not come to terms with the Bundesbank's growing importance.

THE IMPORTANT REALIGNMENTS, 1981–1983

The character and norms that differentiated the EMS from the Snake were established by the realignments between 1981 and 1983. They have been extensively analyzed elsewhere, but a brief reconsideration will help to understand why weaker-currency countries did not exit the regime once they could not change it.[16] The March 23, 1981, devaluation of the lira was unproblematic. The lira had been granted special status by wider bands, and the realignment was universally approved as a simple way to rectify inflation imbalances between Italy and the other members. The important realignments involved the French franc on October 5, 1981, June 14, 1982, and March 21, 1983. The proximate cause of the siege of the franc was the success of the Partie Socialist (PS) in presidential and parliamentary elections in May-June 1981.

Fulfilling their campaign promises, the PS gave their economy a huge fiscal stimulus that further alarmed the currency markets. Although Mitterrand had been advised to devalue the franc as soon as he was inaugurated, he put off the devaluation until it became inevitable in October. A second devaluation was necessary in June 1982, when the international economy did not rebound as quickly as the PS had hoped. The most significant realignment, however, was the March 1983 devaluation because it represented the PS' commitment to a new economic strategy and showed that the EMS could endure even extreme political pressures. A detailed examination of the reasons for the reversal of French policy is beyond the scope of this book, but scholars agree that the French decision to remain within the constraints of the EMS marked the beginning of the new EMS regime.

The French reversal is important in the context of this book because of the role Germany played in Mitterrand's decision to remain in the system. Moreover, the French reversal and the beginning of the EMS regime mark the ascendance of the German—or Bundesbank—norms among the member states.

The October 1981 realignment was worked out exclusively by the French and Germans, much to the dismay of the other members who were presented with a fait accompli.[17] The Germans accepted a 5.5 percent revaluation, and France and Italy devalued 3 percent. The Bundesbank cooperated, spending DM 31 billion in support of the franc until the realignment and lowering its Lombard rate immediately after the realignment.[18] Yet it was highly critical of French policies:

> While efforts were widely being made to fight inflation resolutely, to redress the balance of payments and to consolidate public finance, in France expansionary policies were adopted by the new government, with recourse being taken to dirigiste measures such as price controls and restrictions on outflows of foreign exchange and capital in order to lend support to the new policies. As things stand at present, a greater degree of harmony in the economic policies of the member states is apparently further away than ever.[19]

The Bundesbank blamed the lack of progress toward the institutional stage on the large divergences in economic policies, and by implication on the French. The federal government, by contrast, supported France's realignment and did not openly criticize the policies that had caused the disturbances. The

Franco-German special relationship continued to be paramount. However, the Schmidt-Mitterrand relationship was considerably more distant than the Schmidt–Giscard d'Estaing relationship had been, and privately Schmidt expressed significant reservations about Mitterrand's economic policies.[20] Thus the federal government and Bundesbank positions about the French reflation were in reality much closer than public statements might have led one to believe.

In June 1982 the Germans accepted a 4.25 percent revaluation coupled with a 5.75 percent devaluation of the French franc. The realignment followed a spring of severe currency speculation against the franc. In April, Prime Minister Pierre Mauroy had warned Mitterrand that a second devaluation would be inevitable, and the president began to prepare an austerity plan for the French economy. Privately, Mitterrand resented the pressures from Germany. He told Mauroy that he would wait to devalue until after the June 4 G-7 summit at Versailles, since he did not want to put himself in a position of weakness before the summit. He complained to his prime minister that the economic upturn in France had profited Germany significantly but that "Schmidt and Thatcher would have nothing to do with a concerted action which would permit a less strong deflation."[21] And he noted, "I've stopped believing that I could come to an understanding with Schmidt once I realized that the German economy is not controlled by the Chancellor but by the Banks."[22] After this realignment, Mitterrand implemented significant changes in the domestic economy, including extending a wage freeze and limiting the deficit to 3 percent of GDP, demonstrating that the EMS rules were changing France's domestic policies.[23]

GERMANY DICTATES FRENCH BUDGETARY CUTS

The negotiations leading to the June 14, 1982, realignment mark the beginning of German involvement in French economic policy. State Secretary Manfred Lahnstein demanded policy changes, such as a salary freeze, in return for the German revaluation—a quid pro quo that was repeated before the March 21, 1983, realignment. The Schmidt government and the Bundesbank were in agreement about the cause of the EMS stresses—the Mitterrand experiment—and consequently, there was limited disagreement about the remedy.[24] Germany had to be as uncompromising as possible to make clear to Mitterrand that his policies would bring the EMS and the Franco-German trade to ruin.[25] Notably absent in the 1982 realignment decision was discussion of a French exit of the EMS; it was not seriously considered in France, and it was not used for bargaining advantage in the negotiations of the German revaluation.

This would change in the next realignment. For the PS, remaining in the EMS and adjusting to the 1983 realignment marked a new course of economic policy. Other scholars have investigated why France did not exit the regime and how significant the economic pressures on the government were.[26] It has been documented that the French seriously considered exiting the EMS, and so it was only natural that the French negotiator would use the threat of exit to wring concessions from the Germans.[27] Adding to the crisis atmosphere surrounding the realignment was the fact that in the 1983 negotiations, the new German government was still an unknown quantity, having taken office less than half a year earlier.[28] It was difficult to assess how far the new center-right government would go to help the PS remain in the EMS.

In a January note to Mitterrand, Economics Minister Jean-Louis Bianco stressed the importance of a DM revaluation of 7 percent and suggested that it might be possible to obtain this much of a revaluation if Mitterrand threatened the Germans with an application of an EU clause permitting protection against imports. On March 14, Mitterrand and Mauroy agreed that they would try to convince Kohl to accept a significant revaluation; if he did not, they could envision exiting the EMS. Kohl was willing to press the Bundesbank to agree to a revaluation, and the Bundesbank was not seriously against it. Both the Bundesbank and Kohl, however, refused a unilateral revaluation of the DM. German finance minister Gerhard Stoltenberg told his French counterpart Jacques Delors that Germany would be willing to revalue unilaterally by 5 percent, but the French rejected this as insufficient to correct the inflation differential between the two countries (see Table 4.2). On March 16, Mitterrand, bluffing, told the Germans that he had decided to float the franc. Mitterrand also told Delors to get a combined re/devaluation of 10 percent that would enable the franc to remain in the EMS. Delors, in Brussels to talk about a realignment, insisted that it was up to the Germans to take the larger portion of the realignment.

The final agreement on the realignment did not show the French to have gained much from the threat of leaving the EMS: the DM revalued 5.5 percent and the franc devalued 2.5 percent, approximately what the Germans had wanted. Moreover, getting the Germans to take the larger portion of the realignment had a political cost: Kohl instructed Stoltenberg to go to Paris and oversee a new, more fiscally austere, French financial plan. As Pierre Favier and Michel Martin-Roland stated: "Despite the French denials, it looked like Germany had dictated its conditions to France before making the monetary concessions."[29]

The French decision to remain in the EMS was widely viewed as a defining moment in Franco-German cooperation and marked the beginning of a new era in European monetary cooperation. The EMS had been changed permanently to a system in which the German economic model was institutionalized and other economic policies would not be viable.

Table 4.2 Inflation Differentials (percentage)

Year	Germany	France	Realignment	Difference	Cumulative in EMS
1997	1.4	1.2	—	−0.2	10.4
1996	1.2	2.0	—	0.8	10.6
1995	1.9	1.6	—	−0.2	9.8
1994	2.7	1.8	—	−0.9	10.0
1993	3.6	2.1	—	−1.5	10.9
1992	4.2	2.3	—	−1.8	12.4
1991	3.5	3.2	—	−0.3	14.2
1990	2.7	3.4	—	0.7	14.5
1989	2.8	3.7	—	0.9	13.8
1988	1.4	2.7	—	1.3	12.9
1987	0.2	3.1	3	−0.1	11.6
1986	−0.2	2.7	6	−3.1	11.7
1985	2.2	5.9	—	3.7	14.8
1984	2.4	7.3	—	4.9	11.1
1983	3.3	9.6	8	−1.7	6.2
1982	5.3	11.8	10	−3.5	7.9
1981	6.3	13.4	8.5	−1.4	11.4
1980	5.4	13.6	—	8.3	12.8
1979	4.2	10.7	2.0	4.5	4.5
1978	2.7	9.1	—	6.3	—
1977	3.6	9.5	—	5.8	—

Year	Germany	Italy	Realignment	Difference	Cumulative in EMS
1997	1.4	1.8	—	0.4	—
1996	1.2	3.9	—	2.7	—
1995	1.9	5.2	—	3.3	—
1994	2.7	4.0	—	1.4	—
1993	3.6	4.4	—	0.8	—
1992	4.2	5.1	3.5	−2.6	26.1
1991	3.5	6.4	—	2.9	28.7
1990	2.7	6.5	3.7	−0.1	25.8
1989	2.8	6.3	—	3.5	25.9
1988	1.4	5.1	—	3.7	22.4
1987	0.2	4.8	3	−1.5	18.7
1986	−0.2	5.8	3	−3.1	20.2
1985	2.2	9.2	8	−1.0	23.3
1984	2.4	10.8	—	8.4	24.3
1983	3.3	14.7	8	−3.3	15.9
1982	5.3	16.5	7	−4.2	19.2
1981	6.3	17.8	14.5	−3.0	23.4
1980	5.4	21.2	—	15.8	26.4
1979	4.2	14.7	—	10.6	10.6
1978	2.7	12.2	—	9.5	—
1977	3.6	18.5	—	14.9	—

Source: Commission of the European Communities, *Eurostat,* various years.

THE NEW EMS REGIME

Following the pivotal 1983 realignment, a period of stability resulted from a gradual convergence of economic policies of the EMS member states. With the exception of France, all of the ruling governments were conservative, and France had demonstrated that it too had adopted the norms of disinflation and fiscal austerity. The July 1985 devaluation of the lira was not considered a major change in the workings of the EMS. Indeed, Italy's status as a "special case" made the realignment fairly routine despite the size of the devaluation. As with other realignments involving only one currency, the ministers conferred by telephone, and no significant objections were raised.[30]

Despite the lack of realignments, there continued to be attempts by France and Italy to change the nature of monetary cooperation in Europe. The French took the Council's helm in January 1984, and in his statement of the French program, Mitterrand indicated that

> progress must be made in the monetary field too. We shall be acting in four areas: reinforcement of the cohesion of the European countries in reaction to the movement of the dollar and of interest rates, increasing the ceiling for Community loans, development of the role of the private ECU, and closer relations with the monetary authority of the surrounding countries.[31]

The European Parliament and the Commission also made proposals for progress in monetary affairs. In February 1984, the European Parliament approved the Herman report consolidating the EMS within the existing framework. Among the improvements it suggested were that the EMCF be given control over the ECUs created from the member states' reserves (rather than having them be "lent" to the EMCF on a swap basis) and that the private use of the ECU be encouraged by all members. Both of these suggestions were incompatible with stated Bundesbank positions. The former was an issue from the negotiation of the system itself, and the Bundesbank opposed the latter because of a law prohibiting indexed liabilities, whose value could fluctuate like a basket of currencies. On the whole, the Bundesbank was skeptical of the Herman report and somewhat defensive on the role of the ECU:

> In contrast, questions relating to the role of the ECU involve the danger of distracting attention from the real requirements of lasting cohesion within the EMS. In any event, the attention paid to the ECU in the public discussion is out of all proportion to its significance in the process of monetary policy integration. Above all, any extended use of the ECU, for example, to finance balances arising from intramarginal interventions, must not lead to new obligations for central banks that might make it more difficult for them to conduct a monetary policy geared to stability.

This would not be in line with the objectives behind the EMS either. It was especially these considerations by which the Bundesbank was led in discussing the proposals concerning the further development of the EMS.[32]

The European Parliament's report had little legislative import, since changes to the EMS could only be made by a unanimous vote in the Council of Ministers, an event that did not occur.

The boldest proposal came late in 1985, when the Commission suggested that the EMS be given the full legal authority of the Treaty of Rome. The Treaty of Rome was under revision by an IGC, which would lead in February 1986 to the Single European Act (SEA), and the Commission wanted to include monetary cooperation. The plan was to establish a procedure for creating the EMF, which would give Brussels a greater voice in monetary matters. Since the EMS had been created by the European Council, it was a purely intergovernmental organization; the proposal would have allowed the Commission greater leeway in proposing new initiatives and would have given it a seat on the EMCF board (which included only a representative from each of the central banks). Finally, and most controversially, the EMCF was to be converted into the EMF, although the role of that body was left completely undefined.

France and Italy were enthusiastic. The Bundesbank and the British government immediately opposed the proposal, establishing an alliance that continued to work toward stopping or stalling greater monetary integration. The alliance had mutual benefits. For the Bundesbank, Britain represented a reliable voice that could be counted on to oppose monetary integration in the intergovernmental negotiations from which the Bundesbank was excluded. For the British, the Bundesbank's criticism of the plans lent credibility to the British position.

Finance Minister Stoltenberg was more circumspect about the proposal, reminding his partners that he was obliged to consult with the Bundesbank on these matters. He also listed three outstanding issues that needed to be met before any new proposals should be considered: (1) greater economic convergence, (2) British entry into the ERM, and (3) the elimination of all capital controls.[33] His reluctance to endorse the proposal matched the caution of Foreign Minister Genscher, who said, "It amounts to a leap in the dark and would widen the gulf between hope and reality,"[34] but contrasted with that of his chancellor, who favored the "Europeanization" of the EMS.[35]

On the eve of the December 1985 Luxembourg summit, a compromise of sorts was worked out.[36] In negotiations first between Germany and Britain and then between the Commission and member states, the compromise allowed a new sentence in the Treaty: "[In economic coordination, the member states] shall take account of the experience gained in co-operation in the framework of the EMS and with the ECU, while respecting existing competence." Thus the Commission was allowed to incorporate monetary affairs into the Treaty of Rome. However, the Treaty text also made further development of the EMS more difficult by requiring a unanimous vote in an IGC and ratification by national parliaments (rather than simply a unanimous vote in the Council of Ministers) on any decision affecting monetary policy.[37] This included the establishment of the EMF, a plan that the Bundesbank had long opposed and that was unlikely to pass the German parliament if Bundesbank opposition was made public. It also gave ERM nonparticipant Britain a right to veto further progress in monetary integration, something that was to make the negotiations on the Treaty on European Union more difficult. The Bundesbank was quite clear that its point of view had prevailed and that its autonomy was undisturbed by the SEA:

> At the same time, the new provisions in the Treaty make it clear that existing Community and national responsibilities must not be affected by them. Hence the ability of the Bundesbank to pursue a policy geared to the statutory objective of monetary stability free from instructions from other bodies remains entirely intact.[38]

The assertiveness with which the Bundesbank by now handled both the German government and the governments of other member states indicates that the years of being the anchor in the EMS had changed its role dramatically. Although it remained a German domestic institution, formally subservient to the German parliament, it had become an international actor, and one that could openly contradict the government's stance on monetary issues.

REALIGNMENTS BECOME LESS FREQUENT

Although the pace of realignments had slowed considerably, by April 1986 the new French government wanted a devaluation to compensate for its loss of competitiveness due to the inflation differential with Germany (see Table 4.2).[39] Finance Minister Edouard Balladur wanted an 8 percent devaluation against the DM, a change that Stoltenberg was unwilling to consider.[40] The realignment, however, was not conducted in the crisis-laden atmosphere of the last French devaluation three years earlier. Germany quietly accepted a 5.8 percent devaluation vis-à-vis the franc, and the only surprise in the negotiations was that Italy and Ireland, whose inflation differential with Germany also had risen substantially, did not join France in the devaluation. The Irish punt did devalue 8 percent unilaterally in one of the "informal" devaluations, but the lira survived for another three years.

The slowing pace of realignments resulted in increasing pressures for progress in institutionalizing monetary cooperation. Politicians and academics agreed that the EMS had proved itself the harbinger of stability, and that it could potentially be extended and used, if not as a vehicle to achieve the original goal of economic and monetary union, at least as a stepping stone.[41] A December 1986 IMF report on the EMS noted that "there is a consensus that the existence of the system has encouraged and contributed to the convergence of economic policies and developments."[42] However, the report added that the second (institutional) phase of the EMS "would not be possible on the basis of the EEC Treaty and of existing agreements, but rather would require a new legal framework, that is, an amendment of the EEC Treaty to be ratified by national parliaments and substantial consequent national legislation."[43] This conclusion mirrored the consensus that had been reached during the negotiations of the SEA in December 1985.

UNEASY COMPROMISE: THE BASEL/NYBORG AGREEMENT

After 1986, the Franco-German relationship was strained more often than not because of Germany's economic and exchange-rate policies. The DM appreciation in 1986–1987 (caused mainly by the drop in the dollar) created the conditions for one of the most acrimonious realignment negotiations in the history of the EMS and prompted the federal government to accede to several important changes in the EMS rules.[44] Many observers viewed the Basel/Nyborg agreement as a challenge by the German government to the Bundesbank, since the government was able to agree to seemingly significant modifications of the EMS rules over the objections of the bank. This appearance is deceptive, however, because the Bundesbank continued to interpret its obligations to intervene subject to domestic stability requirements. When push came to shove, the Bundesbank indicated, German domestic stability always came before its EMS intervention commitments.

The genesis of the currency turmoil was the Plaza accord, concluded in New York in September 1985, which resulted in the fall of the dollar vis-à-vis the DM and the yen. A year later, the dollar had fallen to below DM 2.36 from DM 2.85 (roughly 20 percent), and Stoltenberg issued statements that it had fallen enough. As the DM rose against the dollar it created tensions within the EMS, especially with the French franc. Further aggravating the situation was the interest rate policy of the Bundesbank; as had become usual, the Central Bank Council did not allow the rise of the DM to influence its decision not to lower interest rates.[45] French interest-rate cuts became impossible as the French franc languished near the bottom of its DM band at the end of 1986.[46] Currency speculation, fueled by the uncertainty surrounding the January 25, 1987, Bundestag election in

Germany, became the catalyst for the conflict between France and Germany in early 1987.

On January 7, 1987, the French deliberately allowed the franc to slide to the bottom of its band against the DM. They intended to force the Bundesbank to intervene in the markets and to force a revaluation of the DM by as much as 4 percent. French prime minister Jacques Chirac attacked the Germans for not doing enough to stem the rise of the DM: "This is a Mark crisis, not a franc crisis. Let the German authorities do what is necessary. . . . I consider that the German authorities, and particularly the monetary authorities, have not done what they should have. Their behaviour has been a little selfish."[47]

Once again, the Bundesbank refused to consider a reduction of interest rates solely for the purpose of exchange-rate stability and was not yet willing to concede that the German economy was slowing considerably and that, therefore, the inflation risk was minimal. On January 8, in the middle of the currency turmoil, the Bundesbank Central Bank Council refused again to make even a gesture of solidarity by slightly lowering interest rates as the French wanted. For their part, Stoltenberg and Kohl were loath to accept a unilateral revaluation right before an election because the export sector was losing competitiveness, but there was a growing consensus in the Free Democratic Party (FDP) that the economy was slowing and that a fiscal stimulus, planned for later in 1987, should be moved forward and enlarged.

The French position was clear: Chirac refused to devalue, citing the inflation policy that had been implemented in 1983. The French government also pointed to institutional problems the EMS was having in dealing with an exogenous shock. French finance minister Balladur indicated that the workings of the EMS would need improvements, that the composition of member states' currency reserves should be changed, and that the ECU be used more often for settlement of liabilities.

On January 9, the Bundesbank and the federal government met secretly to discuss the currency crisis: the Bundesbank Directorate wanted to make clear to Finance Minister Stoltenberg the cost of the interventions in support of the franc and to impress upon the minister the importance of a realignment. Kohl eventually agreed to the revaluation because, with elections pending, he preferred stable conditions to market uncertainty. In addition, Germany's DM 110 billion trade surplus was growing embarrassingly large. This set the stage for the compromise, reached on January 12, for a 3 percent revaluation of the DM and the guilder and a 2 percent revaluation of the Belgian and Luxembourg franc. France compromised by agreeing that Belgium and Luxembourg could also revalue, in spite of the fact that such a revaluation would put France in the class of weaker currencies with Italy, Ireland, and Denmark.

THE DRIVE FOR REFORM

The January 12, 1987, realignment was the EMS's last realignment until the September 1992 crisis (with the exception of an informal, unilateral, 3.7 percent Italian devaluation in January 1990). For all the calm it created in the currency markets, it also created a strong impetus for institutional reform. The drive for improvements in the EMS was spearheaded by the French; at the January 1987 realignment meeting in Brussels, the EU Monetary Committee received a memorandum from its French members advocating "a more coherent approach by the Community authorities to the US dollar and the yen, and a more symmetrical view of how the EMS should operate, both as regards macroeconomic adjustment and as regards intervention obligations which . . . should be backed by greater resources."[48]

Both the EU Monetary Committee and the Committee of Central Bank Governors helped draft an "understanding," although no formal amendments to the EMS agreement were required. Meeting in Basel, the Committee of Central Bank Governors unanimously agreed on a sixteen-page report outlining technical measures to improve currency intervention. On September 14, 1987, at a meeting in Nyborg, Denmark, the EU finance ministers announced the changes in the operation of the EMS, based on the report of the central bankers. The changes consisted of five broad measures: (1) proper use of interest rate differentials, (2) more flexible use of fluctuation margins, (3) assurance that EMS realignments be as small and infrequent as possible, (4) expanded financing facilities for the EMS, and (5) agreement that price stability be the norm around which the stability of the EMS was to be built. From the bank's earlier objections, it is clear that points 2 and 4 were the most problematic for the Bundesbank. The most controversial part of the package, the intramarginal intervention obligations (2), was phrased vaguely enough to remain open to interpretation.

French leaders called the agreement a victory because intramarginal interventions were now obligatory, whereas the Bundesbank representatives focused on the limits and conditions attached to the obligation. On the issue of repayment of intervention credits with ECUs, the 50 percent ceiling was eliminated experimentally for two years (and later eliminated permanently).

Although the Basel/Nyborg agreement included elements to which the Bundesbank had earlier shown strong opposition, the agreement cannot be viewed as a significant defeat of the Bundesbank because its representatives immediately interpreted the agreement on their own terms. Although Bundesbank president Pöhl conceded that the agreement for greater intramarginal intervention was a "major concession," he insisted that in practice nothing would change and that "automatic short-term financing of intramarginal interventions should not be introduced . . . intramarginal intervention in DM would only be possible if the Bundesbank agreed to it."[49] These remarks contrasted starkly with the interpretation of French finance minister Balladur, who said, "There is a presumption of automaticity," and that of Jacques de Larosière, governor of the Banque de France, who insisted that "the presumption is not challengeable. It is a matter of good faith."[50] In its 1987 annual report, the Bundesbank contradicted the French interpretation again:

> Decisions on economic and monetary policy are not being shifted from the sphere of national responsibility to Community level as a result of [the Basel/Nyborg] decisions. Thus they do not imply any encroachment upon the autonomy of the Bundesbank in applying its instruments of monetary policy; nor do they lead to any obligation that could give rise to a conflict with its stability-oriented monetary policy.[51]

As in earlier conflicts with the Bonn government over international monetary commitments, the Bundesbank had agreed to something that could be regarded as a compromise or internationalization of monetary policy. Once again, however, the bank had an "opt out"; in the words of Pöhl, intervention would not be triggered automatically, and "the main precondition is that it does not threaten price stability in Germany."[52]

The parallel to the Bundesbank's position in the EMS negotiations is clear; the Bundesbank could not prevent (further) cooperation once the federal government had decided it would participate. However, the Bundesbank could set the terms and limits of that cooperation and could even include a warning that under certain circumstances it could defect from cooperation (as in the Emminger letter). Moreover, the Bundesbank was very actively involved in negotiating the changes to the EMS and, through its participation on the Basel Central Bankers Committee, could keep the language in the agreement vague and open to interpretation.

Does the Bundesbank's lack of absolute commitment amount to a rejection of the terms of the Basel/Nyborg agreement? Probably not, since the Bundesbank did comply with its intervention obligations, even during the crises of 1992–1993. However, it does show the limits of the federal government's ability to offer cooperation to its EU partners, and it makes clear the increasing influence of the Bundesbank.

In exchange for the "major compromises" the Bundesbank felt it had made, the bank received an agreement that interest rate levels would be the first course of intervention, thereby minimizing the interventions needed to support a falling currency. As part of the Basel/Nyborg agreement, member states had also pledged that "all partners should pursue in a closely coordinated manner policies that foster stability of domestic prices and costs and external balance as a basis for lasting exchange-rate stability."[53] This institutionalization of the norm of price stability was perhaps just an explicit acknowledgment of the status quo, but it did shape expectations in the EMS toward policies that would be compatible with these mandates. Moreover, it institutionalized the Bundesbank's position in Europe as the model for economic policy. For the Bundesbank as a purely domestic institution, this recognition bestowed an important international legitimacy. In Pöhl's own words, "The Bundesbank has used its negotiating leverage to the point that it can be satisfied with the result. . . . Neither currency stability nor the autonomy of the Bundesbank are endangered through the accord."[54]

These self-satisfied comments are in marked contrast to the warnings and complaints of the Bundesbank during the negotiations of the EMS and later the EMU. Because the agreement had been negotiated by the Bundesbank itself (as part of the Committee of Central Bank Governors meeting in Basel), it is unlikely that the bank perceived the Basel/Nyborg agreement to be overly threatening (especially given its own interpretation of its ultimate obligations). Over time, the EMS regime had established sufficient credibility that the Bundesbank no longer feared huge intervention obligations, as it had in 1978. The other member states had been sufficiently careful not to strain the Bundesbank's willingness to cooperate by making policy adjustments and realignments in a timely manner.

THE BUNDESBANK EXERTS ITS INFLUENCE: THE FRANCO-GERMAN ECONOMIC AND FINANCE COUNCIL

A further episode of conflict between the Bundesbank and Bonn again illustrates the significant impact of the Bundesbank on the *content* of monetary cooperative arrangements negotiated by the federal government. In late 1987, German chancellor Kohl and French president Mitterrand negotiated a treaty that was to be signed in January 1988, commemorating the twenty-fifth anniversary of the signing of the Franco-German Friendship Treaty. The Franco-German Economic and Finance Council was established to promote closer coordination of interest-rate policy between France and Germany, which the French saw as a means to encourage greater expansionary policies in Germany. In Germany, however, there was dissent among the actors.

France's position was promoted by the Chancellor Kohl and Foreign Minister Genscher and opposed by Finance Minister Stoltenberg and the Bundesbank. For Kohl and Genscher, the importance of the council was to give the French a concession in monetary cooperation. The institutional changes resulting from the Basel/Nyborg agreement had been insufficient to appease the French since the agreement did not really loosen the effects of Germany's tight monetary policy. As Kennedy noted, "[French] policy-makers

. . . hoped to achieve through inter-European cooperation what they had not secured alone or in bilateral negotiations: access to policy-making in the Bundesbank itself."[55] Kohl and Genscher were naturally inclined to try to appease the French, whereas the finance ministry—often a conservative ally of the Bundesbank—saw any concession as a dangerous "Trojan horse" into Germany's independent institution.

The Bundesbank was concerned that its policymaking autonomy not be compromised and was irritated that, once again, it had not been consulted in the negotiations of a monetary cooperation treaty. Not only had the Bundesbank been told of the agreement only days before the signing, but also the nature of the treaty, which had been assumed to be intergovernmental, was to be internationally binding. Although the treaty was signed on January 22 as planned, the language of the treaty, which was to be ratified by the Bundestag and the French parliament, was now open to negotiation. The Bundesbank insisted that a preamble be included in the treaty, stating unequivocally that its autonomy was not to be infringed by the agreement. The foreign ministry insisted that such a preamble would weaken the political impact of the treaty. In the Bundestag, new legislation to protect the Bundesbank's independence was discussed,[56] showing the institutional importance *to the Bundestag* of the Bundesbank.[57]

The issue was resolved in October when the Bundesbank agreed to the French and German finance ministries' compromise that a memorandum be inserted into the treaty stating explicitly that the Franco-German Economic and Finance Council would be a consultative rather than a decisionmaking body. In this way, the statutory autonomy of the Bundesbank was safeguarded, and the Bundesbank again avoided having to take international criteria into account in its monetary policymaking. Though the treaty was signed, the content had been significantly altered by the Bundesbank.

CONCLUSION

The EMS's evolution from a system of theoretical symmetry of obligations to a "hard DM zone" regime paralleled the dissatisfaction of the French and other weaker-currency member states with the regime. Given the institutional changes promised to EMS members at the signing of the EMS by the member governments, it is difficult to explain the virtual absence of progress without considering the Bundesbank's role and influence.

In addition, the increasing frustration of the non-German member states at the lack of movement toward institutional changes explains the French and Italian proposals to change the regime again. As Chapter 5 shows, the proposals for changes in the EMS regime turned into proposals for a new regime altogether and were unexpectedly successful.

The question of why the dissatisfied weaker-currency member states simply submitted to the EMS constraints rather than exiting the regime requires a nuanced answer, as this chapter has shown. On the one hand, it is true—as many scholars have argued—that weaker-currency member states wanted to use their membership in the EMS to impose economic austerity on domestic groups in the name of European cooperation.[58] On the other hand, weaker-currency members desired disinflationary policies that amounted to a *convergence* of inflation (meaning stronger-currency members would expand their economies at the same time that the weaker-currency economies contracted). It was never their intent to fix a regime on the Bundesbank standard. Only if one understands this distinction can one make sense of the continuing quest of the weaker-currency countries for improvements in the regime.

Why did the weaker-currency countries continue to press for institutional innovation in the EMS? The simple explanation that countries wanted to wrest control over setting their monetary policy from Germany is insufficient. The weaker-currency countries were fundamentally concerned with the speed at which the European economies should grow. Throughout the 1980s, there was a consensus in the weaker-currency countries that they needed slower growth with more attention to prices. Chapter 6 shows, however, that the consensus disappeared in the 1990 recessions, causing the rupture of the EMS that had been avoided in the 1980s.

For the Bundesbank, the 1980s and the success of the EMS regime proved highly formative. The EMS rules had laid the groundwork for a system that the Bundesbank could now accept, but there had been uncertainty whether or not the new system would be more successful than the Snake had been. As the EMS's track record improved, the rules were enhanced with norms supporting the Bundesbank's position as the system's anchor. Market forces established the Bundesbank's role in the system, but the other member states internalized that hierarchy, and the Bundesbank became the dominant central bank in Europe. Moreover, the Bundesbank increasingly became involved in international negotiations—either through its contacts on the Committee of Central Bank Governors (which drafted the Basel/Nyborg agreement) or through the use of the Bundestag as its agent, in the Franco-German Economic and Finance Council. Increasingly, in issues of international monetary cooperation, the stature of the Bundesbank was equal to that of the federal government.

NOTES

1. Emminger (1986), pp. 448ff. Blaming the government's fiscal policies was also the Bundesbank's defense during the 1992 crisis.

2. See Rossi (1981).

3. Deutsche Bundesbank, *Annual Report,* 1979, p. 59.

4. Ibid., p. 58.

5. Ibid., p. 59.

6. Deutsche Bundesbank, *Annual Report,* 1980, p. 62.

7. Van Ypersele and Koeune (1985), p. 97.

8. Author's interview with Jean-Yves Haberer, March 1994.

9. *Bulletin of the European Communities,* November 1981, press conference of October 13, 1981, p. 94.

10. Van Ypersele and Koeune (1985), p. 106.

11. Deutsche Bundesbank, *Annual Report,* 1981 p. 84.

12. Author's interview, March 1994.

13. "Oral Statement" (1982), p. 96.

14. *Financial Times,* November 8, 1985.

15. *Le Monde,* November 26, 1982 (emphasis added).

16. For analyses of the political and economic choices of the French government, see Cameron (1995a); Favier and Martin-Roland (1990); Hall (1987); Loriaux (1991); Fonteneau and Muet (1985).

17. See Gros and Thygesen (1992), p. 75.

18. Deutsche Bundesbank, *Annual Report,* 1981, pp. 75–7.

19. Ibid., p. 79.

20. Schmidt (1990), p. 290.

21. Favier and Martin-Roland (1990), p. 415.

22. Ibid., p. 417.

23. See Gros and Thygesen (1992), p. 81.

24. Lahnstein recognized that Germany had benefited from the growth of the French economy and therefore accepted a revaluation beyond the limits given by the Bundesbank. See Favier and Martin-Roland (1990), p. 426.

25. Schmidt wrote: "Without the EMS and the loss of prestige of the franc devaluations caused by the French fiscal and monetary policies, Mitterrand would probably have continued his original expansionary, inflationary course, which would in the end have resulted in monetary and trade protectionism." Schmidt (1990), p. 263.

26. See Cameron (1995a) and (1995b); Loriaux (1991).

27. See Favier and Martin-Roland (1990), esp. pp. 465–479; and Cameron (1995a).

28. The SPD/FDP coalition fell on September 17, 1982, and was replaced by a CDU/CSU/FDP coalition on October 1, headed by Helmut Kohl.

29. Favier and Martin-Roland (1990), p. 476.

30. Gros and Thygesen (1992), p. 83.

31. *Bulletin of the European Communities* (1984), January, p. 94.

32. Deutsche Bundesbank, *Annual Report,* 1984, p. 10.

33. *Financial Times,* November 8, 1985.

34. *Financial Times,* December 3, 1985.

35. The true position of Kohl is uncertain: publicly he supported the inclusion of monetary matters, but he seems to have told Thatcher privately that he opposed inclusion. See Thatcher (1993), p. 554.

36. *Financial Times,* December 4, 1985.

37. Ibid.,

38. Deutsche Bundesbank, *Annual Report,* 1985 p. 74.

39. The March 1986 French parliamentary elections gave a victory for the

RPR. The new prime minister, Jacques Chirac, presided over the first "cohabitation" (PS president, RPR prime minister) government in the Fifth Republic.

40. *Financial Times*, April 7, 1986.

41. See, for example, de Grauwe and Papademos (1990); Tsoukalis, quoted in Guerrieri and Padoan (1989).

42. Ungerer et al. (1986), p. 1.

43. Ibid., p. 10.

44. See Henning (1994), pp. 203ff; Solomon (1995).

45. Indeed, Henning noted that the Plaza accord and the February 1987 Louvre accord were significant episodes of conflict between the Bundesbank and the federal government. See Henning (1994), pp. 204ff.

46. Solomon wrote that the situation "helped foster a secret French alliance with [US Treasury Secretary James] Baker. 'We tried to move the Bundesbank with the support, intellectually and tactically, of the U.S. administration,' reveal[ed] French deputy minister Daniel Lebegue, who described frequent phone calls over tactics. . . . 'French interests were the same as the United States' for different reasons.'" See Solomon (1995), p. 306.

47. *Financial Times*, January 7, 1987.

48. Monetary Committee of the European Communities (1988), p. 6.

49. *Financial Times*, September 14, 1987.

50. Ibid.

51. Deutsche Bundesbank, *Annual Report,* 1987, p. 65.

52. Ibid.

53. Reuters News Service, September 14, 1987.

54. *Financial Times*, September 14, 1987.

55. Kennedy (1991), p. 95.

56. Ibid., p. 97.

57. This point is important for the argument in Chapter 8 that the Bundestag considers the Bundesbank's opinions very seriously.

58. See, for example, Woolley (1992).

5

Negotiating the Monetary Union

As Chapter 4 showed, the earlier attempts to reform the EMS regime were largely unsuccessful because of the Bundesbank's unwillingness to countenance any changes that would transfer monetary policymaking ability to another organization. The major issue, then, is why the Bundesbank and the federal government would allow monetary union, which did just that. Put more precisely, why did the Bundesbank and the chancellor agree to cede monetary sovereignty to a new supranational institution, the ECB, by the year 1999, when the EMS was so favorable to Germany?

In this chapter I explore that question in detail, tracing the roots of the proposals that would eventually become the Treaty on European Union (Maastricht Treaty). If one considers the 1988 French and Italian calls for further monetary integration in light of all the calls and proposals of the previous eight years, it is all the more remarkable that anything concrete came of those proposals. In addition, the Maastricht Treaty presents a challenge to virtually all theories of behavior that posit a gains/power maximizing rational actor maximizing gains and power. Why would Germany give up its primus inter pares position in the EMS?

To fully understand why Germany agreed to monetary union, the interplay between the federal government and the Bundesbank must be examined closely. It is important to recognize the turning points in the negotiations and what the constellation of Bundesbank-government positions was at those points. This chapter delineates the preferences and constraints in Germany to show how they changed so as to make international agreement on further monetary integration possible.

THE AGENDA AFTER THE BASEL/NYBORG AGREEMENT

The changes to the EMS implemented at Basel/Nyborg represent an important watershed in European monetary history because they mark the beginnings of institutional change. As Chapter 5 showed, the impetus for change had come from the French in the person of Finance Minister Edouard Balladur. French prime minister Jacques Chirac supported the efforts of his finance minister, but initially was leery of tying his political fortunes too closely to institutional progress in monetary matters. Once the Basel/Nyborg agreement had been concluded, Balladur continued his crusade for a European monetary authority. He was supported by EU Commission president Jacques Delors, another former French finance minister, who was riding a wave of political success due to the SEA. Both men took their cue from the (re)commitment to economic and monetary union that the member state governments had made as part of the SEA. According to former British chancellor of the exchequer Nigel Lawson, the reference to EMU in the SEA had been inserted at the last moment at the behest of Jacques Delors before the European Council meeting to approve the new treaty.[1] Nevertheless, it gave the necessary political impetus to make new proposals in this issue area.

Scarcely three months after the signing of the Basel/Nyborg agreement in September 1987, Balladur suggested that the time was right for further progress toward monetary union. In addition to initiating the Franco-German Economic and Finance Council in mid-November 1987, Balladur put pressure on Germany for further institutional progress in a memorandum,[2] stating that "the European Monetary System should resist the influence of countries with the most restrictive monetary policies."[3] He proposed that the EU create a new single European currency and a European Central Bank to administer it.

The economic context for these initiatives was the continuing rise of the DM against the dollar, brought on by the 500-point fall in the U.S. stock market in October 1987, which put pressure on the French to raise interest rates. In November, the French had borrowed under the expanded financing facilities to support their interventions against the DM, and in November and December, the Bundesbank had bowed to international pressure and quietly lowered interest rates slightly (see Table 5.1).[4]

Despite these concessions to currency stability by the Bundesbank, Prime Minister Chirac endorsed the Balladur proposal and also chastised the Bundesbank for its recent failure to consider the needs of its European partners in its battle with the weakening dollar. He argued that the EMS worked to France's disadvantage because it did not impose equal discipline on all member states and complained that the Bundesbank's interventions on the foreign exchange market were exclusively concentrated on the DM-dollar rate.[5] Such interventions were not compatible with the spirit of the EMS. "In crisis conditions we support burdens we cannot control. At least the Bundesbank could buy francs. Things cannot continue like this, so we must reform the system."[6]

Table 5.1 Interest Rate Decisions by the Bundesbank

Date	Discount Rate	Lombard Rate
January 19, 1979	—	4.00
March 29, 1979	4.00	5.00
May 31, 1979	—	5.50
July 13, 1979	5.00	6.00
October 31, 1979	6.00	7.00
April 30, 1980	7.50	9.50
September 18, 1980	—	9.00
February 19, 1981	—	12.00 (introduction of "special" Lombard rate)
October 8, 1981	—	11.00
December 3, 1981	—	10.50
January 21, 1982	—	10.00
March 18, 1982	—	9.50
May 6, 1982	—	9.00 (end of "special" Lombard rate)
August 26, 1982	7.00	8.00
October 21, 1982	6.00	7.00
December 2, 1982	5.00	6.00
March 17, 1983	4.00	5.00
September 8, 1983	—	5.50
June 28, 1984	4.50	—
January 31, 1985	—	6.00
August 15, 1985	4.00	5.50
March 6, 1986	3.50	—
January 22, 1987	3.00	5.00
November 5, 1987	—	4.50
December 3, 1987	2.50	—
June 30, 1988	3.00	—
July 28, 1988	—	5.00
August 25, 1988	3.50	—
December 15, 1988	—	5.50
January 19, 1989	4.00	6.00
April 20, 1989	4.50	6.50
June 29, 1989	5.00	7.00
October 6, 1989	6.00	8.00
November 1, 1990	—	8.50
January 31, 1991	6.50	9.00
August 15, 1991	7.50	9.25
December 19, 1991	8.00	9.75
July 16, 1992	8.75	—
September 14, 1992	8.25	9.50
February 4, 1993	8.00	9.00
March 18, 1993	7.50	—
April 22, 1993	7.25	8.50
July 1, 1993	6.75	8.25
July 29, 1993	—	7.75
September 9, 1993	6.25	7.25
October 21, 1993	5.75	6.75
February 17, 1994	5.25	—
April 14, 1994	5.00	6.50
May 11, 1994	4.50	6.00
March 30, 1995	4.00	—
August 24, 1995	3.50	5.50
December 14, 1995	3.00	5.00
April 18, 1996	2.50	4.50

Sources: Financial Times, various years. Compiled by author.

In Germany, both the Bundesbank and the federal government tried to dispel French claims that Germany was not cooperating fully in the EMS while resisting U.S. pressure to do more to expand the economy. There was some disagreement among the Bundesbankers and government ministers as to whether Germany could do better than the small interest-rate cuts that the bank had made in the fall. But there was widespread agreement that the more important partner to appease was France. The French presidential election was scheduled for April 1988, and Kohl's friend Mitterrand faced RPR candidate Chirac in the race. Germany needed to send a cooperative signal to France, and the increasing trade surpluses with France (see Table 5.2) were becoming an embarrassment.[7] In one November meeting that included Economics Minister Martin Bangemann, Bundesbank president Pöhl, and vice president Schlesinger, the topic was,

Table 5.2   Germany's Balance of Trade, 1970–1997 (U.S.$ billions)

Year	France	Italy	United Kingdom	United States
1970	0.4	0.1	0.1	(0.2)
1971	0.3	(0.4)	0.3	0.2
1972	0.4	(0.4)	0.8	1.0
1973	1.6	0.4	1.2	1.1
1974	2.4	1.4	1.8	1.3
1975	1.6	(0.4)	1.3	(0.5)
1976	3.1	0.0	1.4	(1.3)
1977	2.7	(0.9)	1.9	0.4
1978	3.3	(1.9)	2.4	1.4
1979	3.7	(0.7)	2.1	0.3
1980	5.5	1.6	0.1	(2.3)
1981	5.2	1.7	(0.6)	(1.1)
1982	7.1	1.5	1.7	(0.0)
1983	4.4	0.2	3.2	1.9
1984	5.4	1.2	2.6	5.5
1985	5.0	1.5	3.1	8.1
1986	7.0	2.2	6.9	13.2
1987	9.0	3.8	9.5	13.6
1988	10.4	6.5	12.7	9.4
1989	12.7	7.8	13.1	4.5
1990	11.5	4.9	10.8	6.1
1991	5.3	0.8	4.9	(0.7)
1992	6.9	2.4	5.3	0.3
1993	5.7	(0.2)	9.7	4.0
1994	6.5	(1.2)	9.0	6.5
1995	11.4	1.2	12.4	6.8
1996	8.6	1.5	10.7	7.4
1997a	(4.5)	1.8	6.5	4.1

Source: IMF, *Direction of Trade Statistics.*
Notes: Parenthesis indicate a German trade deficit in that year.
a. Based on extrapolation of actual second-quarter data.

"what can we do to keep the economy growing and to meet the demands of 'some'—French—people?"[8]

In this foreign policy context, it is perhaps explicable that Foreign Minister Genscher had a favorable reaction to the Balladur proposal for reforming the EMS, a plan that would ultimately lead to a single currency.[9] Unlike Chancellor Kohl, who had a somewhat reserved reaction to the proposals, Genscher wholeheartedly supported the idea.[10] Finance Minister Stoltenberg, though not interested in the idea of monetary reform, was willing to trade progress in monetary reform for the achievement of an agreement on full capital liberalization. This agreement was reached at the ECOFIN meeting in June 1988.[11]

It is necessary to explain Genscher's interest in putting monetary union on the agenda. Three factors coalesced to produce a favorable response from Genscher: (1) his genuine interest in a more federal Europe, which would, in any case, not reduce the competencies of the federal government but rather be at the expense of the Bundesbank; (2) his desire for an ambitious agenda for the German Council presidency, which began on January 1, 1988; and (3) the necessity to appease French unhappiness with EMS workings.

One should not underestimate the importance of the idea of European integration for Genscher and Kohl. Most German leaders born before the war consider the tight integration of France and Germany a political necessity. In the case of monetary union, however, the motivation of Genscher to give up monetary control did not necessarily contradict realist theories of power-maximizing, self-interested actors since the federal government did not have control over monetary policy. Another factor that made the potential ceding of real sovereignty easier was the virtual invisibility of the process. At the time that Genscher put monetary union on the agenda and throughout the negotiations of EMU, little public attention and debate focused on the results of this course, and so there seemed to be little consideration by Kohl or Genscher of the electoral consequences of giving up the DM.

In his January 20, 1988, speech to the European Parliament setting out the German agenda, Genscher stated:

> The EMS is one of the great successes of the European unification process. Even those who were initially skeptical have in the mean time become convinced of its crucial importance for the achievement of the goal of economic and monetary union. The conditions for its further development are favourable, perhaps better than at any other time in the history of the Community.[12]

To those supportive of monetary union, it was probably irrelevant that the EMS had not been created as part of the drive toward EMU but rather as an intergovernmental agreement when all EU-sponsored drives for EMU had failed. Genscher was interested in harnessing the success of the EMS.

> We must develop the European Monetary System further. In the wake of the important decisions by the Governors of the Central Banks and Finance Ministers at Basel and Nyborg, the question arises as to how much scope there now remains for further progress in strengthening the EMS without new institutional arrangements. Possibly there is only little scope left, so that any objectives over and above this raise the question of institutional responsibilities. Senior figures in business, the Central Banks and the Governments of the member states are pressing for speedy progress.[13]

But Genscher knew that the most serious constraint to institutional innovation lay in the Bundesbank, and therefore he added, "It is crucial that this monetary union should lead to a Community of stability."[14] By setting the agenda in such a way that the Bundesbank was unable to reject the proposal out of hand, Genscher ensured that the proposal would be considered seriously during the German presidency. Bundesbank president Pöhl, commenting on the Genscher agenda, said he was not hostile to monetary union but added to the requirements, saying that monetary union would be a very long process and that the central bank would have to be independent.

On February 3, the cabinet of Chancellor Kohl passed a resolution on EMU: "The longer term goal is economic and monetary union in Europe, in which an independent European Central Bank, committed to maintaining price stability, will be able to lend effective support to a common economic and monetary policy."[15] Within the ministries of the federal government, there was tentative agreement on monetary union, even if the agreement on the part of the Finance Ministry was lukewarm and highly conditional. On paper, at least, the Finance Ministry's stand was echoed by the Bundesbank, which was required to support the government's position.

In the weeks leading to the Hannover summit in June 1988, there was disagreement as to who should be on the EU Committee to research steps toward monetary union. Foreign Minister Genscher and the French wanted a panel of academic experts, whereas Kohl, Stoltenberg, Pöhl, and the British supported a committee of central bankers (who would, presumably, be more skeptical about the viability of monetary union).[16] The compromise settled on was a committee of central bankers chaired by Commission president Delors, who would be given the mandate of *how* to reach monetary union rather than whether or not to attempt it. In the end, the twelve governors of the EU central banks, three independent experts, and one Commission member would form the committee, with Delors as chairman, to draft "concrete stages leading towards [economic and monetary] union."[17] The Delors Report was requested in time for the following year's European Council meeting in Madrid.

THE DELORS REPORT

In shaping the institutions of EMU, the Bundesbank played a far more active role than it had during EMS negotiations. David Cameron showed that the role of central bankers in the negotiations leading to the Maastricht Treaty was substantial.[18] Their role during the discussions leading to the Delors Report was the most extensive and substantive of all the actors (although each of the central bankers was on the committee in an ex officio capacity). Moreover, their role did not end after the release of the report. Their conclusions in the Delors Report laid the foundation for the TEU and should be considered an important contribution to the EMU. Once the Delors Report was released, the central bankers' lobbying became more intense, and their drafts of the ECB and European System of Central Banks (ESCB) statutes were adopted directly, without any changes by political actors, as the protocol of the Treaty.

As with the Werner Report and the EMS, several technical issues called forth serious disagreement among the Delors Committee members. The most divisive of these issues were (1) whether to converge the economies first and then fix the currencies, or vice versa (the old "monetarists versus economists" debate); (2) at what stage monetary authority should devolve to the ECB from the national central banks; (3) what the role of the ECU during the different stages should be; and (4) what the role of the ECB should have with respect to member states' fiscal policy. As it had with the EMS, the Bundesbank—through Pöhl on the Delors Committee and through the public statements of Pöhl and Schlesinger during the political discussions following the release of the Delors Report—continued to dominate the discussions of feasible monetary arrangements.

The Bundesbank's position, stated in its 1988 annual report, was that monetary union was completely unnecessary given the EMS's success. "In monetary terms, the EMS in its present form would then provide sound underlying conditions for the internal market to function smoothly."[19] To those aware of the earlier Bundesbank skepticism about the EMS, the bank's newfound support of the regime was somewhat ironic. The Bundesbank, meanwhile, mobilized to ensure that if monetary union occurred, it would be on the bank's terms. In the discussions among committee members leading to the release of the Delors Report (June 1988–April 1989), Pöhl influenced the debate on the first two points of conflict by insisting that stability be the main objective of the ECB, and that the new monetary authority be independent of political influence from member states and EU institutions. These were the minimum criteria for receiving the Bundesbank's approval. In addition, Pöhl demanded that the transfer of monetary authority not be given to the ECB according to a set timetable, but rather when the economies had converged sufficiently to make the linking of currencies possible. Any hopes the French and Italian finance ministries had harbored that EMU would be more accommodating to other objectives such as growth, employment, or third-country currency stability were dashed during the initial discussions with Pöhl. Moreover, in contrast to the EMS negotiations, the federal government seemed to be in close agreement with the Bundesbank's views: both Kohl and Stoltenberg voiced misgivings about monetary union based on anything less than sound money principles.[20] Pöhl maintained the same argument throughout the Delors Committee discussions:

> From the German point of view it is essential to ensure, in the discussion about the future design of a European monetary order, that monetary and credit policy is not geared to stability to a lesser extent in an economically united Europe than is the case at present in the Federal Republic of Germany.[21]

Implicit in the statement was a threat: if the other central bankers on the Delors Committee overrode the German point of view and incorporated other objectives in the mandate of the ECB, it was doubtful that Pöhl would sign the report and virtually certain that Germany would not allow it to be used as a blueprint to monetary union.[22] According to one source in contact with Pierre Bérégovoy, the French finance minister during the Delors Committee negotiations, "It was power politics. If the institutions were not created to the liking of the Bundesbank, there would be no Eurofed, and a European Central Bank would have been impossible without the Bundesbank. This was made explicit to Bérégovoy."[23] Germany presented its partners with a take-it-or-leave-it proposition.

The Delors Report was released in its final form on April 17, 1989. Before the report was released to the public, Pöhl indicated his satisfaction with it, saying, "I am quite happy." One member of the committee said that the report contained "a lot of German thinking," and another indicated Pöhl "had good reason to look happy."[24]

Substantively, the Delors Report proposed the following schedule: the first stage of EMU would begin on July 1, 1990. During the first stage, all EU member states would join the ERM and strengthen their economic and monetary policies. All obstacles to financial integration and the private use of the ECU would be removed. A European Reserve Fund that would foreshadow the future ESCB was under consideration by some member states. It would have a permanent structure and staff and manage pooled reserves.

During stage 2, the ESCB would be created from the Committee of Central Bank Governors and given the key task to begin the transition from the coordination of independent national monetary policies to a single EU-wide monetary policy. How that transition would be implemented was left vague and provided grist for further Franco-German conflicts in the negotiations.[25] More concretely, in stage 2 the margins of fluctuation within the ERM would be narrowed, in light of progress made in economic convergence. Parities could still be changed, but only as a last resort. Finally, in stage 3 exchange rates would be locked, and the ESCB would be responsible for EU-wide monetary policy. The issue of fiscal policy, referred to in nine paragraphs of the report, was an important point for the Bundesbank but was opposed by the British.[26] At issue was whether monetary convergence should involve certain fiscal policies that would erode even further a state's sovereignty. Even the German government was less than enthusiastic about relinquishing the broad outlines of its fiscal policy before full political union was accomplished.[27] However, the Bundesbank's view that fiscal constraints be required prevailed in the final report, and fiscal policy remained an issue of contention throughout the treaty negotiations.

THE MADRID SUMMIT

The threat of a Bundesbank exit from the process of EMU negotiation was made explicit by Pöhl after the publication of the Delors Report. Although the Delors Report had recommended paths to EMU that were compatible with the Bundesbank's preferences (progress in stages, a convergence of the economies before merging the currencies, and an insistence on price stability and independence), there was still uncertainty over whether or not the Delors Report would be the basis of concrete proposals to create monetary union. Fortunately for the Bundesbank, the press and the Commission focused more on the British criticisms of the report and the loss of sovereignty that the report implied than on the Bundesbank's more restrained complaints. Yet the Bundesbank's calls for caution were probably more important than Margaret Thatcher's strident criticisms of the plan (especially in light of the fact that Britain received an opt-out for EMU).[28]

The first institutionalized forum in which the Delors Report was considered was an informal meeting of the twelve finance ministers in S'Agora, Spain, on May 20, 1989. In the communiqué issued after the meeting, the ministers did not endorse the Delors Report explicitly and agreed only to begin work on the first stage. British chancellor of the exchequer Lawson takes credit for the lack of endorsement of the Delors Report and the detachment of stage 1 from stages 2 and 3, but it is doubtful that he was the only one against the EMU process at the meeting.[29] The fact that Britain continuously argued against progress and that progress was in fact later accomplished suggests that perhaps the German and Dutch finance ministers played a key role in preventing endorsement of the Delors Report. German support or lack of support for institutional changes seems to be the important variable in the outcome, and the Bundesbank's coalition with Britain was useful but not essential.

Significant progress was made at the European Council meeting in Madrid on June 26–27. This progress is all the more remarkable in light of the widely divergent preferences of the member states.[30] On the one hand, the member states that were skeptical of monetary union (Britain, Denmark, the Netherlands, and Luxembourg) argued forcefully against the Delors plan, saying that it proposed such a unique loss of sovereignty that they were unable to commit to its contents or timetable. On the other hand, the pro-EMU countries (France, Italy, Spain, Belgium, and—to some extent—the German government) argued that the EU member states had committed themselves to EMU long ago in the Treaty of Rome, the Werner Report, and most recently the SEA. It was time to act. They were joined by the EMU-agnostic states (Portugal, Greece, and Ireland), which recognized that there were financial advantages to agreeing to the process.

It is unclear how widespread German enthusiasm for EMU really was. As always, Chancellor Kohl tread a fine line between the pro-EMU foreign ministry and the anti-EMU finance and economics ministries and the Bundesbank. At the Madrid summit he was cautious about moving too fast to EMU (thereby rejecting Delors's plan that EMU be timed to coincide with the 1992 reforms).[31] Moreover, if one considers Kohl's later ambivalence about stipulating the beginning of stage 2,[32] it is possible that Kohl himself had problems with paragraph 39 of the Delors Report, which states that "the creation of an economic and monetary union must be viewed as a single process . . . the decision to enter upon the first stage should be a decision to embark on the entire process."[33]

Yet it was Kohl who proposed the compromise that salvaged progress at the summit.[34] In exchange for agreeing that the first stage should begin on July 1, 1990, as proposed in the Delors Report, and for instructing the relevant committees to begin planning the IGC, it was agreed that the Delors Report represented *a* process (not *the* process), to monetary union and that dates for beginning the IGC and stages 2 and 3 would be decided only after "full and adequate preparations" were completed (as decided by the EU Monetary Committee, the General Affairs Council, the Committee of Central Bank Governors, the Commission, and the ECOFIN).[35]

Setting the date for beginning the IGC had been a matter of some conflict between Chancellor Kohl and President Mitterrand. Mitterrand, anxious to reach monetary union quickly, preferred that the IGC begin as soon after the beginning of stage 1 as possible. Kohl preferred a later date, not only because he did not want to rush the preparations for EMU, but also because he did not want to begin the IGC before the December 1990 German federal elections. The far right party, the Republikaner, had been gaining support throughout Germany, and Kohl did not want to give them a public issue around which they could mobilize the right-of-center voters on which his center-right coalition depended. By stalling the date of the IGC until "full and adequate preparations" had been completed, Kohl had triumphed.

Even the Bundesbank found something to cheer in the compromise. The European Council's communiqué confirmed that the "realisation [of EMU] would have to take account of the parallelism between economic and monetary aspects," meaning that progress on economic convergence would be necessary before stage 2 or 3 could begin.[36] Furthermore, as Cameron pointed out, agreeing to stage 1 meant only agreeing to further economic convergence while putting off any steps that would encroach on the Bundesbank's domain.[37]

SETTING A DATE FOR THE IGC

In August the chancellor formed a committee to present a common German position in the negotiations.[38] With members from the chancellor's office, the Finance and Economics Ministries, and the Bundesbank, the group attempted to unify some of the disparate views within the German government (although the absence of the Foreign Ministry's views would seem to have underrepresented the EMU enthusiasts). The group released its report, titled "The German Basic Position on EMU," in November 1989,[39] and it became the basis for the German negotiating position (the German draft treaty) presented in the IGC.[40]

At the informal ECOFIN meeting in Antibes in September 1989, the first step toward preparations for the IGC was made. Finance ministers agreed to set up a committee of EU finance and foreign ministers to review and comment on the Delors Report. The meeting was largely overshadowed by British chancellor of the exchequer Lawson's release of a competing plan to achieve monetary union. His plan—to create competition among currencies to arrive at monetary union when only one currency was left—was widely regarded as a red herring at the time, and Lawson admitted as much in his memoirs.[41]

During the meeting, there was discussion on two issues from the Delors Report: the issue of central control over national fiscal policies and the issue of democratic controls on the central bank. The Commission was prepared to compromise on the first issue, allowing voluntary coordination of budget deficits. On the issue of oversight of the central bank, a number of suggestions were discussed, including giving the European Parliament a role in approving the board of governors of the ECB. The discussions were tabled until the formal ECOFIN meeting on November 13.

During the summer, French foreign minister Roland Dumas had selected a group of national finance and foreign ministers under the tutelage of Elisabeth Guigou to prepare questions for the IGC. On October 6, the Guigou Report was finalized and released. Its "findings" were presented as a series of questions that largely reviewed the contents of the Delors Report. Daniel Gros and Niels Thygesen hypothesized that the main purpose of the Guigou Report may have been to politically legitimize the Delors Report, which had been written by a group of central bankers acting in an ex officio capacity.[42] The November ECOFIN meeting took note of the Guigou Report and of the British report on an evolutionary approach to EMU. The only concrete progress of the ECOFIN, however, was to approve two stage 1 Commission proposals concerning the attainment of progressive convergence of economic performance during stage 1 of EMU and increased cooperation between the central banks of the member states.[43] Most of the difficult decisions were left to the European Council meeting in December. As always, progress depended on bargains between the heads of government.

This historical juncture is noteworthy for the Bundesbank's reaction to the dilemma of having to support publicly a plan that it did not endorse privately. During the period leading to the Strasbourg summit, the Bundesbank increased the pressure on other member governments to consider the Delors Report the precise blueprint for EMU without weakening any of the elements contained therein at the insistence of the bank. In several public speeches and interviews, Pöhl and Vice President Schlesinger reiterated their argument that Germans would only relinquish their DM for an equally stable European currency.[44] The threat to exit the negotiations if the Bundesbank's minimum criteria were not incorporated into the plans for EMU was also made explicit in the Bundesbank's annual report for 1989:

> In the Bundesbank's view, stringent demands in terms of stabilisation policy must be met by any European central banking system. *It is only on this condition that it would be acceptable for EC member states with stable currencies to relinquish their national monetary policy sovereignty.* One major requirement would be that the guidelines on monetary policy are unequivocally geared, at Community level, with binding effect for the entire currency area, to the priority of the target of price stability.[45]

Pöhl used every forum available to the Bundesbank to publicize its position that only an institution with a clear mission of price stability and with safeguards against political intrusion would be acceptable to the Bundesbank. Working within its institutional constraints, the Bundesbank did shape the German position considerably and, in a new role for the bank, communicated its hard-line position to the other member states, thus having a significant effect on the outcome. The legal constraints on the Bundesbank to support government policy, however, made it impossible for the bank to reject outright the idea of monetary union.

The Bundesbank's dilemma is shown clearly by contrasting Thatcher's position with that of Pöhl. The two were allied on such issues as slowing the pace toward monetary union and resisting the creation of a central bank and a common currency.[46] Thatcher's praise of Pöhl, in fact, generated some consternation in Bonn, which did not want to see Germany linked to the obstructionist tendencies of the British. It would have been impossible for Pöhl to completely agree with Thatcher, however much he may have personally wanted to, and therefore he continued to support the idea of eventual monetary union, but only on the Bundesbank's terms.[47]

Pöhl assumed that creating ECB institutions to be identical to those of the Bundesbank might prevent agreement on monetary unification. The *Financial Times* cited him as warning that

> no West German government would accept the Delors report's proposal for a new European central banking system unless it was given safeguards at least equivalent to those enjoyed by the statutorily independent Bundesbank . . . *[and I doubt] whether other European governments are prepared to accept those conditions.* The economies of the member states were too divergent to make a European central bank more than a distant prospect.[48]

If the Bundesbank's strict interpretation of monetary union was a deliberate strategy to halt the progress, the attempt failed because all the other member states agreed to the Bundesbank's demands.

During the week before the December 8–9, 1989, meeting in Strasbourg the main subject of contention between France and Germany—the timing of the IGC—was not yet resolved. On the eve of the summit, Kohl's office put out a statement that "Bonn was relying on French agreement to the bid to delay until 1991 the start of an Inter-Governmental Conference on EMU."[49] However, France and Commission President Delors maintained that preparations for the IGC could be completed in a year and that waiting longer or—as Kohl had evidently suggested earlier—making progress on EMU contingent on progress on institutional reform was an unacceptable stalling tactic.[50]

Only a day later, Kohl agreed with ten other EU ministers (Thatcher alone dissented) to begin the IGC in December 1990 as the French had wanted (albeit after the German election). This decision can be counted among the more important ones leading to the Maastricht Treaty and therefore must be scrutinized. Given Kohl's interest in pushing the IGC into 1991 or later, why did he suddenly agree to an early IGC? In doing so, he maintained France's frenetic pace toward EMU, which was counter to the preferences of almost all the German actors. To understand why Chancellor

Kohl backed down in Strasbourg, it is essential to look at the other bargain Kohl made at the summit.

A New Bargaining Chip: German Unification

Only four weeks before the Strasbourg summit, the Berlin Wall suddenly and unexpectedly came down, and the German Foreign Ministry found itself in a situation that not even the most farsighted analysts had foreseen.[51] Kohl used the forum of a November 28 address to the Bundestag to present a "10-Point Program" that consisted of a plan for a German confederation that would eventually lead to German unification. The plan was radical in two respects: (1) it entertained the hope that Germany would be unified, and (2) it had not been cleared with any other heads of state (or even Genscher) prior to the Bundestag address. In points 6 and 7, Kohl was very specific that the EU retained its primacy in the diplomatic relations of Germany:

> The development of intra-German relations remains embedded in the pan-European process, that is to say in the framework of East-West relations. The future architecture of Germany must fit into the future architecture of Europe as a whole. Here the West has shown itself to be the pacemaker with its concept of a lasting and equitable peaceful order in Europe. . . . The attraction and aura of the European Community are and remain a constant feature of pan-European development. We want to and must strengthen them further still.[52]

However, he concluded with point 10, which was somewhat ambiguous about the role of other states in decisions about German unification: "With this comprehensive policy we are working for a state of peace in Europe in which the German nation can recover its unity in free self-determination. Reunification—that is regaining national unity—remains the political goal of the Federal government."[53] Only ten days earlier, at a hastily convened informal European summit in Paris, Kohl had heard both Thatcher and Mitterrand express their reservations about German unity and changing borders.

Kohl's 10-Point Plan did nothing to reassure Britain, France, or the USSR. On December 6, 1989, Mitterrand visited Mikhail Gorbachev in Kiev and cautioned Kohl (through press conferences) about unification and the dangers of tampering with the existing international order.[54] At the Strasbourg summit, Mitterrand and Thatcher met privately to discuss their reservations about German intentions to unify.[55] In short, there was a very realistic perception by Kohl that important allies might try to prevent unification. The domestic political dynamism of the situation, however, persuaded Kohl that he should do whatever it took to leave open the possibility of unification.

> European officials said that it quickly became clear that if Kohl maintained that position [of holding a later IGC] in Strasbourg, it would confirm French fears that Bonn was now more interested in German reunification and in opportunities in Eastern Europe than in its links with the Community.[56]

Thus, with regard to the French, the price of receiving Mitterrand's blessing for German unification was quickening the pace to the IGC.

> There were times before and during the two-day meeting when disagreements on this sensitive issue [German unification] between Chancellor Helmut Kohl of West Germany and some of his partners—not least Mr. François Mitterrand, the French President and chairman of the conference—threatened completely to dominate the agenda. France is not alone in believing that the liberalisation of Eastern Europe calls for an acceleration of the Community's internal development, so as to anchor West Germany more firmly to its Western moorings. In spite of all the official denials, therefore, it was plain how a deal could be made. In return for German agreement to a date for the inter-governmental conference on economic and monetary union—albeit very late in 1990 to allow the West German general election to take place—the French would accept a declaration on German unity which, in spite of the heavy conditionality attached to it, broadly meets Mr. Kohl's domestic concerns.[57]

Only in the context of German unification does Kohl's decision to set an early date for an IGC without first getting a commitment for further political integration make sense.[58]

PREPARATIONS FOR THE IGC

Having agreed that the IGC should open in December 1990, the member states spent much of 1990 making the necessary preparations for the conference. In addition to the two scheduled European Council meetings, the Irish and Italian presidents also decided on special meetings to deal with the preparations. During ECOFIN's February 12 meeting, the finance ministers agreed to implement economic surveillance measures during stage 1, which was set to begin July 1, 1990.

This period saw an important power struggle between the Bundesbank and the federal government, one that foreshadowed the larger role the Bundesbank would play in the IGC and after the Maastricht Treaty had been signed. In Germany, both institutions were preoccupied with the problems of uniting with East Germany and, specifically, the flow of people from East Germany into the Federal Republic. Preparations were continuing for the March 18, 1990, elections in East Germany and, as part of the political campaign of the Christian Democratic Union (CDU) to help its electoral fortunes in the Eastern states, Kohl (without consulting the Bundesbank) announced an offer of monetary union with East Germany on February 6. The import of this development was considerable: it did eventually lead to German monetary union on July 1, 1990, which paved the way for political union. It also created great resentment at the Bundesbank, caused a rift in Bundesbank–federal government relations, and resulted in the early retirement of Pöhl on May 16, 1991.[59] Finally, it created the concern among EU member states that Germany was henceforth going to concentrate on domestic matters and stall further integration.

Largely in response to this fear, Italian prime minister Giulio Andreotti proposed accelerating the date of the IGC from December to July to coincide with the beginning of the Italian presidency of the Council. French president Mitterrand supported this idea, making an explicit link between events in the two Germanies and the integration of Europe: "I think that the acceleration of the inter-German process should be accompanied by acceleration of the European process."[60] The idea was soundly rejected by Kohl, who insisted that the original timetable be respected.

In March, Commission President Delors presented the first of two Commission working papers on EMU. The paper described the economic rationale for and design of the system and included several issues that were important to the Bundesbank:

> 1) the realization of EMU should take account of the parallelism between economic and monetary aspects, respect the principle of subsidiarity and allow for the diversity of the economic situations as requested by the EC in Madrid; 2) monetary union should have as its objective price stability. However, in pursuing this objective, it should support the general economic policy objectives set at Community level; 3) the major role played in this respect by the ECB system or EuroFed; 4) ECU is at the center of the system; and 5) while it is vital to have a single monetary policy, it is not a requirement that there should be a single economic policy.[61]

The Bundesbank's preferences were even more evident in the outcome of the informal meeting of finance ministers and central bankers at Ashford Castle on March 31, 1990:

> There was broad agreement on the overall design: on the monetary side, the participants supported an independent and federally structured central banking institution that was democratically accountable and on the economic side, while the system should be more decentralized, it would provide for *close cooperation on macroeconomic and budgetary policies* (including rules proscribing the monetary or compulsory financing of

budget deficits and the automatic bailing-out by the Community of any member state in difficulties).[62]

In the various technical committees charged with working out the details, the Bundesbank worked in tandem with the German Ministry of Finance to ensure that the Bundesbank's preferences be incorporated. Kohl and Genscher were largely uninvolved in this stage of the negotiations and were, in any case, distracted by the politics of German unification. This presented an opportunity for the technocrats to put their mark on the various Committees' work.

The special meeting of the European Council in Dublin on April 28, 1990, was notable for two decisions, neither of which had a direct bearing on EMU but both of which had an indirect influence: the EU heads of state reached unanimous agreement on a common approach to German unification and discussed the proposal of Kohl and Mitterrand on political union. The former decision was important in the context of Germany's negotiating position; once German unification had been agreed upon, there were fewer incentives for Kohl to make politically unpopular decisions related to the EMU process. The discussions of Kohl's and Mitterrand's proposals for political union were parlayed into a decision at the next Dublin summit to convene a second, parallel IGC to work on an Internal Security Policy and a Common Foreign and Security Policy (which became pillars II and III in the Maastricht Treaty).

THE BUNDESBANK ASSERTS ITSELF

The Bundesbank, having been humiliated by the lack of consultation in the German monetary union policy, rallied to ensure that its voice be heard in the EMU negotiations. In August 1990, the second Commission working paper was unveiled by Delors. It followed the Delors Report fairly consistently but angered the Bundesbank by dropping references to central control of budget policies and including dates for the start of stage 2.[63] During the Delors Report negotiations, Pöhl had inserted the paragraphs pertaining to central control over budget deficits and prevented Delors from making specific proposals about the timing of the stages. Pöhl had publicly criticized plans to let the markets sanction lax fiscal policy, and Delors's sudden conversion to market-based regulation was unwelcome. The inclusion of a date—January 1993—for the beginning of stage 2 was seen by the Bundesbank as an unacceptable attempt by Delors to quicken the pace again. In a September 3 speech, Pöhl questioned the necessity of EMU and decried the Commission's proposals that the member states could move to stage 2 without progress on converging their economies.[64]

The September 9 meeting of the finance ministers in Rome produced an immediate setback for the Commission's plan to begin stage 2 in January 1993. Supported by the Dutch and British, German finance minister Theo Waigel indicated that rushing into stage 2 was not prudent and that economic convergence was more important than setting deadlines. On this, the German finance ministry was completely in agreement with the Bundesbank.

In its September 19 Central Bank Council meeting, the Bundesbank spelled out its essential conditions and warned Kohl not to compromise away these elements in the name of political expedience.[65] The Bundesbank advised that

> the points listed above [were] indispensable, not optional requirements. The Bundesbank considers it necessary for the German delegation to advocate these principles strongly at the intergovernmental conference. The viability of . . . [EMU] must not be endangered in the above mentioned key respects *by the acceptance of compromises during the negotiations.*[66]

Among the elements the Bundesbank wanted contractually safeguarded was that EMU be based on economic union. The bank also demanded that binding rules and sanctions be employed to ensure the fiscal responsibility of EMU member states. The Bundesbank revealed some of the statutory elements it felt should be in the ECB draft treaty:

> In EMU's final stage, monetary policy will have to be formulated by a European Central Bank System (ECBS), which must:
> a. give priority to pursuing monetary stability;
> b. have guaranteed independence;
> c. largely include EC national banks as integral parts. These should no longer follow their own policies;
> d. have a Council (to set monetary policy targets) and an executive board (to implement them). The council should comprise the national central bank governors and the board members.
> e. have all the necessary monetary policy instruments;
> f. have sole responsibility for foreign exchange market intervention;
> g. be under no obligation to lend to public authorities.
>   Because of the far-reaching political implications, the ECBS statute and the rules on budgetary discipline should be specified in the Treaty.[67]

The Bundesbank warned that to reach the final stages of EMU, "a lengthy transitional process" would be needed. It set the following criteria for stage 3:

> 1. Anti-inflation policy must have converged so that price differences have been largely stamped out, budget deficits reduced to a tolerable level, and capital markets rates virtually harmonized.

2. EMU members must have participated fully in the EMS exchange rate mechanism and have liberalized capital movements.
3. National central bank statutes must be harmonized so that they can become integral parts of the ECBS. This would include monetary policy instruments.
4. The contractual arrangements on budgetary discipline in all member states must be adopted at Community level.
5. The single market program must have been realized fully, including the dismantling of border controls.[68]

The Bundesbank's demands are quoted here at length because they evince the Bundesbank's preferences so clearly. They also demonstrate the Bundesbank's uncompromising stance and, when compared to the Maastricht Treaty, show that all but the last point were incorporated in the Treaty. The assertiveness of the Bundesbank vis-à-vis the federal government shows that the bank was far more involved in specifying the terms of agreement than it had been in the Werner Report discussions about EMU. This statement of the Bundesbank also shows that to explain the bank's role as a "ratifier" is too passive, since it was involved at every point and was sometimes the main negotiator of the German position.

The Bundesbank did soften its opposition to dates for the second stage in a paper it circulated among the central banks. The paper, entitled "Compromise proposal for the Second Stage of EMU," included the concession that stage 2 could begin by January 1, 1994 (the date suggested by Spain), provided that strict conditions be met.[69] The paper had the desired effect of causing Kohl to shift his opinion on the date for stage 2. On October 17, 1990, Kohl publicly endorsed the 1994 date, and Delors congratulated him on accepting a "reasonable compromise."[70] It was uncertain, however, how committed Kohl was to the date. Whereas in the Franco-German bilateral summit in April, Kohl had endorsed the proposal to achieve political and complete monetary union by January 1, 1993,[71] before the October 27–28 European Council meeting in Rome, he

> took a surprisingly soft line . . . about his intentions [on a date of stage 2. He] suggested that perhaps the conclusions of the special Council could say something about a "consensus building around the idea" of a specified starting date for Stage 2. But [British foreign secretary Douglas Hurd] recorded his impression that the German Chancellor was not set on seeking even this much, and that he might be open to persuasion to drop references to any date.[72]

In the summit, Kohl kept his promise to support the January 1994 date despite Hurd's earlier impressions. Progress was made not only in setting the conditions for stage 2 but also in formulating a negotiating brief on the IGC for the December 1990 meeting. Agreement also was reached on the starting date for a second IGC on political union, an outcome Kohl had wanted.

Parallel to the political discussions, the Committee of Central Bank Governors had quietly reached agreement on the technical details for the statute of the new ECB in a November 13 meeting.[73] The details were revealed by Pöhl in speeches to industry groups and, unsurprisingly, reflected the Bundesbank's views on most issues.[74] The Committee of Central Bank Governors was united on many of the technical details since the members shared a similar educational background, a common career path, and a conservative conception of central banking. Moreover, the statutes also included a special sweetener—a mandate to give any dependent central banks political autonomy from their member states before the beginning of stage 2.

In late November, the question of a two-speed EMU was resolved in Germany. The Bundesbank and the Finance Ministry concluded that, given the leaders' agreement at the Rome I European summit to a finite period between the beginning of stage 2 and stage 3, a two-speed Europe was all but inevitable.[75] The issue of two-speed EMU was and continued to be a divisive subject among the member states. The reports of Bundesbank and federal government agreement on the desirability of a two-speed Europe spurred the Commission and the French to incorporate into the Maastricht Treaty language they hoped would prevent the fragmentation of the process.

THE BUNDESBANK AND THE GOVERNMENT AGREE

The European Council meeting in Rome on December 15, 1990, is noteworthy not only for formally inaugurating the two IGCs, but for the role played by the finance ministers. The biggest surprise was the sudden intransigence of the finance ministers of Germany, the Netherlands, Spain, and France on issues related to EMU.[76] Delors accused them of "giving the impression of reneging on their governments' commitment to economic and monetary union" and, more ominously, said "I am no longer so sure that Britain is the biggest menace."[77]

Delors indicated that Waigel had "violently attacked" the Commission's draft EMU treaty on the grounds that "it diminished rather than increased the chances of reaching accord on remaining 'open' questions in the EMU negotiations."[78] Delors' chief complaints were that he had been lulled into a false sense of security by the agreements at the Rome I summit and that the progress he had counted on had been reversed.

Three issues resurfaced during the December 1990 meeting: (1) the EU's role in controlling fiscal rectitude, (2) the concrete steps that stage 2 would entail, and (3) the length of stage 2. These issues were hammered out during the monthly IGC meetings. The IGC on EMU was notable for the fact that, for the first time in the EMU negotiations, all parties in Germany (with the possible exception of Foreign Minister Genscher) had the same objectives with respect to EMU. The government had adopted the Bundesbank's positions. The Finance Ministry and the Bundesbank agreed that Germany should avoid pledges to make any major changes at the beginning of stage 2. There was agreement that some form of fiscal control had to be incorporated, and there was a consensus that moving slowly was the appropriate course. The alliance that the federal government would build with the British government in the spring reflected that new, cautious approach. At their meeting February 11, 1991, Kohl suddenly supported British prime minister John Major's "slow" approach to EMU, and later in the month, Kohl rejected Mitterrand's attempts to move quickly to greater monetary cooperation. The most important example of Kohl's stalling on EMU was his call to link progress in the IGC on political union with that of the IGC on EMU. Since progress in the EMU IGC was considerably further along because it had been discussed for nearly two years, this could only mean a slowing of the EMU negotiations.

At the second IGC meeting, January 28, 1991, France and Spain presented the IGC negotiators with draft treaty proposals. The Spanish memorandum contained support for the earlier British proposal for a "hard ECU" and was widely dismissed as another red herring to postpone or derail negotiations on EMU. The French draft was received more favorably by the Commission and other member states. The proposal included sanctions for excessive budget deficits, a provision the German negotiators applauded, but it also contained the creation of the ECB at the beginning of stage 2 and gave it a central role in coordinating national monetary policies during stage 2. Both of these latter provisions were anathema to the Bundesbank.

The next document to emerge was the Luxembourg Council presidency document, which reflected Luxembourg's attempt to find compromise positions among the member states rather than promote its own preferences.[79] The draft included guidelines on economic policies of member states, sanctions for exceeding the criteria, and a "no bail-out" clause but was silent on the divisive issues of timing and monetary control.

In the third IGC session, February 25, 1991, the Germans arrived with their own treaty draft. In presenting the draft, German negotiator Horst Köhler explicitly stated that the proposal had the support of the Bundesbank. The German version fixed the start of stage 2 on January 1, 1994, in accordance with the Rome I communiqué but created an interim structure composed of the Committee of Central Bank Governors, instead of the final ECB. More important, monetary policy making authority would remain with the member states until stage 3. Germany wanted a unanimous vote by the member states before moving to stage 3. It also stipulated that a majority of the member states must meet three criteria (price stability, low interest-rate differentials between the member states, and reduction of national budget deficits) in order to be eligible for the single currency.[80]

The draft was publicly criticized by a spokesman for Delors: "The [German] plan does not conform to the conclusions of the Rome European Council . . . which anticipated, notably, that at the beginning of the second phase of economic and monetary union the new institution would be created."[81] The German Finance Ministry, knowing that the draft represented a consensus between the federal government and the Bundesbank, responded only with the comment that the criticism was "incomprehensible and in this form unusual because it was made in public and during the ongoing negotiations by the government delegates."[82] The willingness of the Finance Ministry to risk antagonizing Delors speaks volumes about its new alliance with the Bundesbank. Since the institutional conflict had been laid to rest, the German position became much more powerful internationally. Germany's preferences would now become consistent and would dominate the negotiations on the major points of contention.

By the end of April 1991, Luxembourg presented a second compromise draft treaty that incorporated more of the German preferences. Specifically, the draft contained the German proposal that a "council" of the national central bank governors could be established, to become the ECB later. This concession was linked to the blueprint that the ECB be created on January 1, 1996, unless member states agreed unanimously to set it up earlier. The German delegation rejected the "automaticity" of the compromise draft, and the Luxembourg presidency could report no further progress on the difficult stage 2 issues at the end of its term in June. On one other important issue, however, the member states were able to agree: the issue of an "opt-out" for Britain. Following up on a consensus reached in a May ECOFIN meeting, the member states agreed that no member state could be forced to enter the single currency, and conversely, no member state could prevent the others from forming EMU. This breakthrough essentially solved the problem of Britain. During the Council presidency of the Netherlands, in the second half of 1991, the influence of Britain in the IGC on EMU negotiations was negligible, and Germany lost an ally in its cautious approach to EMU.

SLOW PROGRESS ON THE BUNDESBANK'S TERMS

At the first IGC meeting of the Netherlands Council presidency, September 9, 1991, the Dutch finance minister Wim Kok presented the Netherlands's "technical paper." Unsurprisingly, given that the Dutch currency had consistently been a strong currency pegged to the DM, the draft was much closer to German preferences than the Luxembourg drafts had been. The draft endorsed a two-speed approach to currency union, stipulating that if only six members met the strict economic criteria by 1996, they could proceed to monetary union. Delors ruled out the proposal immediately, and the weaker-currency states all opposed the concept. Kok was forced to concede defeat, saying that "we should not be creating the impression that certain member states would be left behind more or less indefinitely."[83]

There was progress on related issues, however: the member states agreed to establish the European Monetary Institute (EMI) at the beginning of stage 2 and were able to agree in principle on convergence criteria that would be used to judge entry into the single currency. By October, there was progress on the issue of the two-speed approach favored by Germany and the Netherlands and the mandate for stage 2. Although billed as a compromise, the proposal reflected more of a compromise on the parts of France, Belgium, and the Commission than on that of Germany. Germany's compromise was the acceptance of a firm date for the beginning of stage 3, a concession the Bundesbank and finance ministry had been against since the Delors Committee. In return, however, the other member states agreed to strict convergence criteria to be eligible for stage 3, the need for sanctions to enforce those standards once EMU had been achieved, and the creation of the ECB only at the beginning of stage 3 (with an institutional mandate for independence that exceeded even the Bundesbank's).

Moreover, the Bundesbank gave another position paper on November 7, 1991, to the German government in advance of the Maastricht summit.[84] The paper expressed satisfaction that many of the important points in its September 1990 position paper had been incorporated in the draft treaty. It noted, however, that since the other member states could be counted on to try to negotiate the treaty in their self-interest, certain points still had to be seriously considered in the final negotiations. The first of the three points concerned the responsibilities of the EMI: it was essential that no real decisionmaking power go to the EMI before the beginning of stage 3 and that no reserves be transferred before stage 3. Furthermore, EMI presidents and vice presidents could only be drawn from the ranks of central bankers. The second point was the need for convergence to take precedence over considerations of timing, and the third issue concerned specific rules for the ECB, which would give voting rights only to members in compliance with all responsibilities.

By November 25, 1991, the bargains were firmed up: the convergence criteria were stipulated, and the Committee of Central Bank Governors attached its draft document about an independent central bank to the treaty draft. The final bargain was struck at the Maastricht European Council summit in December. Mitterrand and Italian prime minister Andreotti worked out an alternative plan because of their fear that an insufficient number of member states would be able to meet the convergence criteria by the date planned for stage 3, thereby consigning this EMU to the same fate as the Werner Report's EMU. The plan accepted a two-speed Europe rather than the abandonment of the single currency and is a testament to Mitterrand's commitment to EMU at any cost. Their proposal set stage 3 to begin in 1997 if a majority of the member states were ready to join, but required stage 3 to begin at the latest by 1999, when a single currency would be created by only those countries that met the criteria. In retrospect, this proposal was one of the most important elements in making EMU a reality. As Mitterrand and Andreotti had correctly foreseen, a majority of member states did not meet the criteria by 1996, and thus it was only their addition to the Maastricht Treaty that actually resulted in monetary union. We should ask, however, why Kohl would be willing to agree to a last-minute proposal without consulting his ministers? Here, it becomes clear that Kohl was personally predisposed to make EMU irreversible.[85] There can be no other explanation: if Kohl had wanted to prevent monetary policy, or even if he was indifferent, he would not have accepted the Franco-Italian proposal. He was, of course, anxious to reach agreement on further political reforms, and he knew that the Bundesbank would be unable to argue that Germany's stability policies had been compromised. But, ultimately, one man had ensured that cooperation would inevitably occur.

CONCLUSION

The Maastricht Treaty, signed December 5, 1991, incorporated all of the Bundesbank's significant demands. It enshrined stability as the sole mandate, giving the ECB more political independence from member governments than even the Bundesbank has from Bonn. It also instituted prohibitions against budgetary overdrafts covered by the central bank and fiscal and economic convergence criteria to be met by all governments before monetary union could be achieved. Short of preventing monetary union altogether, the treaty was everything the Bundesbank could have wished. As one scholar observed, "Far more significant [for the outcome of the EMU negotiations] was a renewed assertiveness of the Bundesbank and clear evidence that Germany's bargaining positions in the IGC were being strongly influenced by it."[86]

Germany's participation in EMU was a necessary condition to that venture's success, and this explains the Bundesbank's ability to act as more than a ratifier and impose strict conditions on resigning monetary sovereignty. But perhaps more puzzling are the questions, why did the Bundesbank allow the initiative to gain momentum initially, and how was that momentum maintained during the thirty-two months after the release of the Delors Report? The questions can be answered by considering two factors: EU member states' acceptance of German unification and Kohl's ultimate decision to support EMU and to make it irreversible. Certainly the former explanation accounts for how the momentum was maintained up until April 1990 (when the European Council formally gave its blessing for German unification). How did the negotiations continue after German unification had been achieved? This explanation hinges on the role of Kohl and the institutions in the EU. The initial impetus for EMU had to come from the European Council, but once the mandate had been given, the Commission was able to maintain a steady stream of mandates to the various institutional bodies of the EU to make compromise and progress possible. At various intervals, it is true, the bargains and compromises required ratification from the heads of state, but under the circumstances, since the ultimate result had been agreed upon, it was politically difficult for reluctant participants to renege on the commitment.

In the interinstitutional rivalry in Germany, the IGC on EMU was a pivotal event because it required the federal government and the Bundesbank to work together. The new status of the Bundesbank internationally made it impossible for the federal government to attempt to negotiate the Treaty without the input of the Bundesbank. The Bundesbank's membership on many of the relevant committees required the federal government to incorporate the bank's preferences in its positions. Thus the Kohl government was in the situation of taking a hard line in the negotiations of the terms of EMU while, at the same time, keeping the talks on EMU from foundering.

Although the newfound, albeit reluctant, cooperation between the Bundesbank and the federal government proved a significant benefit to the German position during the international negotiations of the Treaty, it did not last long. Almost before the ink on the Maastricht Treaty was dry, the two institutions would engage in their next conflict, a battle that almost destroyed the EMS.

NOTES

1. Lawson (1993), p. 894.
2. See Balladur's memorandum of December 29, 1987, reproduced in Krägenau and Wetter (1993), pp. 337–338. The memo comprised three sections: "I. More Progress Is Necessary"; "II. Realizable Progress"; and "III. Creation of a Zone with a Single Currency." The third section consisted mainly of questions that would need to be addressed rather than proposals. Balladur gave an indication of

these plans publicly in a television interview. See also *Financial Times,* January 7, 1988.

3. *Financial Times,* December 7, 1987.

4. Solomon (1995), p. 382.

5. For more on the problems with the falling dollar and Bundesbank's resistance to "target range" proposals, see Henning (1994).

6. *Financial Times,* January 8, 1988.

7. Since the inception of the EMS, Germany's trade surpluses had almost tripled from $3.3 billion in 1978 to $9 billion in 1987. By 1989, the surplus reached a record $12.7 billion. The effect of the EMS can also be seen in Germany's trade surplus data with Italy. Whereas Germany traditionally ran a deficit with Italy before the EMS, it switched to surpluses during the years that Italy was in the EMS and then reverted back to deficits after Italy left the EMS in 1992. Interestingly, the exit of Britain from the EMS did not have the same salutorious effect on the German balance of trade with Britain.

8. Solomon (1995), p. 382.

9. For more on Genscher's views, see Krägenau and Wetter (1993), pp. 309–310.

10. *Financial Times,* January 15 and 21, 1988.

11. Gros and Thygesen (1992), p. 315.

12. *Bulletin of the European Communities* (1988), 1–88, January, p. 87.

13. Ibid.

14. Ibid.

15. *Financial Times,* June 23, 1988.

16. Thatcher (1993), p. 740. It is clear she counted on Pöhl to derail the plans: "I hoped that . . . the sceptical Herr Pöhl would manage to put a spoke in the wheel of this particular vehicle of European integration."

17. Committee for the Study of Economic and Monetary Union (1989), p. 3.

18. Cameron (1995c).

19. Deutsche Bundesbank, *Annual Report,* 1988, p. 11.

20. *Financial Times,* June 23, 1988.

21. Committee for the Study of Economic and Monetary Union (1989), p. 131.

22. As it was, even the Treaty's strict provisions for monetary union were challenged before the German Constitutional Court. See Chapter 7.

23. Author's interview, March 1994.

24. *Financial Times,* April 13, 1989.

25. The report noted that "at this juncture, the Committee does not consider it possible to propose a detailed blueprint for accomplishing this transition." Committee for the Study of Economic and Monetary Union (1989), p. 38.

26. *Financial Times,* July 18, 1989; *The Economist* July 7, 1990.

27. Schönfelder and Thiel (1994), p. 53.

28. For more on Thatcher's criticisms, see Thatcher (1993), chap. 24.

29. See Lawson (1993), p. 920.

30. For more on the preferences of the states, see *Financial Times,* June 26, 1989; *The Economist,* July 1, 1989.

31. Kohl made his approval for an IGC on EMU conditional on two things: the IGC could only start after stage 1 had started on July 1, 1990, to coincide with removal of all capital controls, and preparations for stages 2 and 3 would also have to be "sufficiently far advanced" for substantive negotiations. See *Financial Times,* June 27, 1989.

32. Thatcher records that Kohl might have been open to dropping references to any date for stage 2 to begin from the Rome communiqué. See Thatcher (1993), p. 765.

33. Committee for the Study of Economic and Monetary Union (1989), p. 31.

34. See Cameron (1995c), p. 54.

35. *Financial Times,* June 28, 1989.

36. *Financial Times,* June 28, 1989.

37. See Cameron (1995c), pp. 54ff.

38. *Financial Times,* October 30, 1989.

39. Deutscher Bundestag (1990), p. 31.

40. The draft treaty, which was presented in the IGC on February 25, 1991, is reproduced in Krägenau and Wetter (1993), pp. 331–334.

41. Lawson (1993), p. 938ff.

42. Gros and Thygesen (1992), p. 323.

43. *Bulletin of the European Communities* (1989), 11–89, November, p. 12.

44. See for example, *Financial Times,* July 1, 1989, August 18, 1989, October 30, 1989, November 20 and 27, 1989, and December 15, 1989.

45. Deutsche Bundesbank, *Annual Report,* p. 6 (emphasis added).

46. *Financial Times,* July 1, 1989.

47. In a July 1, 1989, *Financial Times* interview, Pöhl indicated that "the Bundesbank can live very well with the status quo."

48. *Financial Times,* November 20, 1989 (emphasis added).

49. *Financial Times,* December 8, 1989.

50. Ibid.

51. For interesting poll results on the unification question before 1989, see Merkl (1993), pp. 120–126. For an overview of the EU's response to the question of German unification, see Feldman (1991).

52. Speech reprinted and translated in James and Stone (1992), p. 38.

53. Ibid., p. 40.

54. Hamalainen (1994), p. 88.

55. Thatcher (1993), p. 796.

56. *Financial Times,* December 8, 1989.

57. *Financial Times,* December 11, 1989.

58. Other scholars also support this interpretation. See Pond (1993); Zelikow and Rice (1997).

59. Kohl did not consult Pöhl in advance about German economic and monetary union and also ignored the Bundesbank's advice about the terms of that unification. Thus, although the Bundesbank recommended a 2 ostmark/DM exchange, the government converted at 1:1 for the first 4,000 ostmarks in savings and all wages and 2:1 for savings above 4,000 ostmarks. In the final event, the weighted average was approximately 1.8:1. See Marsh (1992), p. 216; Tietmeyer and Guth (1990).

60. *Financial Times,* February 15, 1990.

61. *Bulletin of the European Communities* (1990), 3–90, March, p. 8.

62. *Bulletin of the European Communities* (1990), 4–90, April, p. 14 (emphasis added).

63. *The Economist,* August 25, 1990.

64. *Financial Times,* September 4, 1990.

65. Deutsche Bundesbank (1990), *Monthly Report,* pp. 40–44; *The Economist,* September 22, 1990.

66. Deutsche Bundesbank (1990), *Monthly Report,* p. 44, [emphasis added].

67. *Financial Times,* September 21, 1990.

68. Ibid.
69. *Financial Times,* October 8, 1990.
70. *Financial Times,* October 19, 1990.
71. *Financial Times,* April 20, 1990. This commitment was probably more of a show of political goodwill before the European Council meeting about German unification on April 28.
72. Thatcher (1993), p. 765.
73. *Financial Times,* November 14, 1990.
74. The only issue that wasn't resolved entirely to the Bundesbank's liking was the question of whether the ECB would be the lender of last resort for Europe. See *Financial Times,* November 21, 1990.
75. *Financial Times,* November 26, 1990.
76. *Financial Times,* December 18, 1990.
77. Ibid.
78. Ibid.
79. *The Reuter Library Report*, February 22, 1991.
80. *The Reuter Library Report*, February 26, 1991.
81. *The Reuter Library Report*, February 27, 1991.
83. *The Reuter Library Report*, September 9, 1991.
84. See Krägenau and Wetter (1993), p. 334.
85. See Sandholtz (1993b), p. 137.
86. Dyson (1994), p. 154.

6

The EMS Crises

By the late 1980s, the EMS had evolved to look less like a crawling-peg system and more like a fixed-rate regime. As a consequence, some Europeans began to consider the EMS a forerunner of a European monetary union. The functioning of the regime remained asymmetrical, with the Bundesbank setting the monetary policy for all EMS member states. The other states' monetary policy, however, had generally approached the German standard, and realignments in the system had become infrequent—in fact, none had occurred since January 1987. The understanding that the EMS had become a stepping-stone to monetary union was confirmed by the Maastricht Treaty's inclusion as a criterion that a member state's currency should observe the normal fluctuation range of the ERM for at least two years without devaluing against the currency of any member state. However, ten months after the signing of the Treaty on European Union in Maastricht on December 5, 1991, the EMS suffered the greatest setback in its thirteen-year history with the exit of the British pound and the Italian lira. And little more than another ten months later, the system all but fractured completely when the fluctuation bands were widened to ±15 percent.[1] Was the EMS doomed to failure, or had the regime dynamics been altered by the Maastricht Treaty?[2]

The crises of the EMS were, in large measure, caused by Germany. A careful reading of the facts shows that the Bundesbank's relationship with the federal government was the underlying source of the crises, but their conflicts were compounded by the other member states' unwillingness to take the traditional remedy of a general realignment. Their resistance to the necessary realignments were based on the perception that the markets would consider them unfit for the single currency, and thus the safety valve of the regime was disconnected by the member states themselves.

It is inaccurate to refer to a *single* EMS crisis in 1992; there were several points during the year when the system was under strain. The first crisis culminated, however, on "Black Wednesday," September 16, 1992, when the United Kingdom and Italy allowed their currencies to float, thus effectively exiting the EMS framework. Additional European currency turmoil after September 1992 resulted in the devaluation of the Spanish peseta, the Portuguese escudo, and the Irish punt as well as the abandonment by Sweden, Norway, and Finland of their unofficial exchange-rate pegs to the EMS currencies. Until August 1993 there was speculation that the Danish krone and the French franc would also be devalued, which forced the central banks to intervene massively to counter speculative capital inflows. Only after the August 2 decision by the EU Monetary Committee to widen the bands to ±15 percent did stability return to the remnants of the EMS. We might ask, what factors were responsible for this turbulence, and specifically, how did the Bundesbank–federal government internal *domestic* conflict affect the *international* relations among the EMS partners?

GOVERNMENT-BUNDESBANK CONFLICT DURING GERMAN MONETARY UNION

The storm clouds on the EMS horizon first became visible with German unification. The domestic stresses that accompanied the July 1, 1990, German monetary union spilled over into the international arena because of the steps the Bundesbank had taken to deal with rising inflation.

The decision to unify the currencies of and West Germany even before legal unification involved considerable open conflict between the Bundesbank and the federal government.[3] With electoral considerations in mind, on February 6, 1990, Chancellor Kohl suddenly announced a pending monetary union between East and West Germany without consulting Bundesbank president Pöhl. Prompted by the flow of East Germans into West Germany, Kohl wanted to bring the DM into East Germany to staunch the flow of "refugees." The conversion rate was critical: too high and it would create inflation in West Germany; too low and it would cause a recession in East Germany and alienate many potential CDU voters in the GDR. Pöhl and the Central Bank Council proposed a rate of 2 ostmarks to 1 DM in order to reduce the risk of imported inflation. On April 23, Kohl announced the more generous rate of 1:1, basically ignoring the advice of the Bundesbank. Kohl's final affront was his decision to finance unity through borrowing with only minimal tax increases, thus overburdening the monetary policy of Germany.[4] These slights created tension between Kohl and Pöhl and ultimately led to Pöhl's May 16, 1991, resignation from the Bundesbank. The conflict was also perceived as a setback to the power of the Bundesbank because the federal government had received but ignored the Bundesbank's advice and seemingly had not suffered any loss of esteem in the public's eye.[5] This setback to the Bundesbank's position, however, was temporary and only served to strengthen the bank's institutional resolve not to be subordinated by the Kohl government again.

As Germany lurched toward higher inflation and, later, recession, the "I told you so" of the Bundesbank was only part of the punishment the Bonn government had to endure. Much more damaging were the high interest rates that the Bundesbank had raised to finance the borrowings of the government and to quell burgeoning inflation. The soaring interest rates were condemned both domestically and internationally, causing the Bonn government much consternation throughout 1991–1992 and eventually breaking up the EMS regime.

EMS MEMBERS RESIST REALIGNMENT

In 1990, German monetary officials discretely canvassed the other EMS participants as to whether they would consider a general EMS realignment to damp the inflationary impact of German unification.[6] Such a realignment—the first since January 1987—would have revalued the DM against all the other currencies in the EMS and thereby held in check the inflationary pressures stemming from German unification by keeping import prices down.

In July 1990, there could and probably should have been a general realignment of the EMS currencies (or at least a revaluation of the DM) to coincide with German monetary union. Italy's January 1990 devaluation of 3.7 percent should have made it clear that, in the later words of a senior Bundesbank official, "we are not in a fixed exchange rate system yet."[7] Realignments were becoming more infrequent, but the economies had not converged to the point at which realignments were unnecessary. However, many of the member states were avoiding realignments, lest they be seen as unable to keep their commitment to price stability mandated by the Maastricht Treaty.

Although Chancellor Kohl was not necessarily averse to a general EMS realignment, French authorities were completely against severing the DM-franc parity that had been the basis for France's *franc fort* policy since 1984. Moreover, since they were afraid of imported inflation, they would not even consider the idea of a realignment. Could the Germans have pressed the French harder? At the time of the January 1990 Italian devaluation, France had made clear to its EMS partners that it would not consider realignment; as Pöhl commented after the Italian devaluation, "A realignment of the EMS is not on the agenda because the major players in that system do not want it."[8]

German pressure for an EMS realignment in 1990 probably stemmed more from Pöhl and the Bundesbank than from Kohl. German economic officials were engaged in serious negotiations with the French about a quick approach to European monetary union, culminating in EMU as early as January 1, 1993. In the context of the ongoing and delicate EMU negotiations, it is unlikely that either Chancellor Kohl or German finance minister Theo Waigel wished to strong-arm French finance minister Pierre Bérégovoy into considering a realignment that included a de facto franc devaluation, despite the franc's relative weakness in the EMS at the time. The German government was keenly aware that maintaining the franc's parity to the DM was politically essential for the French and thus did not push them. The Bundesbank, however, was less concerned with the niceties of Germany's ties to France than with the misalignment of central rates to several EMS member states and wished to correct the imbalances. The bank, not having the institutional mandate to initiate conversations with its partners on the subject, could therefore only obliquely hint that it would have preferred a general realignment.

Other EMS countries also rejected a comprehensive EMS realignment because of the political implications of a de facto devaluation, and thus a formal realignment proposal was never discussed within the EU's Monetary Committee.[9] Had the EMS been functioning as it did in its earlier years—as a fixed but adjustable exchange-rate system—it should have been possible to achieve a comprehensive EMS realignment while minimizing the political stigma of devaluation. Given that German unification was an exceptional historic event, it should not have been difficult to justify a realignment within the EMS (even in France, with its emphasis on the *franc fort*) by which all currencies moved down vis-à-vis the DM. A comprehensive realignment of all EMS currencies, brought about by German monetary union, would have better positioned the EMS to avoid the subsequent upheavals of 1992 and 1993.[10]

A second storm cloud appeared in October 1990, when the United Kingdom began participating in the ERM with a DM-sterling parity of DM 2.95. The British government had already trespassed one of the norms of the EMS regime by announcing the parity publicly rather than negotiating it with its partner states. Moreover, in the view of German—especially Bundesbank—officials, this rate was too high and would eventually cause strains within the EMS.[11] The British nonetheless insisted that DM 2.95 was a reasonable parity for sterling, and throughout 1991, they appeared to be correct.[12] The EMS seemed to be functioning reasonably well; European monetary discussions in 1991 focused on the proper course to EMU without questioning the stability of the EMS. Although German interest rates steadily edged upward, prompting criticisms from Germany's EMS partners who were trying to maintain their EMS links to the DM, 1991 was a year of long-range planning in which the transition path from EMS to EMU was mapped out and agreed upon, with the Maastricht Treaty signed in December. The stability and viability of the EMS itself did not come into question.

Within Germany, however, economic strains related to the costs of unification were becoming apparent. The Bundesbank began to criticize openly the Federal Republic's subsidies for inefficient firms in the former East Germany on the grounds that the subsidies were irresponsibly inflationary and undermined the tools available to the Bundesbank for monetary control. German inflation was rising: by April 1991, the inflation rate in Germany had overtaken that of four of its EMS partners, and the German money supply consistently exceeded the Bundesbank's monetary growth targets. German interest rates continued to rise: by July 1992, the Bundesbank had raised the German discount rate to 8.75 percent and the Lombard rate to 9.75 percent.[13] Reports of disagreements between Germany and its EMS partners over the Bundesbank's high interest rates began to appear regularly in the press.[14]

When the Danish electorate rejected the Maastricht Treaty on June 2, 1992, the stresses on EMS currency links increased substantially. For exchange market speculators, any indication of economic policy disagreement or of a weakened commitment to EMU raised the possibility that national monetary authorities would be unwilling to undertake and maintain the difficult domestic sacrifices (e.g., sustaining damagingly high interest rates) necessary to keep to their EMS parities. These sacrifices had become especially painful for Britain and Italy, where interest rates were kept high in order to attract and retain capital and thereby remain within their DM bands. Although by some measures inflation in the UK during the summer of 1992 was lower than in Germany,[15] British interest rates remained at 10 percent, notwithstanding the most severe recession in Britain since the 1930s.[16] EMS parity stresses were compounded by the sharp fall in U.S. interest rates over the 1991–1992 period. As U.S. rates fell in response to economic recession there, capital flowed out of the United States in search of a better return in Europe.[17] However, this capital inflow was not evenly distributed across EMS countries; as usual, the DM experienced strong upward pressures vis-à-vis the dollar. This tended to drag the other EMS currencies up with it, but because they were not as strong as the DM, they consistently languished at the floor of their DM band. With the currency markets aware of the economic pain that accompanied high British interest rates, sterling was consistently the object of market speculation during the summer, notwithstanding the unequivocal rejection of any sterling devaluation by British authorities.[18]

When the Bundesbank Central Bank Council met on July 16, 1992, and agreed on a rise in the discount rate to 8.75 percent, Germany's EMS partners were stunned. By ignoring many signals that the German economy itself was slowing, the Bundesbank deliberately sent a signal to the markets, the federal government, and the EMS partners: the Bundesbank's aversion to inflation had not weakened, nor would interest rate policy be determined by political pressures. Several participants, including some at the Bundesbank, later opined that the increase was less a decision justified by market conditions than a signal that the Bundesbank was not the federal government's lapdog.[19] Indeed, in retrospect, the increase was a mistake because the bank had considerably misjudged the strength of the German economy, and the rise was causally linked to the September EMS crisis. The Bundesbank, however, had made its point.

THE BUNDESBANK'S UNPOPULAR POLICIES

When German monetary policy tightened beginning in the late 1980s, the Bundesbank was lauded for taking precautionary measures. Despite slowed economic growth, German inflation in 1992 nonetheless neared 4 percent, and German monetary targets were consistently overshot. By 1992, however, the reaction of Germany's EMS partners to the Bundesbank's monetary tightening had ceased to be favorable. High German interest rates in practice set the floor beneath which other countries' interest rates could not sink while still maintaining their exchange-rate commitments in the EMS. As economic growth slowed across Europe in 1992, interest rate reductions to stimulate domestic economic growth were held in check by the floor set by the Bundesbank's tight monetary policy.

It is clear that Bundesbank interest-rate policy was widely unpopular both domestically and internationally, not merely because it constituted traditional and painful discipline, but because many within Germany and in other European states believed that it was the wrong policy for the given circumstances. Indeed, perhaps never before had Bundesbank policy alienated so many different sectors and interest groups simultaneously. The degree of both international and domestic opposition to the Bundesbank's high interest rates suggests that pressures for lower German interest rates might have been accommodated to a greater degree than they were. At the very least, the Bundesbank could have seen fit to shave off more than 0.25 percent from its Lombard rate following the Italian devaluation of September 14, 1992. Even if the federal government had been predisposed to accede to its EMS counterparts' (and domestic interest groups') demands for interest rate relaxation, the Bundesbank Central Bank Council had the only means to do that, and it stubbornly kept German interest rates high.

By August 1992, the Bundesbank's interest rate policies were coming under attack both externally and within Germany. Franz Steinkühler, head of Germany's largest union, IGMetall, characterized the Bundesbank's agenda as paying excessive attention to inflation while neglecting the Bundesbank's other legal and economic responsibilities (i.e., employment, steady economic growth, and foreign trade balance considerations). In a similar vein, the German Institute for Economic Research (DIW) accused the Bundesbank of pursuing a self-defeating and misguided monetary policy that threatened to undermine the entire restructuring approach in East Germany. In response, Bundesbank president Helmut Schlesinger chided German politicians for creating the domestic economic conditions that necessitated a tight German monetary policy.[20]

In the week of August 24, another wave of selling pressure hit the dollar. With the German currency experiencing sharp upward pressure against the dollar, sterling and the lira sagged against the DM. As one senior UK official commented, "Sterling's fate is out of our hands. The future of the pound depends on what happens to the dollar and the DM."[21] Stresses in the EMS were compounded with renewed doubts about the future of European monetary cooperation in light of the upcoming September 20 French referendum on the Maastricht Treaty; public opinion polls in France showed the French electorate narrowly defeating the Treaty. Markets had become extremely nervous about the outcome of the referendum; they also had lost confidence in the accuracy of public opinion polls, which had been so wrong in the case of the Danish referendum.[22] By Thursday, August 27, the Bank of England had reportedly spent approximately £1 billion in support of sterling on the exchanges.

There were indications from the Bundesbank Central Bank Council—an advance text of a council member speech included references about the "potential" for EMS realignment—that the Bundesbank desired a general EMS realignment.[23] On August 28, after a turbulent week in European currency markets, the lira had fallen through its EMS floor against the DM, and sterling was in danger of following suit.[24] At the behest of the United Kingdom (which occupied the Council presidency), EU finance ministers issued a joint statement ruling out any EMS realignment.

> The member states of the EC are committed to economic and monetary stability in the EMS, which is an important element in European prosperity. The governments of member states agree that a change in the present structure of central rates would not be the appropriate response to the current tensions in the EMS. They welcome the activation of the Basel/Nyborg agreement on intramarginal intervention and the respective cooperation among the European central banks. The authorities of Community member countries are actively pursuing economic policy cooperation and stand ready to enforce their cooperation to ensure an appropriate functioning of the EMS.[25]

Currency market speculators, however, were unconvinced, and pressures on the EMS rates continued into September.

European central banks found themselves engaged in an almost daily struggle to maintain currencies within the EMS fluctuation bands. On September 3, British officials announced an ECU 10 billion ($14.5 billion) three-year foreign currency credit line to be used for sterling support; Italy raised interest rates to 15 percent in an attempt to ease pressure on the lira. In Germany, Bundesbank officials were especially dismayed by the pressures on sterling and the lira. The 1987 EMS Basel/Nyborg agreement had established a "presumption" that financing within specified limits would be extended from strong-currency central banks to weak-currency central banks for purposes of intramarginal intervention.[26] As sterling and the lira came under pressure, the British and the Italians drew upon Bundesbank DM financing to support their currencies. But heavy central bank intervention in DM had the effect of adding to the inflationary pressures within the German economy because the DM sold in support of sterling and the lira were immediately recycled back into Germany. EU finance ministers were scheduled to meet in Bath, England, over the weekend of September 5–6, 1992, and a face-to-face meeting held out the possibility of arriving at a common view among EMS participants on how to respond to the ongoing currency stresses.

THE BATH SUMMIT AND ITS REPERCUSSIONS

In retrospect, the Bath summit appears to be a classic case of misperception and misunderstanding. Each of the participants came to the meeting with their own agenda on how to address the crisis, and there was little agreement across the table. Three positions emerged. The French were completely opposed to a general EMS realignment (especially one that would come so close to the September 20 French referendum on the Maastricht Treaty), but they were indifferent to the individual realignments of other countries. The British were opposed to any EMS realignment and simply wanted the Bundesbank to lower interest rates. The Germans preferred a general realignment but would accept individual ones. Because of the statutory independence of the Bundesbank, however, the federal government representatives were unable to make an explicit bargain of a realignment for lower interest rates. Schlesinger actually came close to making a quid pro quo offer at Bath when he privately suggested that a general realignment with a significant DM revaluation would make the exorbitantly high German interest rates unnecessary.[27] However, the British, who were uninterested in any realignment, controlled the agenda at the meeting. Jean-Claude Trichet, French *Directeur du Trésor* and chairman of the EU Monetary Committee, never broached the subject of a realignment to the British; hence, a general EMS realignment was never even formally discussed at Bath. The countries in favor of a general EMS realignment—Germany, the Netherlands, Belgium, and Italy—did not have the opportunity to coordinate a position among themselves, and time ran out before other specific proposals could be considered. The statement issued at the close of the Bath summit reflected the "lowest common denominator" of agreement that the participants could reach:[28]

> In the face of the tensions in the exchange markets the following decisions have been taken.
>
> 1. The August 28 agreement not to proceed to a realignment in the European Monetary System has been confirmed.
>
> 2. The governors stand ready to intervene in the exchange markets to counter tension in those markets, exploiting as fully as necessary the means and instruments provided under the EMS for member states.
>
> 3. The ministers and governors have also examined the present economic situation in the Community and in this context they emphasized the importance of early and full implementation of strict convergence programmes, in particular to consolidate fiscal positions and to keep under control wage and other cost pressures. They particularly welcomed the recent policy decisions by the Italian government, and its firm commitment to achieve a substantial primary budget surplus in 1993.
>
> 4. In the light of a slowing of the growth prospects of their economies, and insofar as the disinflationary process allows it, they have decided to take advantage of any opportunity to reduce interest rates. They welcomed the fact that the Bundesbank in present circumstances has no intention to increase interest rates and is watching the further development of the economy.[29]

Following the meeting, UK chancellor of the exchequer Norman Lamont[30] strongly implied that the EU finance ministers had wrung a concession from the Germans with the statement that "the Bundesbank . . . has no intention to increase interest rates."[31] However, this implication was quickly repudiated by Bundesbank president Schlesinger the following day, when he stated that the Bath communiqué "represented no change in policy" for the Bundesbank, thus appearing to distance himself from the no-realignment agreement.[32]

Currency markets were unimpressed by the evident lack of agreement at the Bath meeting of finance ministers. As soon as markets opened on Monday, September 7, heavy speculation commenced in anticipation of a sterling and lira devaluation.[33] By Friday, September 11, the lira was again trading below its EMS floor, notwithstanding intervention by the German and Italian central banks. That evening, German chancellor Helmut Kohl, Finance Minister Theo Waigel, and State Secretary for Finance Horst Köhler paid a secret visit to the Bundesbank, where President Schlesinger and Vice President Hans Tietmeyer showed the ministers the burden of the bank's foreign exchange interventions—DM 290 billion on the week, according to one account[34]—and the undermining effect DM intervention had on the bank's tight monetary policy. They discussed that evening how to achieve a general realignment in the EMS and the degree to which German interest rates could fall in response to an EMS realignment. At the end of the evening, Kohl decided to send Köhler and Tietmeyer first to Paris and then to Rome to discuss a realignment.

There was considerable telephone activity among the EMS participants during the weekend of September 12–13, with discussion of EMS realignment in both general and specific terms. Trichet did not, however, tell the other members that the Germans wanted a general realignment. In light of the fact that repeated central bank intervention and interest-rate increases had not brought the lira back within its EMS fluctuation band, the Italians had accepted the necessity of a lira devaluation. The Germans were against the lira devaluing unilaterally, but also knew that the French authorities would certainly be unwilling to devalue the franc only a week before their September 20 Maastricht referendum. Köhler therefore proposed a general realignment in which the British, Italian, Spanish, Portuguese, Irish, and Danish currencies would move down against the German, French, Belgian, and Dutch currencies. The British, however, rejected this proposal because it linked sterling with the weakest currencies in the system. In fact, the only proposal that could be agreed upon by all participants over the weekend was that the lira would be devalued by 7 percent and that the Bundesbank would lower interest rates.

The size of the German interest rate cut—a 0.25 percent cut in the Lombard rate (to 9.5 percent) and a 0.5 percent cut in the discount rate (to 8.25 percent)—disappointed other EMS members and currency markets, which had expected that the German action would be more significant. Accordingly, on Tuesday, September 15, the pound was again at its EMS-defined DM floor, and senior British Treasury and Bank of England authorities met to discuss alternatives. The consensus among the participants was for heavy central bank intervention on Wednesday, September 16, to be followed by an increase in British interest rates if heavy central bank intervention failed to bolster sterling. During the course of this meeting, the news arrived of Bundesbank president Schlesinger's interview in the German business paper *Handelsblatt*. Schlesinger was quoted as saying that the tension in the EMS was not over yet and would not be over until there was a comprehensive realignment. Although Schlesinger did not specifically mention sterling, it was clear to the British and the markets that sterling was the target of the remark. At the behest of UK chancellor of the exchequer Lamont, Bank of England governor Robin Leigh-Pemberton repeatedly pleaded with Schlesinger throughout the evening to repudiate his remark. Schlesinger finally did so, but the *Handelsblatt* editor threatened to go public with an audiotape of the interview, and

Schlesinger could only say that the release of the EMS-portion of the interview had been "unauthorized."[35]

When Schlesinger's *Handelsblatt* interview appeared the following morning, Wednesday, September 16, 1992, sterling was already trading beneath its floor of DM 2.7780. Lamont issued yet another public statement to assure the markets that Britain intended to hang on: Britain "will take whatever measures are necessary to maintain sterling's ERM parity."[36] After massive central bank interventions did not nudge sterling upward, the prime minister agreed in the morning to announce a rise in British interest rates from 10 percent to 12 percent—the first British interest rate increase since the UK had joined the EMS almost two years earlier. When 12 percent interest rates did not stem the sterling sell-off, a further increase to 15 percent was authorized and announced in the afternoon. Nonetheless, the pound closed the day beneath its EMS floor. In the evening, Lamont announced that sterling's membership in the EMS would be suspended, that the pound would be allowed to float freely, and that the second of the two interest rate increases (from 12 percent to 15 percent) was reversed. At a hastily convened meeting of the EU's Monetary Committee in Brussels late in the evening, British officials tried unsuccessfully to obtain agreement to suspend the EMS until after the French referendum, which was still considered by the British as the primary destabilizing factor in the EMS; the French opposed the British proposal and reaffirmed their intention to keep the franc closely linked to the DM in the run-up to the referendum.[37]

By the following day, sterling had sunk significantly beneath its now-suspended EMS floor, and the lira had become the new object of currency speculator attention. Notwithstanding the previous week's 7 percent devaluation, the Italian currency was again trading below its lower EMS band because it was still overvalued relative to the DM. During the evening of September 17, the Italian government reluctantly followed the example set by the British and suspended Italy's EMS membership. The Spanish peseta, which had also been trading near the lower band of its range, was devalued by 5 percent, albeit within the EMS framework.

German support for British efforts to maintain sterling at its EMS parity had been less than 100 percent enthusiastic, especially when contrasted with the efforts made on behalf of the French franc in the weeks that followed Black Wednesday. The *Financial Times* explained the German attitude vis-à-vis sterling in part by the UK's failure "to act fully in the spirit of the EMS."

> While the Germans accept that the French franc should be pinned to the
> D-mark for political as much as economic reasons, they have watched
> with disquiet how governments have aspired to fix currencies such as
> sterling, the peseta, and the escudo to the D-mark. . . . There has also

often been resentment among the other ERM members at the way the UK has frequently appeared reluctant to take the unpleasant medicine sometimes associated with EMS membership. If [British chancellor of the exchequer Norman] Lamont has in recent weeks frequently emphasized how Britain would base its defence of sterling on the so-called 1987 Basel/Nyborg agreement, he has until yesterday [September 16, 1992] been unwilling to use the main weapon in the Basel/Nyborg armory, which is to change domestic interest rates. Those different approaches reflect the UK's long absence between 1979 and 1990 from a club in which other members were adapting to each other's ways.[38]

Britain and Germany nearly had a diplomatic incident in the aftermath of the crisis. Matters became personalized after Schlesinger released a letter in early October 1992 presenting his view of the EMS crisis and laying the blame for Black Wednesday squarely on Britain's refusal to devalue sterling within the EMS. To counter claims that the Bundesbank had been insufficiently supportive during the crisis, Schlesinger revealed how much the Bundesbank had contributed to the defense of sterling and the lira. The British were outraged at the release of Schlesinger's letter. A minister of state at the British Foreign Office expressed "the government's concern at the deliberate decision to disclose Dr. Schlesinger's letter, and [made] clear the government's view that the release of the document was unhelpful,"[39] and the German ambassador to the United Kingdom was called into the Foreign Office to receive an official message registering the complaint. The Bundesbank was at the center of the international diplomatic and monetary crisis, notwithstanding the fact that it was nominally a German domestic institution.

THE AFTERMATH OF BLACK WEDNESDAY

Despite a narrow victory in favor of the Maastricht Treaty in the September 20, 1992, French referendum, the franc continued to trade near the bottom of its fluctuation band.[40] However, in notable contrast to the evident lack of cooperation and consensus between Germany and Britain, German authorities issued timely statements about the appropriateness of the franc's parity and stressed German resolve to defend the existing franc-DM rate. On September 23, the French and German finance ministries and the Banque de France and Bundesbank issued a joint statement that the DM-franc parity "correctly reflect[s] the real situation in their economies" and that no justification for a change existed.[41] By the end of the trading day, the Banque de France had bought FFr 160 billion, the largest intervention to date in the history of the bank. The Bundesbank had also intervened publicly for the first time since the EMS crisis had begun and provided a secret swap line to the Banque de France.

All of Europe waited for the Bundesbank to begin to reverse its interest rate increases, taking note of the declining economy in Germany. Lower German interest rates would practically guarantee the salvation of the EMS, and Germany's partners hoped it would happen sooner rather than later. Within Germany, former leaders, cabinet members, commercial bank directors, and economic institutes began voicing complaints about German interest rates. As former German chancellor Helmut Schmidt argued in October, 1992:

> The Bundesbank has been trying to use high interest rates to keep money supply under control—without success, because high D-Mark interest rates have attracted considerable amounts of foreign liquidity. The Bundesbank has thus itself contributed to the increase in the money supply and has also brought the D-Mark under revaluation pressure. . . . The Bundesbank council must now concede that its tight money policy has been counterproductive. Germany's monetary watchdog has bitten its own tail.[42]

The Berlin-based DIW economics institute warned that the Bundesbank would hurt the German economy and its own reputation if it did not relax its hard-line campaign against inflation. At year-end 1992, DIW and other research institutes were predicting a 1 percent fall in gross domestic product (GDP) for 1993, 3.5 percent inflation, and increases in unemployment to 5.5 million.[43] Ulrich Cartellieri, a director on the board of Germany's largest bank, argued that the Bundesbank

> was partly to blame for September's turbulence in the currency markets, through its controversial decision to increase interest rates in July [1992]. . . . It was obvious for months that above all Britain, but also France, needed lower interest rates in order to enliven their economies.[44]

Cartellieri warned that the resulting currency turbulence had damaged Germany's industry by increasing the value of the DM against other currencies. Under present circumstances there was a real danger of a downwards spiral of devaluation, with negative and threatening consequences for jobs, investment, and economies across Europe. Even Köhler could not refrain from public criticism of the Bundesbank when he made the off-the-cuff observation that world growth and high unemployment should be considered more often in the Bundesbank's council meetings. The Bundesbank remained impervious to such criticisms; the specter of a decline in its inflation-fighting credibility if it lowered interest rates too quickly was more fearsome to the bank than its international unpopularity. It continued to act as a domestic institution, even though its stature had by now in fact changed to make the Bundesbank a quasi-international institution.

RENEWED SPECULATION IN THE CURRENCY MARKETS

By November 1992, the worst of the EMS crisis seemed to be over, even without a further cut in German interest rates: the French franc was trading well above its EMS floor, and interest rates had come down to pre-crisis levels in France and Spain. In the middle of the month, however, currency speculators created unrest in the system again, this time by speculating on the Swedish krona. The krona had been pegged to the ECU since May 1991 in order to show Sweden's commitment to becoming a member of the EU. That peg was dropped on November 19 after raising overnight interest rates to 500 percent had not quelled the speculation. The EU Monetary Committee had rejected Sweden's efforts to link its currency with the EMS as an associate member, which would have entailed intervention obligations. Bundesbank president Schlesinger criticized Sweden for pegging to the ECU rather than the DM, calling the ECU "a currency which doesn't really exist" and stating that a "natural currency" would have been better.[45]

At the same time, the currencies of Spain, Denmark, Ireland, and Portugal all came under renewed speculative attacks.[46] On November 22, in a face-to-face meeting in Brussels, the EU Monetary Committee agreed to a 6 percent devaluation against the DM for the escudo and the peseta. The krone and the punt continued to trade near their floors, leaving the impression that more realignments were to come. Notably, however, like France, neither Ireland nor Denmark's economies betrayed a fundamental misalignment of the parities.

In the wake of the Bundesbank's refusal to cut interest rates at its December 10 meeting, Norway was forced to drop its official peg to the ECU, as Sweden had been forced to do.[47] The international community expressed its disappointment with the Bundesbank, and even conservative voices signaled their disapproval of the Bundesbank's tough line. Finance Minister Waigel indicated that cuts in interest rates would be the single most effective means to reviving the faltering German economy. Cooperation between the Finance Ministry and the Bundesbank, which had been useful in the Maastricht negotiations, had ended because of differences over the Bundesbank's interest rate policy.

The markets again tested France's commitment to its *franc fort* policy, and on December 20 the franc closed at its lowest level since the September crisis. This time, traders pointed to anxiety about the March 1993

French elections, which included candidates such as Charles Pasqua and Philippe Seguin, who had argued that the franc's level against the DM was unsustainable. "The influence of men like Pasqua creates insecurity in the markets. The weakness of the franc is political, not economic," said Stefan Collignon, director of the Association for European Monetary Union in Europe.[48]

At year's end, senior EU policymakers began a verbal campaign in support of existing EMS parities. Tietmeyer said there was no reason to change the parity between the DM and the franc, whereas the EU commissioner for economic and financial affairs said he expected no change in the value of the Irish punt and the Danish krone. In early January 1993, with the franc continuing to trade near its EMS floor, the French and German central banks joined forces again, issuing a communiqué that they would "pursue their close cooperation in order to ensure the proper function of the European exchange rate mechanism."[49]

In a January meeting of the EU Committee of Central Bank Governors, the participants maintained that the EMS crisis had abated and that there was no longer an economic reason for realignments. Economic fundamentals had, of course, never been particularly relevant to the markets, and the Irish punt continued to be sold. At one point, the Irish government even resorted to increasing overnight lending rates to 100 percent and one-month rates to 60 percent. Clearly, Ireland was doing everything within its power to maintain its DM parity; a Bundesbank interest-rate cut would have secured the parity by allowing Ireland to cut its interest rates. The markets, however, believed Ireland's close economic ties to Britain made the interest-rate differential unsustainable in the long run. Moreover, they saw no imminent Bundesbank gesture to lower interest rates for the sake of its EMS partners. The punt was able to hold out until January 30, 1993, when it was devalued by 10 percent. The franc and the krone did not join Ireland in the realignment because both had recently recovered some ground against the DM.

Within the framework of the EMS, the devaluation of the punt had all the animosity of the British exit. Finance Minister Bertie Ahern complained:

> We had hoped that the multilateral aid that we were requesting from the Community and particularly from the Bundesbank . . . would happen. Instead [there was] bilateral aid for the French which worked against us. . . . One of the great difficulties with the ERM is that not only is there not equal help for all members but the larger members seem able to negotiate side agreements.[50]

The Irish had tried unsuccessfully to orchestrate an overall realignment two weeks earlier but had been rebuffed by France, which wanted to maintain its *franc fort* policies.

As if to add insult to Irish injury, the long-awaited cut in German interest rates occurred less than a week later, on February 4, when the Bundesbank lowered its discount rate to 8 percent and its Lombard rate to 9 percent. Both the French and the Danish central banks commented that the cut was sufficient to ward off another round of realignments.[51] Only a day earlier, the Danish central bank had raised its discount rate by a full 2 points to 11.5 percent in order to deter speculators. The cuts in the German rates allowed Denmark to lower its rate by a point in late February.

Three days before the first round of French parliamentary elections on March 21, the Bundesbank suddenly lowered the discount rate again by 0.5 percent. It is unlikely that this was a prearranged political gesture to France, however, because the French did not take advantage of this reduction to lower their interest rates. Nonetheless, the French elections were important to the German government. Although all mainstream parties affirmed their support of the *franc fort* policy, there was room for doubt to what extent the new government would continue to sacrifice the needs of the domestic economy to its international commitments. The new prime minister of France, Edouard Balladur, began cautiously reducing French interest rates soon after his March 28 election victory. The French interest-rate cuts, widely expected, did not have a significant impact on the franc. Indeed, the franc unexpectedly strengthened against the DM in May and June.

The hopes that the speculative crises in the EMS were finally over were dashed on May 13, when Spain and Portugal again devalued (8 percent and 6.5 percent, respectively). The devaluations came five days before the second Danish referendum on the Maastricht Treaty and again highlighted the uncertainty in the markets with respect to EMU's desirability and achievability. Yet, during the period leading to the second referendum, the currency speculation did not center on the franc, and the franc even strengthened.

Far from undermining the EMS, the devaluations of the peseta and escudo reinforced the system by showing that orderly devaluations could be achieved within the existing rules and that the EMS remained a "fixed but adjustable" system. This perception was confirmed by two reports in May that examined the causes of and responses to the September 1992 crisis. The Monetary Committee, meeting in Kolding, Denmark, spread the blame for the crisis among all the member states because they had not followed the rules of the EMS. The report concluded that nothing was fundamentally wrong with the EMS. The Committee of Central Bank Governors' report on the EMS echoed the sanguine conclusions of the Monetary Committee's report.[52] Together, the reports painted a picture of a crisis that could have been avoided had the rules been followed more closely. Scarcely two months later, however, the EMS had its greatest crisis, one that cast into doubt its very survival.

THE BUNDESBANK FORCES THE EMS TO WIDEN THE BANDS

June 1993 was a period of relative calm in the currency markets, especially with respect to the volatile franc-DM rate. The DM weakened
against most currencies, due to fiscal budget woes in Germany and Bundesbank interest rates that had been judged inappropriately high by Germany's six leading economic institutes. The Banque de France continued
to cut interest rates, and by the latter part of June had lowered its intervention rate to 0.25 percent below Germany's discount rate, which traditionally set the floor of the EMS. This was the first time in twenty-six
years that French interest rates were below those of Germany. On June 22 the
Banque de France's head of research told an audience of senior economists:
"The French franc is sharing the duty of anchoring the [European exchange
rate] mechanism. . . . The D-Mark is impossible to avoid as an anchor but
other currencies will share the responsibility." Delors agreed that the franc
might temporarily take over the DM's anchor role inside the ERM.[53]

Perhaps emboldened by the franc's new strength and position, French
finance minister Edmond Alphandéry publicly called on the Bundesbank
to lower interest rates. Calling the routine meeting with Waigel a forum for
"joint discussion of the conditions for a concerted reduction in French and
German rates," he added that "we are going to speak equal to equal. . . .
That was not the case a few months ago. . . . Today the franc can support
itself, perhaps better than the D-Mark."[54] His remarks so angered Waigel
and the Bundesbank that Germany canceled the talks. Possibly, Alphandéry's comments caused the Bundesbank to harden its resolve as a
way of showing the French that they were a long way away from being the
EMS's anchor or coanchor. More than one observer mentioned this possibility as the cause of the July turbulence in the franc-DM rate.[55] If true, it
reinforces the image of a Bundesbank that, although it opposed the EMS at
the beginning, had grown to like the regime that gave the bank such importance internationally.

In any case, it is true that the end of June marked the end of the
strength of the franc against the DM. Following a July 1 Bundesbank discount rate cut of 0.5 percent, the Banque de France lowered its intervention rate by 0.25 percent on July 2. However, a week later, the Banque de
France had to intervene in the markets again to support the franc, and two
weeks later, the franc and the Danish krone were again at their DM floor.
Despite Bundesbank intervention (as required by the Basel/Nyborg agreement) and Waigel's statement that the fundamentals of the French economy were healthy and that Germany would support the franc-DM parity,
the franc continued to trade just above its floor.

The French and German central bankers and finance ministers met secretly in Munich on July 22 to try to coordinate interest-rate policies and

to increase the DM-franc swap line, which had been created after the spec-ulation in the fall. On July 23, France raised its key overnight borrowing rate to 10 percent, and the two governments issued a joint statement pledg-ing their support for the existing DM-franc rate. The currency speculation continued unabated in anticipation of the July 29 Bundesbank meeting.

As in September, the Bundesbank's stubbornly conservative interest-rate policy was again the catalyst for the crisis in the EMS. At its July 29 Central Bank Council meeting, the debate was whether to further decrease interest rates for the sake of Germany's EMS partners, in particular France. Schlesinger, as in the July 1992 Central Bank Council debate on the same issue, argued for maintaining interest rates at their current levels to avoid undermining the Bundesbank's credibility. There would be no "political" rate reductions while he was president. However, Vice Presi-dent Tietmeyer argued in favor of solidarity with the EMS partners and for a wider European interest.[56] Further, he thought a gesture was necessary in light of the informal agreement that the French and German central bankers had made in Munich. The outcome of the Council vote—a 0.5 per-cent reduction in the Lombard rate and an off-the-record plan to lower the money market rate[57]—was supposed to be a compromise of sorts between the two positions; instead it paved the way for more serious speculation on the French franc. The decision to leave the more significant discount rate unchanged was viewed by many traders as a betrayal of France by Ger-many. George Soros, the trader who had almost single-handedly forced sterling out of the EMS in September 1992, said dramatically, "For France to stay [in the EMS] after the Bundesbank action would be like for a bat-tered wife to go back from the hospital to her husband."[58]

In hindsight, it is not difficult to see why this particular Bundesbank decision might have been the proverbial straw that broke the camel's back. The decision showed yet again that the Bundesbank was almost com-pletely unwilling to subordinate the needs of the domestic economy to the needs of its partners—even its most important partner. The fact that this time France, rather than Britain, was the object of the speculation seemed to make no difference to the Bundesbank. The markets were also some-what surprised that the Bundesbank did not help the franc, given that it agreed there were no fundamental economic disequilibria undermining the DM-franc rate (as there had been with Britain).[59] Three weeks of specula-tion had weakened the French reserve position, and now the markets ques-tioned the Balladur government's commitment to the *franc fort* policy at any cost. By not lowering interest rates, the Bundesbank was sending a signal that it did not care about the consequences for the franc or the EMS. Since the Bundesbank would be on vacation in the month of August, the markets knew that the next chance to lower interest rates would be in Sep-tember, and enough people were willing to speculate that the franc could not hold out that long.[60]

The following day, the French and German central bankers and finance ministers met again secretly at Bercy to discuss their options. At the meeting, Banque de France governor Jacques de Larosière demanded that the Bundesbank lower its interest rate at least for the next week and that the bank intervene in unlimited amounts to stop the franc from dropping to the floor of its DM band. The DM 30 billion DM-franc swap line had been completely used, and the franc continued to drop. During the Bercy meeting, the franc fell below its floor and thereby required the Germans to intervene in unlimited amounts in any case. The amount of intervention at the end of July was estimated to be twice the £16 billion that the Bank of England had spent before its exit on Black Wednesday,[61] and the Bundesbank was interested in finding another solution to the problem. The Bundesbank proposed lifting the obligation to intervene until after the weekend's EU Monetary Committee meeting. As it was already 11:00 A.M. on a Friday, this would not have been a long period of floating, but it did require the assent of the other EMS members. The French were adamantly against this proposal since it would be interpreted as a defeat of the *franc fort* policy. They responded with a counterproposal that the Germans leave the ERM, but this was rejected by Waigel on the grounds that it would label the DM as the cause of the monetary disturbances.

That Friday night, Waigel, Schlesinger, Tietmeyer, and Köhler's replacement, Gerd Haller, all flew to Kohl's Austrian vacation home to discuss their strategy for the upcoming Monetary Committee meeting. Contrary to the Bundesbank's expectations, however, Kohl did not try to persuade the Bundesbank to lower interest rates in solidarity with the French, but rather agreed to the Bundesbank's idea of widening the EMS bands to ±6–8 percent. The Bundesbank had already discussed widening the bands months earlier, when the EMS turbulence had not subsided after Black Wednesday. The five German officials agreed that this would be their proposal at the EU Monetary Committee meeting the following day.

The Monetary Committee meeting on Sunday, August 1, 1993, lasted until 2 A.M. on Monday, an indication of how divided the EMS members were about the best course for the EMS. The Bundesbank began aggressively: President Tietmeyer greeted his colleagues with a "bonjour," and when asked why he was speaking French he reportedly replied, "apparently we are all now required to speak French in the EMS."[62] The French had evidently also come with their own strategy. Their opening proposal was to send the DM on a *petite congé* (a short holiday) since it was the German policies that were out of alignment with the policies of the rest of the EMS members. According to one account, the Germans were not opposed to this proposal. "To the surprise of the French, Germany readily agreed to this plan, an attitude which probably meant that Germany no longer considered the ERM a credible system and did not mind being blamed for its collapse."[63] However, interviews with participants on the

French and the German side seem to support another version: the Bundesbank rejected the French proposal of a *petit congé* because it would look as though Germany was at fault for the disturbances in the currency markets. One Bundesbank representative said that the bank had a leadership role in the EMS and could not leave for that reason, and a French participant indicated that the Bundesbank was against the *petit congé* because the system needed Germany as the anchor.[64] All accounts agree that the problem with the plan to have the DM leave (whether or not the Germans would have complied) was that the Dutch had already reached an agreement with the Bundesbank to keep the guilder tied in the ±2.25 percent DM band, and the Benelux states also decided to go with the DM rather than remain in the EMS with France.

Once this fact was established, all parties concurred that widening the bands was the only remaining option. The Bundesbank had planned to widen the bands to ±6–8 percent, but the French objected, saying this would only incite the speculators. The Belgians requested that the bands be temporarily widened to ±15 percent, which was the final outcome after many more hours of negotiating. The Bundesbank was not much concerned with the width of the band—any increase above the 6–8 percent it had requested was going to virtually eliminate the Bundesbank's intervention obligations, something the bank had always favored. Chancellor Kohl was less sanguine about the size of the bands, since it was difficult to credibly maintain that the EMS still existed and that this was not a major blow to European monetary cooperation.

Other member states were largely satisfied with the outcome. For Britain and Italy, the crisis and outcome was a vindication that, contrary to the May reports of the Monetary Committee and the Committee of Central Bank Governors, there were indeed deep "fault lines" in the EMS. Further, there was thinly disguised gloating that even the French, with their hallowed special relationship to Germany, had failed to convince speculators that the DM-franc parity was correct or to wrest a concession from the Bundesbank. In light of the perceived lack of support from Germany for the pound, lira, and punt over the past year, there were those who reveled in France's comeuppance.

CONCLUSION

As we have seen, complex interactions between EMS norms, market expectations, Bundesbank norms, and Maastricht requirements were important sources of the EMS crises. Four interrelated factors helped bring down the EMS: (1) no general EMS realignment in 1990, (2) high German interest rates, (3) the Maastricht referenda and criteria, and (4) rivalry between the German government and the Bundesbank. Each of these factors highlights points at which the crises might have been averted.

Despite the widely acknowledged inflationary potential of West and East German monetary union in 1990, the German government did not insist upon a general EMS realignment. Although it was foreseeable that the exogenous shock of German unification and the way it was financed would create problems for the EMS, it was impossible to coordinate a comprehensive realignment.[65] One participant indicated that the norms of EMS realignments required that realignments be based on actual, not expected, misalignments. For that reason, the idea of a proactive realignment was out of the question in 1990.

The soaring interest rates of the Bundesbank were important because they were not entirely necessary and showed that the Bundesbank was deliberately conservative. The bank maintained its high interest-rate policy in 1991–1993, despite global criticism and contrary to the advice of senior German economists, bankers, industrialists, and politicians. This intransigence can be traced to the vestiges of ill-will from the German monetary union policy conflict with the government. It also demonstrated the bank's institutional importance to all of Germany's partners. At the same time, however, it showed that the Bundesbank was not going to act in a way consistent with its new international role. Time and again, the Bundesbank refused to lower interest rates for the benefit of its EMS partners. This course would have been economically beneficial for Germany as well, since high interest rates pushed the German economy into a recession. Indeed, lowering interest rates solely for the purpose of its partners would not have been unprecedented: as we have seen, the Bundesbank was willing to subordinate its domestic stability efforts to international commitments in the early 1970s.

In addition, the Maastricht Treaty's requirement that potential EMU members not devalue in the system, coupled with the uncertainty surrounding the Maastricht referenda in Denmark and France, caused the currency markets to test the commitments of the governments. Moreover, these Maastricht-related factors also caused the member states to decline options like realignments that had been the most important elements of the EMS's stability to that point.

Finally, the rivalry between the Bundesbank and the federal government over international monetary cooperation is essential to explaining the bank's actions during the crises. The Bundesbank had always resisted the EMS's mandatory intervention obligations, and widening the bands to ±15 percent in the July 1993 crisis virtually ensured that the Bundesbank's obligations would be small in the future. From an institutional perspective, the prolonged crisis in the EMS demonstrated how important the bank had become. The EMS, built on the Bundesbank's anchor role, had enhanced the importance of the Bundesbank by making it an international actor rather than simply a domestic institution. With this stature, the Bundesbank showed the other EMS participants that *it,* and not the federal government, was now the important player in monetary regimes.

NOTES

1. With the exception of the DM-guilder rates, which continued to be able to move only in ±2.25 percent bands.

2. See Eichengreen and Wyplosz (1993).

3. In addition to Marsh (1992), see Burda (1990); Pohl (1991); and Tietmeyer and Guth (1990).

4. The exact consequences of the German unification financing strategy were large fiscal deficits, which caused the German Finance Ministry to borrow large sums. The massive increase in borrowing in turn forced the government to raise interest rates to attract capital and to damp inflationary pressures from large-scale deficit spending. High interest rates then caused a recession in the EMS member states.

5. Surprising many, Kohl's CDU did very well in the March 18, 1990, elections in East Germany, receiving 40.8 percent of the votes cast to the SPD's 21.9 percent and the PDS's 16.4 percent.

6. Author's interviews, March 1994.

7. *Financial Times,* July 13, 1992.

8. *Financial Times,* January 10, 1990.

9. See *Le Monde,* January 7–8, 1990; *Financial Times,* January 10, 1990.

10. See Eichengreen and Wyplosz (1993); Cameron (1993).

11. See Pöhl (1992), p. 6.

12. Britain's inflation rate was only 2.4 percent above Germany's in 1991, and the currency markets did not test the parity.

13. The Lombard rate is the rate at which the Bundesbank extends credit to commercial banks to bridge temporary financing gaps. The discount rate is the rate at which the Bundesbank lends to banks through "rediscounting" trade bills and Treasury bills falling due within three months and is the more significant rate internationally because it sets the floor of the EMS. See Marsh (1992), pp. 5–6, and Table 5.1.

14. See, for example, *Financial Times,* July 9, 1992, July 16, 1992, July 30, 1992, August 19, 1992, and August 24, 1992.

15. *Financial Times,* July 18, 1992. Eurostat reported in 1992 that German inflation was 0.4 percent *above* British inflation.

16. *Financial Times,* July 10, 1992. High interest rates in the UK were particularly painful because mortgage rates are tied directly to the base rate, and most mortgages are variable rate.

17. The interest rate differential between the United States and Germany rose to 6.75 percent in July 1992.

18. At the July 1992 G-7 summit in Munich, UK chancellor of the exchequer Lamont stressed that there was "no question of an alteration of sterling's exchange-rate value vis-à-vis European currencies" (*Financial Times,* July 9, 1992). The Italian lira was also the object of market speculation, in part because of budgetary difficulties facing Italian authorities.

19. Author's interviews, March 1994.

20. The strong rise in bank lending (much of it to finance investment in the former East Germany) was one of the main reasons for the steep increase in the German money supply. Since eastward investment was heavily subsidized, the constricting effect of Bundesbank interest-rate increases on monetary growth in Germany was muted.

21. *Financial Times,* August 24, 1992.

22. Author's interview, October 1993.
23. *Financial Times*, August 27, 1992.
24. *Financial Times*, August 29, 1992.
25. Ibid.
26. Directorate-General for Economic and Financial Affairs (1989), pp. 11–12.
27. *The Guardian*, November 30, 1992.
28. Ibid.
29. Reprinted in the *Financial Times*, September 7, 1992.
30. Lamont had apparently so irritated Schlesinger during the Bath meetings that at one point Schlesinger had to be restrained from walking out of the meeting. See *Financial Times*, December 11, 1992.
31. *Financial Times*, September 7, 1992.
32. Ibid.
33. Non-EMS currencies also suffered; on September 8, the Finns, who had unofficially linked the markka to the EMS currencies, were forced to abandon the link. Sweden, also with an unofficial link to the EMS currencies, raised short-term lending rates to 24 percent and then to 75 percent to defend the Swedish krona; overnight rates in Sweden were raised to an unprecedented 500 percent to combat the speculation.
34. *The Guardian*, December 1, 1992.
35. *Financial Times*, December 11, 1992.
36. *Financial Times*, September 17, 1992.
37. *The Guardian*, December 1, 1992.
38. *Financial Times*, September 17, 1992.
39. *Financial Times*, October 2, 1992.
40. The outcome was 51.1 percent in favor of ratifying the Treaty.
41. *Financial Times*, September 24, 1992.
42. *Financial Times*, October 9, 1992.
43. *Financial Times*, December 10, 1992, December 11, 1992, and January 7, 1993.
44. *Financial Times*, December 9, 1992.
45. *Financial Times*, November 21–22, 1992.
46. The Spanish government had been requesting a 5 percent devaluation from the EU Monetary Committee since the beginning of November. See *Financial Times*, November 21–22, 1992.
47. Norway had also pegged against the ECU in October 1990 in a political decision attributed to the government's desire to apply for membership in the EU.
48. *New York Times*, December 21, 1992.
49. *Financial Times*, January 6, 1993.
50. *Financial Times*, February 1, 1993.
51. *Financial Times*, February 4, 1993.
52. *Financial Times*, May 25, 1993.
53. *Financial Times*, June 23, 1993.
54. *Financial Times*, June 26–27, 1993.
55. Author's interviews, October 1993 and March 1994.
56. *The Sunday Times*, August 1, 1993.
57. *Financial Times*, December 23, 1993.
58. Ibid.
59. The following section is based on the accounts of the July 1993 crisis in *Financial Times*, December 23, 1993, and *Times* (London), August 12, 1993.

60. *Financial Times,* December 23, 1993.
61. Ibid.
62. *Times* (London), August 12, 1993.
63. Ibid.
64. Author's interviews, March 1994.
65. Author's interview with a Bundesbank official, November 1993.

7

The Ongoing Importance
of the Bundesbank

As we have seen, the Bundesbank was actively involved in the negotiations of the Treaty on European Union and had had most of its preferences incorporated into the Treaty. The Bundesbank clout can best be explained by its ability to act as the domestic ratifier to the government's initiatives. Thus, before the government could commit to a regime, the bank's preferences had to be addressed. Surprisingly, however, the Bundesbank managed to influence almost all EMU implementation decisions *after* the signing of the Maastricht Treaty as well, despite having limited institutionalized means to make its preferences heard. I now examine how the Bundesbank was able to persuade the other member states to accept its preferences in the EMU implementation decisions after the Treaty had been ratified.

In the first section of this chapter I detail some of the technical decisions that were implemented during the 1992–1998 period. Surprisingly, given the limited role of the Bundesbank in the decisionmaking process, the majority of the issues were resolved in a manner consistent with the preferences of the Bundesbank. In the second section I discuss a new actor in the debates about monetary cooperation in Germany—the political parties. In order to make sense of the deference to the Bundesbank's preferences after the Maastricht Treaty ratification, one must understand the complex relationship between the 1993 German Constitutional Court decision on the Treaty, the Bundesbank, and the political parties in the German parliament.

In October 1993, the German Constitutional Court had finished hearing various challenges to the Maastricht Treaty and issued its opinion.[1] The Court ruled on October 12, 1993, that the Treaty was legal and could be signed.[2] There was, however, also a significant victory for the anti-EMU forces in Germany; the Bundestag and Bundesrat obtained the right to evaluate whether all of the conditions for entry into the single currency

had been met before Germany joined the single currency.[3] The Court ruled
that there was nothing automatic about the transition to the third stage; the
convergence criteria would have to be met exactly and could not be
changed or weakened without another decision by the German government.[4] This gave the supporters of a "hard" interpretation of the convergence criteria ammunition that continued to be used in the EMU-implementation decisions. The Court's ruling cleared the way for the signing of
the Treaty by Germany, and on November 1, 1993—nearly a year later
than scheduled—the Treaty entered into force.

Up to this point, a discussion of domestic political parties was missing
in this (and most other) accounts of EMU negotiations because the political parties were not relevant to the outcome of cooperation in monetary
matters. First, monetary political negotiations were "high" politics, which
involved mainly the elites, with little or no political party or interest group
participation. Second, the German mainstream political parties' positions
on monetary integration were so close as to be virtually indistinguishable.
Finally, we can discount the possibility that links between the parties and
those elites who controlled negotiations could somehow have transmitted
interest group preferences: no evidence of any such links exists. Chancellor Kohl certainly supported EMU enthusiastically, not because the mass
public support for EMU filtered up to the chancellor's office but rather because of a personal conviction that was not universally held within the
CDU/CSU (Christian Democratic Union/Christian Social Union).

Another key aspect of the debates over monetary cooperation was its
hidden nature, politically speaking. Because monetary integration was carried out almost exclusively by governmental elites out of view of the public, there were few domestic electoral consequences in the EU countries.[5]
This, however, dramatically changed in the years between the signing of the
Maastricht Treaty and the May 2, 1998 decision to merge the currencies.

The debates over European integration initially became visible and
highly contentious during the Maastricht ratification process, perhaps because the "democratic deficit" had become more apparent. As the member
states were proposing to transfer even more responsibilities to the supranational level despite the deficit, the Treaty faced public scrutiny, skepticism, and, in the case of Denmark, outright rejection. Whereas previously
the EU had been a fairly impenetrable bureaucracy operating generally
with the tacit approval of the public, the publicity surrounding the referenda brought many divisive issues into the open. As the opinions of the
public about Maastricht grew more diverse, even mainstream parties became interested in capitalizing on the disaffected voters.

When confronted with the fact that their leaders had negotiated the
elimination of the DM, the German people began withholding their support for EMU. However, no German mainstream party adopted a position

critical of, or in opposition to, EMU or Maastricht. Despite the attempts by several senior politicians to raise the issue of EMU in political debate, it is striking how often the parties united to censure these politicians. In fact, throughout the 1992–1998 period, rising popular opposition to EMU was not captured by any mainstream political party. It was left to institutions outside the political sphere—primarily the Bundesbank and the Constitutional Court—to spearhead the German opposition to EMU.

CONTENTIOUS ISSUES IN EMU IMPLEMENTATION

The Calm After the 1993 EMS Storm

The EU member states spent the months of August and September 1993 reappraising the EMS and reassessing plans for monetary union. Initially, it was uncertain whether the EMS still really existed, given that a 30 percent fluctuation margin was the de facto equivalent of floating for most currencies. There were also questions about how quickly France and other member states with depressed economies would lower interest rates and what effect that would have on the exchange rates. Finally, no one knew what the widening of the bands meant for Article 109(j) of the Treaty, which stipulated that each member state had to fulfill "the observance of the normal fluctuation margins provided for by the Exchange Rate Mechanism of the European Monetary System, for at least two years, without devaluing against the currency of any other member state."[6] Given that the bands had been only "temporarily" widened, there was uncertainty about exactly how long the bands were to be held at ±15 percent. However, it seemed clear in 1993 that eventually the members would return to the narrow bands since the wide bands could not be described as "normal" by any stretch of the imagination.

The EU finance ministers took the first step back toward the status quo by vowing to continue on with the Maastricht timetable at their September 14, 1993, meeting. Negotiations also continued regarding the location of the EMI, the ECB's precursor. Behind the scenes, Kohl pressured all of the member states to allow it to be located in Frankfurt, and failing that, Bonn. The decision to locate the EMI in Frankfurt had been blocked by the British at the June 1992 Lisbon summit, but Kohl continued to insist that locating the ECB in Germany was essential to receiving the German public's support for EMU. According to a confidential Dutch memo, Kohl went beyond cajoling his partners: he threatened to block the candidacy of Ruud Lubbers for Commission president unless Lubbers dropped his opposition to Frankfurt.[7] At the October 29, 1993, Brussels informal summit, the decision was made to locate the EMI in Frankfurt.

Redefining "Normal" Bands

At the December 1993 European Council summit, the member states agreed to more of the Bundesbank's agenda. The leaders debated legally binding macroeconomic guidelines, including lower interest rates, wage restraints, lower budget deficits, and reductions in government debt as required by the Treaty. French objections to the level of detail of the guidelines delayed formal adoption of the proposals at the meeting. Nevertheless, the guidelines were later formally adopted by EU finance ministers. Germany (and Britain) successfully resisted Commission President Delors's suggestion that the EMI's role should be enhanced.

A few days after the summit, the Bundesbank scored a major victory. Henning Christophersen, commissioner for economic affairs of the EU, stated that EMU did not depend on the member states returning to the EMS's ±2.25 percent bands. The Bundesbank had been the driving force behind the widening of the bands during the August 1993 crisis, and Bundesbank president Tietmeyer continued to support the wider bands because they deterred currency speculators and virtually eliminated the Bundesbank's intervention obligations. By stating that EMU did not require a return to the smaller bands, Christophersen had contradicted EMI president Alexandre Lamfalussy's position and made the status quo politically viable at a time when no member states—with the possible exception of Denmark—were anxious to return to the former bands.

The issue of a return to the narrow bands was raised several times again in 1994; in February, eleven EU finance ministers voted against a Danish proposal to return to the narrow bands, and in April, Lamfalussy told the European Parliament that he had changed his mind about the need to revive the former bands, thus solidifying and legitimizing the status quo.

At their December 1994 meeting, EU finance ministers officially endorsed an EMI proposal that member states could enter EMU without having been in the narrow EMS bands for the required two years. The decision marked the complete legitimization of the status quo and represented a victory for the Bundesbank's position that a return to the narrow bands before the economies had converged would invite currency speculation. Although the finance ministers avoided calling the wider bands "normal" in deference to the Commissions's wishes, one minister indicated after the meeting that if monetary union were to occur on January 1, 1997, the wide bands could retroactively be deemed normal.

January 1, 1994, marked the beginning of stage 2, which included the establishment of the EMI and the surveillance of the member states' economies by the EU Monetary Committee. Though the Treaty had a provision allowing the member states to transfer reserves to the EMI, Tietmeyer ruled out such a transfer, preferring to transfer control over reserves only at stage 3 when required.

Bundesbank Objections to the Exemption for Ireland

The Bundesbank almost immediately became involved in other technical EMU debates that involved interpretations of the Treaty. At their September 10–11, 1994, informal meeting, the EU finance ministers considered the question of which member states should receive an excessive deficit warning about their budgets as required by the Maastricht Treaty, and whether to make the EMI's excessive deficit recommendations public.[8] Meeting in Lindau, their first order of business was to decide whether to agree to the Commission's recommendation to exempt Ireland from the Treaty rules on government debt. According to the Maastricht Treaty, member states had to keep their annual budget deficits to less than 3 percent of GDP and their total government debt to less than 60 percent of GDP. However, an ambiguity in the Treaty allowed member states to join EMU even if their ratios were not exactly at the Treaty reference levels. The precise text of Article 104(c) of the Maastricht Treaty is worth quoting at length:

> The Commission shall . . . examine compliance with budgetary discipline on the basis of the following two criteria:
> (a) whether the ratio of the planned or actual government deficit to gross domestic product exceeds a reference value, unless
> —either the ratio has declined substantially and continuously and reached a level that comes close to the reference value;
> —or, alternatively, the excess over the reference value is only exceptional and temporary and the ratio remains close to the reference value;
> (b) whether the ratio of government debt to gross domestic product exceeds a reference value, unless the ratio is sufficiently diminishing and approaching the reference value at a satisfactory pace.[9]

The vagueness of the Treaty, which helped get it signed and ratified by member states, once again required interpretation in its implementation, and the Bundesbank and German Finance Ministry used every opportunity to stress the importance of the strictest interpretation of the ratios. At the Lindau meeting the finance ministers were well aware that granting an exception to the most conservative interpretations of the ratios for Ireland would create a precedent for such exceptions. Negotiations were therefore quite heated.

At issue was whether Ireland should receive a warning from the EMI or whether it, like Luxembourg, met the Maastricht criteria. The case for a generous interpretation of Ireland's condition had merit and had already been approved by the Monetary Committee. However, in that committee France had supported the Bundesbank's reservation about considering the convergence criteria flexible. Germany preferred to disregard entirely the caveats in Article 104(c) and to use only the ratios as the final determinants. In the end, the Monetary Committee backed the Commission's proposal to exempt Ireland. Ireland had kept its budget deficit below 2.5 percent and had reduced its government debt from 114 percent to 90 percent of GDP in the past two years. Ireland could thus credibly make the argument that its ratio was "sufficiently diminishing and approaching the reference value at a satisfactory pace."

Tietmeyer's failure to block agreement on Ireland in the Monetary Committee created problems within the Bundesbank. Reimut Jochimsen, a Bundesbank Central Bank Council member known to be hostile to EMU, attacked the attempts to relax the terms of EMU. Jochimsen feared that the other EU member states were beginning a campaign to soften the convergence criteria. He also stood behind the Bundesbank's position that in the long run, monetary union required political union. "If we want to take this powerful step of EMU we will need a federal order in Europe . . . no one wants a superstate, but unless we have the right framework it might be necessary, as a last resort, to give up this project."[10]

At the Lindau finance ministers' meeting, the ministers followed the lead of the Monetary Committee and agreed not to sanction Ireland. Germany's compliance was brought about by the promise that in the future, EU Monetary Committee and Commission members would be more explicit about explaining why they choose to censure certain states and not others. Tietmeyer responded that "from my point of view it is to be welcomed that the Council of Finance Ministers has resisted a general softening of the budgetary criteria, although I have some difficulties in understanding why the Irish case was not addressed critically."[11]

Germany's representatives had a similar reaction when Denmark did not receive an excessive deficit recommendation in June 1996. At the finance minsters' meeting in Luxembourg, Germany formally objected to allowing the Danes to join Ireland and Luxembourg as eligible states because Denmark's debt ratio was 71.9 percent.[12] Germany was again outvoted in the committee.

There was another question about the excessive deficit recommendations made by the EMI against member governments not meeting the convergence criteria. Although the Maastricht Treaty stipulated that these recommendations would remain private during stage 2, some finance ministers wanted to make them public even at that stage. Waigel was among those pressing to make the recommendations public on the grounds that public pressure would help convince delinquent member governments to take unpleasant corrective action. This point of view prevailed, and the finance ministers agreed informally that the EMI's recommendations be published in time for the first EMI council meeting.

The Possibility of EMU in 1997

Within Germany, a consensus between the Bundesbank, the federal government, and the parties was emerging that EMU was unlikely to occur before 1999 and that the convergence criteria had to be enforced as strictly as possible. The SPD, CDU/CSU, and FDP all agreed that the convergence criteria could not be loosely interpreted. In November 1994 the Bundesbank went one step further, stating that it was not enough for the member states to meet the criteria only during an economic growth period, but that even in recessions, economic ratios must meet the standards: "It is crucial that entry into EMU is open only to those countries which meet the criteria in full."[13] The unanimity between the parties' and the Bundesbank's positions may have been due to the increasing percentage of the German public that voiced its unhappiness and fears about EMU to pollsters. A *Der Spiegel/Financial Times* poll published in December 1994 showed that even fewer Germans (24 percent) were in favor of a single currency than Britons (33 percent),[14] and *Eurobarometer* results showed more Germans were against the single currency than for it.[15]

The December 6, 1994, EU finance ministers meeting had deemed that member states did not need to rejoin the narrow EMS bands. Although this decision did not rule out the possibility of EMU in 1997, the Bundesbank and other realists considered it unlikely that a majority of the soon-to-be fifteen member states would be able to meet the convergence criteria by then. In contrast, the French president and the Italian prime minister both believed that the earlier date was still feasible. Tietmeyer's statement that he was "convinced that monetary policy integration in Europe can only be the outcome of a lengthy process," was designed to counter French and Italian optimism.[16] As late as January 1995, Mitterrand called on the member states to continue trying to converge their economies in order to create EMU by 1997. Jacques Delors, speaking for the Commission in the last few months of 1994, also did not want to eliminate the possibility of EMU in 1997.

The May 1995 French election sealed the fate of the Commission's proposal to leave the 1997 date open. Aside from the fact that only a minority of states would probably have been in a position to enter in 1997, the new Chirac government was considerably less eager to push for EMU at the earliest date. Without the French impetus, the Commission—led as of January 1 by Jacques Santer, a consolidator rather than a visionary like Delors—was forced to agree to the plans of the more conservative states. In June 1995 the finance ministers met again in Luxembourg and agreed once and for all that the 1997 date could no longer be realized. The formal decision was made at the June 26–27 meeting of the European Council in Cannes. For Germany, this represented a stay of execution for the DM, something both the government and the Bundesbank had wanted.

What's in a Name?

The extent of Germany's dominance in the EMU-implementation process is nowhere more apparent than in the question of what the single currency should be named. On the face of it, the question seems trivial, and indeed some member states thought the issue had been resolved in 1978 when Helmut Schmidt agreed with Giscard d'Estaing that the currency basket be called the ECU. Kohl and Waigel first raised the issue after the signing of the Treaty in December 1991, saying that the final choice of a name had not yet been made. The Bundesbank fully supported this position, believing the German public would not have faith in the single currency if it were named "ECU," since, historically, the value of the ECU had depreciated against the DM. The bank maintained that in order to inspire confidence that the new single currency was as stable as the DM, the new currency must be named something other than "ECU." However, it is far from clear that ordinary Germans were really against the name "ECU." A December 1994 *Der Spiegel/Financial Times* poll showed that, of the respondents who favored a single currency, the top name suggested was "ECU" in Germany (40 percent), followed only distantly by "Euromark" (21 percent).[17]

The French were indignant that Germany was suddenly against the name since it had deep roots as a historical compromise. Former prime minister Balladur was furious about the German government's intransigence on this matter: "I think that the discussion [in Germany] is infantile. I don't see why one should change the name under a German pretext. It's a French word corresponding to an English acronym. I don't want to put the name into question."[18]

The question of the name was to be settled by the end of 1995, and throughout the year Kohl and Waigel stepped up the pressure on their European counterparts to consider another name. In February, Waigel supported Bundesbank claims that the German electorate would find it difficult to accept a currency called "ECU." Again the federal government strategically used the Bundesbank and the electorate's opposition to make its preferences prevail internationally.

In June 1995 the Commission published a green paper detailing its recommendations on the introduction of the Eurocurrency. The paper contained several ideas that closely followed German thinking on the process, including the admission that the question of the name was not settled. In a June 22 speech to the Bundestag, Waigel praised the green paper:

what is positive is that the green paper leaves no doubt that convergence is the cornerstone of the Maastricht Treaty and the unrenouncable precondition to a strong and stable unified currency. The green paper also rightly considers the question of the name of the new currency to be open. The question of the name is a very decisive point for us. The technical term, ECU, is not possible to convey to our citizens. We should agree on a solid name that will receive the acceptance of our citizens.[19]

At the December 15–16, 1995, Madrid summit, EU leaders finally confirmed the new name of the currency: the "euro." Throughout the fall, France had held fast to the name "ECU," and former president Giscard d'Estaing "was said to be furious about the German-led campaign to kill the ECU, the name . . . which he and former chancellor Schmidt created alongside the European Monetary System in 1979."[20] Right before the summit, however, Chirac had changed his tactic and campaigned for an EU-wide referendum on the name. Kohl countered that 80 million Germans would vote for "euro," so there was no point in going through the exercise.[21] Kohl's argument carried the day, and the euro was created.

The Commission's Green Paper

The Commission's June 1995 green paper provided a blueprint for the actual changeover to the single currency. The Commission proposed several features that the Bundesbank opposed, including a recommendation that the changeover have a short transition period for most financial transactions. The green paper suggested three phases leading to the introduction of the single currency as late as 2002. In phase A, the governments would choose which states would participate in the single currency and irrevocably lock exchange rates (this corresponded to stage 3 of the Treaty). In phase B, the ECB would fix the parities and the public debt would be converted to the single currency, which would also be the only currency used with third-party currencies. The final phase C would occur approximately three years after phase A, when national currencies would be phased out, and the euro would become sole legal tender.[22]

The June 19, 1995, finance ministers meeting proved divisive on several points. France and the southern states all supported the Commission's emphasis on the irreversible move to monetary union and the need to enhance the credibility of the euro by having business and banks use it early in the timeline. Austria, Germany, and Britain all resisted. Germany wanted the single currency to become the sole legal tender only once the euro was minted at the end of the transitional phase. Before that point, Germany insisted that businesses, banks, and the federal government be able to use the DM.

In November 1995 the EMI central bankers weighed in with their proposal, which was approved by the heads of state at the Madrid summit in

December. The EMI proposal reflected a great deal of German input—a less than surprising result, not only because of the Bundesbank's position on the EMI council but also because of the nationalities of the EMI staff: 61 of the 192 staff members were German (32 percent), followed by 29 Britons (15 percent), and 18 Frenchmen (9 percent).[23] Tietmeyer expressed his approval of the EMI proposal before it was even announced publicly: "Without wanting to preempt [the EMI's announcement], I may state that the recommendations will take account of significant German concerns."[24]

The document proposed a four-step timetable. During the first stage, which could start as early as 1998, governments would decide which countries were going to join EMU. The EMI would oversee production of the new euro banknotes and coins. In the second stage, beginning January 1, 1999, the euro would be introduced for noncash transactions. New public debt would be issued in euros, and conversion facilities would be established to change national currencies to euros.[25] Member states would have the choice of continuing to transact business in either their national currencies or the euro. Stage 3 would begin by January 1, 2002, at the latest and would involve the introduction of the euro coin and banknote to the public. The final stage would begin July 1, 2002, at the latest and would require the removal from circulation of all national currencies.

The EMI's proposal reflected the Bundesbank's primary concern that the DM remain in use during the transition period. In essence, the proposal had bought the DM three more years before its extinction. France, which maintained that a long transition phase exposed its currency to speculation, argued to no avail against the EMI's plan at the EU finance minister's meeting on November 27, 1995. The ministers endorsed the EMI's proposal, and the heads of state formally approved the plan at the Madrid summit. Once again, German preferences had prevailed.

Waigel Creates Debate

In the final four months of 1995, Waigel's statements about EMU became more incautious, creating a diplomatic furor in one instance. In a September 20 private session of the Bundestag finance committee, Waigel said that Italy and probably Belgium would not be able to meet the targets on budgetary discipline necessary to qualify for EMU.[26] Apparently unaware that he was being reported by the internal Bundestag press service, he also voiced skepticism about France's ability to meet the criteria.[27] When these comments leaked out a day before the Majorca summit, they created a diplomatic quandary for Kohl. On the one hand, Waigel was stating the obvious to most observers, and no one in the German government wanted to create the impression that there could be a relaxation of the criteria for entry. On the other, Kohl did not want to create the impression that the

Germans were guiding the choice of EMU countries too closely. His response was to rally behind Italian prime minister Lamberto Dini, saying only that Germany had no right to judge which countries would qualify for the single currency.

Nevertheless, Dini began exploring alternatives to the EMU time line. Breaking a long-standing taboo against questioning the starting date for EMU of 1999, which Italy had insisted be inserted in the Treaty, Dini said the introduction of a single currency might have to be delayed on political grounds. Dini admitted that Italy would probably not meet the targets. "Then we will have to decide politically if it's in the interests of Europe to have a very small group of countries [in EMU] or whether to wait and start together after a year with a majority group of countries."[28] In 1995, however, there was no serious discussion of Dini's idea of a delay in the timetable.

The Stability Pact

Waigel created greater controversy by proposing a "stability pact" between EMU members. In a September 1995 interview, Waigel called for the "installation of additional measures to secure budget discipline" and indicated that proposals for enhancing the Maastricht Treaty had been discussed in the Bundesbank and finance ministers' meetings for six months.[29] What emerged from the discussions were two proposals: a Commission recommendation that countries running excessive deficits should lose some of their regional aid and Waigel's stability pact. In a November 10 speech to the Bundestag, he described the concept: after 1999, any state with a budget deficit of greater than 3 percent of GDP would be required to place a non-interest-bearing deposit of 0.25 percent of GDP for each additional 1 percent of budget deficit with the ECB. If the deficit was still above 3 percent after 2 years, the deposit would become a fine and would be paid into the EU budget.[30]

Although the French government supported the need for a penalty against governments that run excessive deficits after switching over to the single currency, it was reserved about Waigel's proposal. The harsh nature of Waigel's sanction met with alarm in several member states and seemed to reflect the degree to which Germany distrusted its partners to maintain correct economic policies within the single currency.

By March 1996, Waigel's stability pact had been opposed on both legal and political grounds by all EU member states except France and the Netherlands.[31] When the issue arose again at the Luxembourg meeting of finance ministers in June 1996, Germany was isolated in its position that disciplinary procedures should begin as soon as an excessive deficit existed. The other fourteen states wanted action only when an excessive deficit *persists*. However, the other states conceded to Germany the inclusion of time limits that would give a delinquent state only a finite amount of time to rectify its problems.

In August, State Secretary for Finance Jürgen Stark suggested a softening of Germany's position by proposing that in exceptional circumstances a state could be allowed to exceed the excessive deficit criterion. This led to a tentative agreement, announced after the September 10, 1996, Monetary Committee meeting, that the member states would have nine to twelve months to correct their fiscal imbalances. Thereafter, sanctions would be automatic but would be imposed only by a "stability council" of other EMU participants, first in the form of non-interest-bearing deposits and then as fines. Although the fines were smaller than the Waigel proposal, they were automatic, and a German official indicated that the Germans were "quite happy with the way [the agreement] is evolving."[32] The finance ministers, however, were unable to agree on how "exceptional" circumstances should be defined.

The final terms of the stability pact (renamed the "stability and growth pact" at the behest of the French) were not, however, settled until a marathon negotiating session during the Dublin summit on December 13–14, 1996. Germany remained isolated in the position that the fines be automatic and rejected the French position that some political intervention mechanism was necessary to make the sanctions practicable. "The negotiations on the stability pact were driven by concern about domestic public opinion, and that's a new phenomenon," said a German diplomat.[33] Waigel finally conceded that automatic fines would require rewriting the terms of the Maastricht Treaty's criteria, and Germany felt that rewriting the criteria would be counterproductive. The final version was a compromise between the French and the German positions.[34] Bundesbank director Otmar Issing expressed disappointment with the pact, saying that "unrestrained automaticity would not have been possible, but one cannot be satisfied with a decision mechanism in which potential sinners pass judgment on actual sinners."[35] In the end, Kohl—always a politician more than an economist—settled for a stability pact that was not as strict as the one Waigel had originally proposed. It should be remembered, however, that a fiscal stability pact was not in the Maastricht Treaty, and thus the Germans ultimately added to the requirements of EMU. Moreover, the episode showed that the Bundesbank–finance ministry collaboration to assert the bank's preferences again proved productive in achieving a consensus around Germany's preferences at the international level.

The "Ins" and "Outs"

An issue of concern to both Germany and France was the final relationship between the euro and the currencies not yet participating in the single currency. France's concerns that these countries could achieve a competitive advantage over euro members by devaluing were supported by Germany. Moreover, the British—as yet undecided about whether to use their opt-out—wanted to clarify their position in the event that they chose not to join.

The issue was discussed in the February Monetary Committee meeting, and the member states agreed on a preliminary concept of having a second EMS to link the euro with the other European currency countries. There was debate about how tightly to link the currencies and whether or not to make the link obligatory. Hard currency countries like France, Belgium, and the Scandinavians wanted tight links (for example, the old EMS ±2.25 percent bands) between their currencies and the euro, whereas countries prone to inflation and devaluation like Britain, Spain, Italy, and Portugal were in favor of looser arrangements, with Britain being especially concerned that the arrangement be voluntary. Germany was willing to support the French in their demands for an "EMS II" so long as the ECB's intervention obligations were limited. The position of the Finance Ministry was that, since the other states were trying to converge to the ECB's policies, the ECB's intervention obligations should not be symmetrical (unlike those of the EMS).

In April, Tietmeyer weighed in with his proposals for the EMS II: the president of the ECB should be the decisionmaker for parity changes with the "outs." This would depoliticize realignments and amount to a better guarantee of ECB stability. At the June 1997 Amsterdam summit, the details of the EMS II were agreed. The new EMS would begin with the launching of the euro, and its principles explicitly stated that it would function only insofar as it did not jeopardize the objective of price stability. Participation in the EMS II was voluntary for the member states outside the euro area, but any member state that wanted to join the euro had to first join the EMS. Because the EMS allowed ±15 percent bands, the ECB was unlikely to have to intervene in significant amounts. Moreover, although interventions at the margins were automatic and unlimited in principle, the ECB could suspend intervention if this conflicted with its primary objective. Again, the handiwork of the Bundesbank was quite apparent in the final outcome.

Trust But Verify

Another minor dispute illustrated explicitly the level of German distrust of its partner governments. At issue was the date of the financial statements that would be used to gauge fitness for entry into the single currency. This became the subject of discussion at the November 27, 1995, Finance Ministers meeting, when Waigel insisted that the decision by the member states on EMU entry be made on the basis of actual 1997 data rather than 1997 forecasts or quarterly reports. This meant that the selection of countries could be made as late as May 1998, which, indeed, proved to be the case. The French wanted the decision made well before that date because they did not want EMU entry to become an issue in France's March 1998 parliamentary elections.[36] At their Madrid summit, EU leaders acceded to Germany's demands that the decision be made "as soon as possible in 1998" on the basis of the actual performance in 1997.

Rumors of Delay

At the beginning of 1997, the preparations for the timely launching of the euro began to look inadequate. With twelve months before the final decision was to be made, neither Germany nor France looked likely to be able to meet the 3 percent deficit convergence criterion, and the markets began to believe that a deal might be struck to delay the starting date by two years. Although the Commission continued to project both Germany and France being able to meet the convergence criteria exactly, most other economic analyses projected a higher deficit for both of these important countries (see Table 7.1). Kohl himself admitted that Germany might not make a 3.0 percent deficit, as he had always promised.[37]

Germany's own precarious financial situation made the political question of Italy's membership more problematic. For most Germans, the thought of Italy joining EMU in the first wave of countries was ludicrous and dangerous. Politically, it behooved Kohl to try to strike a deal with Italy that would guarantee its membership in 2000 or 2001. A privately

Table 7.1   Forecasts of Budget Deficits as Percentage of GDP

	France		Germany		Italy		Spain	
	1997	1998	1997	1998	1997	1998	1997	1998
European Commission	3.0	3.0	3.0	2.7	3.2	3.9	3.0	2.7
NatWest Securities	3.1	2.8	3.0	1.6	3.4	3.0	3.2	2.9
Goldman Sachs	3.4	3.0	3.4	3.0	3.6	3.2	3.3	2.9
Economist Intelligence Unit	3.2	3.0	3.5	3.0	4.0	3.0	3.4	2.8
OECD[a]	3.2	3.0	3.4	2.6	3.7	3.4	3.4	2.9

Source: The Economist, June 7, 1997.
Note: a. Organization for Economic Cooperation and Development.

proposed agreement to this effect, however, was angrily rejected by Italian prime minister Romano Prodi, who pointed out that Germany itself did not meet the criteria at present.[38] As rumors of a two-year delay swept the markets, however, Prodi commented that "if Germany was considering asking for a delay, that [was] their business. It [was] possible, but it [was] not an easy thing."[39]

Delay rumors persisted throughout the first part of 1997. In part, they reflected the market's unease with the fact that even Germany did not meet the convergence criteria exactly. Moreover, France, integral to monetary union, looked even more unlikely to achieve the deficit ratio, and German finance minister Waigel continued to make speeches in which he assured Germans that 3.0 percent meant 3.0 percent. Within Germany, isolated voices began to publicly advocate an orderly delay. Herbert Hax, the head of the German government's Council of Economic Advisors,[40] former Bundesbanker Wilhelm Nölling,[41] and Edmund Stoiber rejected the timetable approach to EMU that Kohl increasingly seemed to be using. Kohl himself rejected any suggestion of delay and denied that there was a contradiction between the criteria and the timetable. Time and again, he assured Germans that Germany and its partners would meet the criteria on time. Delay was impossible.

Behind the scenes, it was clear that the government was not so sanguine about the numbers. German growth was rising, but so was unemployment. The gold reserve revaluation plan (discussed in the following section) betrayed the Kohl government's desperation. By fall, however, it had become clear that an orderly delay would not be proposed by the EU leaders, and the markets began to contemplate the euro seriously.

Still, there were no signs that Germany would meet the 3.0 percent deficit criterion and, in October 1997, four respected academics brought a suit in the Constitutional Court asking the court to delay EMU, citing insufficient convergence.[42] The suit was rejected in April 1998, but during the critical phase of deciding which member states met the Maastricht Treaty requirements, it continued to throw doubt on the political process in Germany. Could Kohl commit Germany and then have the Constitutional Court reject that international commitment? Would an eight-person, unelected body really prevent Germany from joining the euro?

There were other last-minute appeals for an orderly delay: in February 1998, a month before the list of member states fit to join EMU was to be announced, 155 German economists published an open letter in the *Financial Times*, urging the Kohl government to postpone the deadline.[43] As with other public calls for a delay, the Kohl government insisted that a delay was unnecessary, and that all the member states had made sufficient progress toward economic convergence to allow a stable euro to be created. Thus, for all the domestic calls for delay from legitimate sources, the

Kohl government steadfastly refused to be drawn into discussions about delay, labeling them "harmful" and "counterproductive." With respect to the economists' letter, there was also a sense that it had come too late to stop the momentum toward the single currency. By October, the markets and the German public sensed the inevitability of the project. Delay was no longer a realistic hope for EMU skeptics.

The Bundesbank-Government Conflict About the Gold Reserves

As the government's fiscal position worsened in the course of 1996–1997, the Kohl government (like the other European governments) began to scrounge for every last bit of revenue that could be used to bring Germany's deficit down to the requisite 3 percent in 1997. The plan to revalue the Bundesbank's gold reserves seemed like the ideal target for getting a boost to the German deficit ratio. Unfortunately for Kohl, however, the plan caused the most public confrontation with the Bundesbank in years and forced him to withdraw the plan in a humiliating about-face.

The Bundesbank had the largest amount of gold reserves of all the EU countries, and the reserves were valued at only 25 percent of their market price.[44] The Maastricht Treaty required a revaluation of the gold reserves to market prices (yielding Germany a paper profit of approximately $23 billion[45]), and in early 1997 Tietmeyer made Kohl's government aware of this requirement. It is unlikely that Tietmeyer deliberately set a trap for the government: when the government initially proposed that the revaluation proceeds be used to bring down the 1997 debt ratio, Tietmeyer was not unduly skeptical. However, when the finance ministry decided to use the proceeds from the revaluation to bring down the government's 1997 *deficit* (and thus easily reducing the German deficit ratio to 3.0 percent), the Bundesbank balked. According to *Der Spiegel*, Tietmeyer not only refused to allow the gold revaluation to be used for 1997's deficit ratio, but he also lobbied Kohl hard for a delay. If Kohl could not meet the convergence criteria without resorting to "accounting tricks" that would undermine the authority of Germany to uphold the standards for EMU entry, perhaps a delay would be better after all? "Wouldn't it be possible, together with France, to delay the beginning of EMU?" he asked.[46]

When word of the government's revaluation plan leaked to Germany's EU partners, reaction was swift and unambiguous. This was a clear confirmation that Germany was itself in trouble, fiscally, and could no longer pass judgment on the other fiscal laggards. Italian finance minister Carlo Ciampi declared his *Schadenfreude*, "now we aren't the black sheep any more,"[47] and others expressed glee that Germany had fallen off its high horse.

Publicly, the Bundesbank responded to the government's plan with a terse five-paragraph position paper detailing its opposition to using the gold reserve revaluation money for the purposes of bringing down the 1997 deficit ratio. In its final point it warned the government not to force the issue:

> If the revaluation [along the lines of the government's proposed plan] is legislated, this would be interference in the monetary policy of the Bundesbank. Such an action would contradict German tradition as well as the conception of the Maastricht Treaty regarding the independence of the central bank.[48]

In the face of domestic and international condemnation of the government's plan, Kohl and the Bundesbank "hammered out what they called a compromise that gave the Bundesbank everything it wanted."[49] The gain from the revaluation would be applied to the 1998 deficit, thus ensuring that Germany still had to meet the 1997 deficit criterion and qualify for EMU without the help of accounting tricks.

The March 1998 Surprises

At the beginning of 1998, anticipation about the various governments' financial statistics grew. EMU was almost a foregone conclusion, but many expected the convergence ratios to be the linchpin of the whole project. If the ratios, especially the politically sensitive excessive deficit ratios, were not sufficiently close to the 3 percent threshold, there could be problems. On February 27, the member states finally released their nationally calculated numbers. To many people's surprise, the national figures showed that all eleven of the states that were interested in joining the euro had met the convergence criteria. Some, like France, had *barely* met the deficit ratio (3.02 percent) but the other ten were at or below the 3.0 percent level (see Table 7.2). For euro-skeptics, this was creative accounting and political manipulation. How could Italy, which only a year earlier had had a deficit ratio of 6.7 percent, bring its figure down to 2.7 percent legitimately?

When the Commission and the EMI released their convergence reports on March 25, 1998, the ratios were exactly the same. This lent credibility to the convergence figures, but most Germans were eager to hear what the Bundesbank report,[50] which came out two days later, would reveal, since the Bundesbank Council had vowed to examine each state's convergence individually, and it was not bound to use Eurostat (the Commission's statistical arm) numbers as the EMI and the Commission had been. If anyone would find the accounting tricks, the Bundesbank would.

To many Germans' surprise, the Bundesbank accepted the Commission and EMI's ratios exactly. Although the Bundesbank's report was more

**Table 7.2   1998 Maastricht Convergence Ratios, Commission Findings Based on
1997 Statistics**

Country	Deficit[a]	Debt[b]	Inflation[c]	Interest Rates[d]
Austria	−2.5	66.1	1.1	5.6
Belgium	−2.1	122.2	1.4	5.7
Finland	−0.9	55.8	1.3	5.9
France	−3.0	58.0	1.2	5.5
Germany	−2.7	61.3	1.4	5.6
Ireland	+0.9	66.3	1.2	6.2
Italy	−2.7	121.6	1.8	6.7
Luxembourg	+1.7	6.7	1.4	5.6
Netherlands	−1.4	72.1	1.8	5.5
Portugal	−2.5	62.0	1.8	6.2
Spain	−2.6	68.8	1.8	6.3
Electing not to join EMU in 1999				
Denmark	+0.7	65.1	1.9	6.2
Greece	−4.0	108.7	5.2	9.8
Sweden	−0.8	76.6	1.9	6.5
UK	−1.9	53.4	1.8	7.0

Source: Comm Doc IP/98/273, Brussels, March 25, 1998.
Notes: a. The reference value for an excessive deficit is 3 percent.
b. The reference value for excessive debt is 60 percent.
c. Inflation could not be more than 1.5 percent above the average of the three best countries, which were Austria, France, and Ireland.
d. Long-term interest rates could not be more than 2 percent above the three best countries, which were France, Ireland, and Austria.

skeptical about the feasibility of Italy and Belgium's joining the euro, its
doubts were predicated on their debt ratios rather than their deficits.

> The debt criterion and its effects on the budgetary politics were often
> unjustifiably ignored in the convergence debates. The Maastricht Treaty
> explicitly requires that the debt ratio be "sufficiently diminishing and
> approaching the refence rate." Although no concrete time horizen is
> given, this should not mean that convergence can be drawn out indefi-
> nitely. The 10-year convergence horizon used in this analyis is not a new
> requirement, nor should it be misconstrued as a projection. The mathe-
> matical examples of budget deficits illustrate concretely, however, the
> level of corrections that are still required by quite a few member states
> to achieve the Treaty's reference ratio within a 10-year time period. . . .
> Although Belgium has made clear progress in the past years, these ef-
> forts do not, in the view of the Bundesbank, suffice to reduce the excep-
> tionally high debt to eliminate significant doubts about the long term vi-
> ability of the public finances. Italy, too, has made impressive
> convergence progress. However, the debt ratio has gone down compara-
> tively little. Italy's progress does not, in the view of the Bundesbank,
> suffice to decrease the exceptionally high debt ratio in such a marked
> way to eliminate significantly doubts about the long term viability of the
> public finances.[51]

Even these Bundesbank reservations, however, were not enough ammunition for EMU skeptic Edmund Stoiber to fight an anti-euro campaign, and he declared that the Bundesbank's report was "just what I wanted to hear."[52] There was a suggestion by the Bundesbank later that the politicians had been too quick to cast aside the serious qualms of the Bundesbank, but the effect was the same: with the Bundesbank's blessing, all the parties, with the exception of the PDS, were able to vote to submit the DM into the euro on April 23, 1997. The lopsided vote in the Bundestag, 575 to 35, was more positive even than a similar vote in the French National Assembly on the same day, where euro-skeptics were outvoted 334 to 49. In Germany's upper house, the Bundesrat, fifteen of the sixteen *Länder* governments voted in favor of EMU, with only Saxony president Kurt Biedenkopf abstaining because there was insufficient control over the debt reduction of Italy and Belgium.

It is interesting to see how the issue of delay was kept off the agenda by all the political parties and thus never had enough momentum to seriously threaten the launch of the euro. I discuss this issue in the section about political parties' responses. Before that, however, I examine the final conflict before the Brussels summit in May 1998.

The ECB President, "Wim-Claude Trichenberg"

The 1998 timetable leading to the decision about which member states qualified for the single currency was tight, and the decision was expected to be highly contentious. However, after the release of the 1997 figures showing that all eleven interested member states met the all-important deficit criterion, the month between the Commission's recommendation and the Brussels summit was one of boredom. The analysts and markets predicted an unproblematic decision and more pomp and circumstance than political infighting. With respect to the question of euro-membership, they were right. However, a long-simmering dispute about the presidency of the ECB added the missing drama to the summit and cast a pall over the political cooperation that the launching of the euro was supposed to symbolize.

The issue of who should run the ECB was not a politically contentious decision in 1993. Initially, EU leaders had difficulty finding any central banker to come in on January 1, 1994, to manage the newly created EMI. Dutch central bank president Wim Duisenberg had been asked but had declined, as had Belgian Alexandre Lamfalussy initially.[53] The Belgian government eventually convinced Lamfalussy to take the helm, but with the stipulation that he be allowed to leave after his three-year term was up. In 1996, Duisenberg made his commitment to the EMI contingent on assurances by the governments (which unanimously elect the ECB president) that he would be selected to be the first ECB president. These assurances were given by all governments except the Italian and French. French central bank president Jean-Claude Trichet blamed the intransigence of his government on his poor relationship with the Chirac government, and wrote Duisenberg a personal note of support. With these assurances, Duisenberg took the EMI job. In early 1997, Chirac told Commissioner Yves-Thibault de Silguy that he had a French candidate for the ECB presidency, and rumors began to circulate that IMF managing director Michel Camdessus would be the French choice to lead the ECB. Camdessus declined, and this left Chirac with Trichet as the French choice for the top ECB job. On November 4, 1997, seven months before the Brussels summit, Chirac formally announced his choice.

Initially, many thought this was to be a bargaining chip. Specifically, France was interested in ensuring that Italy be in the first wave of entrants into EMU, and it also was lobbying Germany to create a new "stability council" that would coordinate the euro-members' economic policies. The French envisioned a political counterweight to the ECB, and this was anathema to the Germans. Thus, when Chirac's Trichet nomination was announced, many people believed Chirac was creating new French chips to be traded in other bargains. The other fourteen member states supported the nomination of Duisenberg for ECB president, and thus the stage was set for the Brussels showdown.

In the month leading up to the May 1–3, 1998, Brussels summit, all sides dug in. With an election scheduled for May 6, the Dutch had no interest in backing down to the French. Moreover, although there had been talk of a compromise that would allow Duisenberg to retire after some specified date, both the Dutch and the Germans were against an explicit deal. The Dutch were opposed because it offended the professional integrity of Duisenberg, and the Germans saw the compromise as political interference with the ECB. This latter complaint became the rationale against any kind of deal, whether explicit or implicit. Reimut Jochimsen, a senior Bundesbank council member, went so far as to say that an agreement to split the term could trigger legal action in Germany's Constitutional Court.

At the last minute, British prime minister Tony Blair used a formula that was transparent to all as a capitulation to the French but that provided a small fig leaf to the Dutch: Duisenberg made a personal, "voluntary" statement that he would take early retirement, but without stipulating the date for his retirement. When the statement was read to reporters, there was spontaneous laughter among the press, to which Chirac responded with an irritated "stop laughing."[54]

The German position had been unified against such a solution and solidly behind the Dutch throughout the summit, and it was only Kohl's willingness to capitulate to Chirac that made this outcome possible.[55] The Bundesbank was forced to come to terms with its new impotence: Klaus-Dieter

Kühbacher, a Bundesbank council member, indicated that although the deal violated the Maastricht Treaty, there was no action the Bundesbank could take in response. "This is up to Governments," he conceded.[56] Any leverage the Bundesbank had had before the April 23, 1998, Bundestag vote was gone.

THE POLITICAL PARTIES AND EMU

Anti-EMU Sentiment: Politically Incorrect?

During the 1993–1998 period the political leadership felt greater scrutiny on European matters from the electorate in many member states, but popular opposition to EMU was especially great in Germany. Net support for EMU remained negative, and increasingly the Germans felt that they had been inadequately consulted before the Treaty had been signed. *Eurobarometer* surveys leave no doubt as to where Germans stood on relinquishing the DM: as early as 1983, Germans had a net negative (−40 percent) response to the question, "Would you be for or against replacing your national currency by one common European currency?"[57] But when discussions of a common currency began at the elite level in the fall of 1988, Germans were slightly (+6 percent) in favor of "a single European currency, the ECU."[58] By the fall of 1990, West German net support for the single currency peaked at +23 percent.[59] In the fall before the signing of the Maastricht Treaty, net support fell to +10 percent,[60] and by June 1992 (after the failed Danish referendum), net German support was negative again (−15 percent) and remained so. A 1996 poll indicated that a division between elites and the mass public on this issue existed. Elites, defined as leaders in politics, economics, and management, were in favor of EMU (83 percent), whereas the mass public opinion about EMU was 58 percent against the single currency.[61] Given these unambiguous opinion poll results, it is all the more surprising that German mainstream political parties did not try to harness these sentiments for electoral advantage.

The history of German criticism of EMU shows that time and again, politicians *did* try to make an issue out of the EMU process but were almost universally condemned by all sides of the mainstream political establishment. Individual politicians from the mainstream parties, with the exception of the Greens, tried to criticize the agreement to relinquish the DM but failed to gather support from either the other party members or the political establishment.[62] As we shall see, this lack of support for those politicians who would speak out against EMU ultimately gave the Bundesbank power as a political force.

The criticism of the Maastricht Treaty began right after the Treaty was signed in February 1992. The first politician to try to exploit the German public's apprehension about Maastricht and especially EMU was Peter Gauweiler, the Bavarian environment minister. A rival to Waigel for the CSU party leadership, he came out against the whole process of European union, calling it a "totalitarian dream of universal redemption" and calling the single currency "esperanto-money."[63] More significantly, the leader of the SPD, Oskar Lafontaine, called for his party to reject the Treaty: "You cannot have a common currency, and a single central bank, while allowing each member state to pursue its own incomes policy, social and financial policies."[64] The SPD rejected his plea and voted in favor of ratification in exchange for a promise that the Bundestag be allowed to decide whether the preconditions for EMU had been met.

Edmund Stoiber, Bavaria's minister-president, criticized the Treaty publicly the day after it took effect. In an interview, he indicated that the CSU no longer considered a federal European state desirable and that he wanted to retard European integration. "I'm not against integration. I am against the speed of the integration. . . . The people can't catch up and therefore we have to take our time to reach the ultimate goal: a permanent European Peace Community."[65] He later accused his fellow politicians of suffering too long from guilt over their national identity and insisted: "We do not want a European nation in the place of nation states."[66] Although the interview was cast in terms meant for domestic (Bavarian) consumption, the statements drew widespread criticism from Germany's EU partners. The baldness of the comments seemed to signal a change in the German attitude toward Europe—particularly because they were coming from a coalition party politician. "A few years ago, nobody [in Germany] would have said these things—not even [Franz Joseph] Strauss," said former Belgian finance minister Henri Simonet.[67]

Stoiber's comments also offended Germans; in the Bundestag, the SPD roundly condemned his statements, as did the FDP. The interview even drew a rebuke from the CSU's coalition partner Kohl, who restated his commitment to the goal of European union in a Bundestag address: "For Germany, there is no alternative to European unity. Securing and continuing the task of European unification concerns the very fate of this continent, but above all of our country."[68] Although only 18 percent of West Germans and 12 percent of East Germans stated that they could see real advantages for the country in EU membership,[69] Stoiber's attempt to capitalize on voter dissatisfaction failed completely, as all parties closed ranks and condemned the statements.

Monetary union continued to be unpopular in Germany, and in January 1994 a small party, the Bund freier Bürger (BfB), was created in Hesse with the platform of preserving the DM.[70] The party was founded by Manfred Brunner, the former *chef de Cabinet* of German commissioner Martin Bangemann, who had been dismissed because of his anti-EMU position.

Brunner had also been one of the challengers of the constitutionality of the Maastricht Treaty. Polls brought the party national attention by indicating that it was expected to get as much as 35 percent of the vote on the basis of its anti-EMU position,[71] but the BfB did not cross the 5 percent threshold, receiving only 1.1 percent of the votes.[72] The party had a small resurgence in late 1995 when it planned to gather signatures on a petition calling for a referendum on EMU. Chancellor Kohl repeatedly stated that he would not subject German EMU entry to a referendum, since there were no provisions in the Basic Law for such an event.

In Germany, 1994 was a *Superwahljahr* (super election year) and one might have expected some party differentiation on European issues. The SPD gingerly tested the anti–currency union sentiment. An SPD economic policy spokesperson said that the 1999 target date should be extended by ten years since Germany and other EU members were unlikely to be able to fulfill economic criteria. Even though his remarks were not particularly anti-European or anti-EMU, he stressed that his comments were not official SPD policy.[73] The issue of a one-speed versus two-speed Europe was thus raised publicly by a party widely expected to be part of the ruling coalition after the June 1994 elections. Yet the SPD did not actually break publicly with any CDU/CSU–initiated policies regarding Europe throughout the months before the election.

In June 1994, Economics Minister Günter Rexrodt was the first senior government minister publicly to question whether or not the single currency could be achieved by decade's end. Saying that EMU might not be reached until 2001, Rexrodt highlighted a split in the CDU between those who thought EMU could be accomplished on schedule, with only a few countries in a "hard core," and those like Kohl who believed that the timetable was less important than including such longtime euro-partners as Italy and Belgium.

The CDU "Hard-Core" Proposal

The split was dramatically revealed one month before the October 16, 1994, Bundestag election. In a strategy paper, the CDU/CSU detailed its vision for EMU: a hard core of five founding EU countries (Belgium yes, Italy no) that was expected to coordinate not only monetary policy but also fiscal, budgetary, economic, and social policy. CDU/CSU parliamentary leader Wolfgang Schäuble presented the five-point plan at the 1996 IGC and indicated that "variable geometry gives us better chances to complete this process, given the different, sometimes competing views. We must accept that not every member can accept every step at the same time."[74] In the plan, Germany and France formed the center of the hard core, but the document also admitted that "[Germany and France's] special relationship faces a stiff test because it too is beginning to show signs of differentiation of interests and perceptions which might cause them to drift apart."[75]

The French government did not fundamentally disagree with the CDU's plan: Prime Minister Balladur had recently also floated the idea of a multispeed Europe, and the CDU's paper did not create an uproar in France. It did, however, significantly strain relations with Italy, Denmark, and Britain, all relegated to the "soft core." Italy's prime minister Silvio Berlusconi telephoned Kohl, and the UK joined a protest from Italy and Denmark about the proposal. The international outcry forced Kohl to distance himself publicly from his party's paper, saying that the proposals were not official German policy. There was speculation, however, that Kohl had unofficially endorsed the paper in order to gauge the reaction to the ideas, and indeed it is difficult to imagine that Kohl was not apprised of the recommendations and did not agree with them.

The paper was also criticized by the CDU's coalition partner. Foreign Minister Klaus Kinkel, the leader of the FDP, condemned the proposal, saying that it had given a "disastrous signal" to Germany's neighbors.[76] Predictably, the CDU's paper also met strong criticism from the SPD. One of the toughest critics of the paper was former chancellor Helmut Schmidt, who objected to its self-righteous tone. "It is a paper in which only Germany appears to be the country that has the right answer to all the questions and is in every case a leading power."[77]

Bundesbank president Tietmeyer joined the debate by questioning whether the multispeed Europe might not divide Europe rather than unite it. The Bundesbank's position was somewhat ambiguous since it had supported the multispeed, "concentric circles" conception of EMU. Tietmeyer's interview suggests that the Bundesbank might have been in favor of amending the treaty to take effect when all EU economies were ready (that is, much later than 1999).

The CDU paper was rejected at a meeting of EU foreign ministers on September 10 and in the European Parliament on September 28. Although the paper's conclusions were overwhelmingly rejected, the debate about the concepts continued—albeit not under the exclusive auspices of the CDU. At any rate, the CDU did not suffer electorally on account of the paper; on October 16, it won reelection by a small margin, confounding the polls that had predicted an SPD victory.[78] Helmut Kohl thus remained the chancellor who would take Germany into EMU despite serious political and economic obstacles.

The SPD Also Questions EMU

The SPD did not try to make an issue of EMU until a year later, when SPD leader Rudolf Scharping disparagingly referred to EMU as "some idea or other."[79] At the time, the reference seemed hardly worth the domestic uproar it created. The heated discussion was further fueled by SPD economics spokesperson Gerhard Schröder's statement that the SPD would make an electoral issue of Germany's EMU commitment.[80] However, Scharping most likely did not mean to unleash the furor with his original comments. He almost immediately tried to downplay the remark, and he retreated from Schröder's statements, calling them "irresponsible" and adding, "we also don't make the death penalty an electoral issue."[81] SPD deputy leader Oskar Lafontaine, by contrast, seemed to relish the opening of the topic, saying the EMU treaty had been badly bargained. Some of the intra-SPD wrangling about EMU was due to the leadership struggle—indeed, at the Mannheim party congress in November, Lafontaine succeeded in unseating Scharping thanks to a rousing speech that included references to the single-currency question.[82]

The debate within the SPD about whether to be more critical about monetary union was denounced as "cheap populism" by Kinkel, and the *Neue Zürcher Zeitung* noted that "the sharp and moralizing criticism which the opposition has heaped on the SPD supports the belief that a fundamental debate about monetary union is 'politically incorrect.'"[83]

In the November 8, 1995, Bundestag debate, the main topic was EMU. After the SPD criticized Kohl for forgetting the needs of ordinary citizens, Kohl retaliated. He called the SPD clueless in its discussions of euromoney and asserted that if the DM was not the core of the monetary union, there could be no monetary union. Moreover, Kohl claimed that the SPD was irresponsibly increasing the resistance of the German people to EMU and thereby irritating Germany's partners. Kohl urged the SPD to drop the harmful discussion of EMU as quickly as possible.[84]

Electoral Apathy over the Euro

The *Land* election of Baden-Württemberg in March 1996 provided an interesting new hypothesis regarding the electoral attitude about EMU: politicians did not make an electoral issue of the single currency because the electoral payoff was nonexistent. Contrary to the expectations of senior SPD officials who had been critical of EMU and who had sought to challenge Kohl's record as the chancellor who gave away the DM, the SPD's share of the vote sank 4.3 percent from its level in the previous election.[85] This result was repeated in the Hamburg election of September 1997, when Henning Vorscherau also attempted a mildly anti-euro campaign. He proposed a referendum on the issue and professed himself to be against the idea. As with its showing in Baden-Württemberg, the SPD failed to do as well as it had in the previous election, and Vorscherau resigned as a result.

These examples of the parties trying to make an electoral issue of EMU showed that in Germany, opposition to EMU was a double-edged sword. On the one hand, the parties were interested in mobilizing popular opposition to EMU, but on the other, the parties were constrained by their historical, interparty consensus about European integration being good for Germany. Moreover, for all the heat that the euro debate in Germany provided, empirical results from *Länder* elections showed Germans unwilling to vote on the issue of the euro when the opportunity arose.

CONCLUSION

This chapter connected two separate, but related phenomena: (1) the EMU implementation decisions that were made at the international level between 1992 and 1998 overwhelmingly incorporated the preferences of Germany, and (2) the German political parties were unwilling or unable to make German participation in the euro an electoral issue. The relationship between these two points is complex and must be examined further.

Why were German preferences so obviously dominant in the outcomes of international negotiations of specific technical points after 1992? The previous chapters revealed that the Bundesbank's ability to act as a domestic ratifier and to threaten to exit the project if the other member states did not incorporate those preferences was the decisive variable in explaining German dominance before the Treaty was signed and ratified.

After the ratification, however, one would expect that the Bundesbank's ratifier role had been eliminated. This, however, was not the case, because of the German Constitutional Court's 1993 decision giving the Bundestag the right to vote before the DM was submitted into the euro. Thus, the German parliament became the domestic ratifier of all post-Maastricht arrangements. However, this domestic ratifier function would only create leverage at the international level if the mainstream political parties would (theoretically, at least) be willing to vote against the euro. Thus the question of Germany's international leverage became an empirical one: would German politicians vote against the euro?

The second part of this chapter would seem to cast doubt on the willingness of the parliament to veto EMU. Time and again, German mainstream politicians did *not* challenge Kohl on this electorally promising issue, and there was little party differentiation among the political parties. No amount of popular opinion against EMU seemed to make any of the mainstream parties take an anti-EMU stance. Why, then, would Germany's EU partners take the parliament's veto threat seriously and capitulate to German demands in decisions on EMU implementation?

The solution to this puzzle is the role of the Bundesbank, which was the only institution that might have been able to persuade the Bundestag members to vote against the euro.[86] The Bundesbank's opinions on the subject of EMU had three advantages over those of the politicians: (1) they were not seen as a renunciation of Germany's European commitments generally; (2) unlike the government's positions, the bank's views on EMU had not varied in twenty-five years; and (3) they were perceived as technical and therefore apolitical. As we shall see, these elements contributed to the credibility of the Bundesbank's pronouncements and therefore continued to influence negotiations at the international level.

To Germany's partners, the situation looked essentially the same after the Treaty was signed as it had before: the preferences of the Bundesbank had to be taken seriously because the Bundesbank's views were taken seriously by members of the Bundestag. A member of the Bundestag was unlikely to vote against EMU entry on the basis of popular discontent with relinquishing the DM. Only 6.6 percent of the Bundestag members considered public opinion an important factor in their decision,[87] but 57 percent indicated that they might be persuaded to do so if the Bundesbank reported that all of the criteria had not been met.[88] Moreover, 80 percent of the Bundestag members reported that information from the Bundesbank was important or very important to their decision.[89] Thus, the Bundesbank's institutional reputation was extremely high in Germany, and its opinions and recommendations about international commitments carried substantial weight. Because of the Bundesbank's domestic stature among members of parliament, the need for Germany's partners to appease the Bundesbank in the post-Maastricht implementation negotiations remained strong until the parliament's vote.

The final confrontation between the French and the Dutch (and Germans) provided some confirmation of this hypothesized relationship. Since the ECB presidency decision was made after the Bundestag and Bundesrat vote about German EMU membership, the Bundesbank's criticisms and threats about the political solution that was adopted were ignored. Kohl was able to agree to a deal that the Bundesbank had publicly opposed because the Bundesbank's leverage had disappeared.

The following chapter will synthesize the various motivations that led to EMU and establish that the Bundesbank-government institutional relationship is necessary to understanding the German position.

Notes

1. The challenges came from a diverse group: four Green Party members of the European Parliament argued that the democratic deficit of Europe required a German referendum, and former FDP member Manfred Brunner argued that the Treaty represented the hollowing out of the German state. A third challenge was from an independent member of the Bundestag, claiming his democratic rights as a member of parliament were restricted. A senior Justice Ministry official and the two main right-wing parties (Republikaner, Deutsche Volkspartei) were also among

the plaintiffs. For more on the Court challenge, see the *Financial Times,* May 18, 1993, and October 6, 1993.

2. For more on the Constitutional Court's decision, see *Süddeutsche Zeitung,* October 13, 1993, and *Neue Zürcher Zeitung,* October 13, 1993. For an analysis of what the decision reflects about the constitutional approach to integration by the German Court, see Weiler (1995).

3. The bill passed in the Bundestag and Bundesrat concerning EMU was explicit about the convergence criteria: "The German Bundestag will oppose any effort to soften the stability criteria which were agreed at Maastricht. It will guard that the transition to the third stage will orient itself strictly on these criteria." See *Entschliessung des Deutschen Bundestages zum Vertrag vom 7. Februar 1992 über die Europäische Union,* December 2, 1992.

4. *Neue Zürcher Zeitung,* October 13, 1993.

5. For an analysis of the salience of EU issues at the national level, see Slater (1982).

6. Council of the European Communities/Commission of the European Communities (1992), Article 109j.

7. *Financial Times,* October 26, 1994. Ironically, even though Lubbers eventually agreed to the Frankfurt location, Kohl did not support Lubbers for Commission president because of Lubbers's earlier opposition to German unification.

8. Council of the European Communities/Commission of the European Communities (1992), Article 104(c)(3).

9. Ibid., Article 104(c)(2).

10. *Financial Times,* September 10–11, 1994.

11. *Auszüge aus Presseartikeln,* September 30, 1994, no. 72.

12. *Financial Times,* June 4, 1996.

13. *Financial Times,* November 5–6, 1994.

14. *Financial Times,* December 5, 1994.

15. *Eurobarometer 42,* spring, 1995, p. B43.

16. *Financial Times,* November 19–20, 1994.

17. *Financial Times,* December 5, 1994. However, the percentage of German respondents supporting a single currency was quite low (24 percent) compared to those who opposed the single currency (53 percent).

18. *Financial Times,* June 23, 1992.

19. *Auszüge as Presseartikeln,* June 26, 1995, no. 46.

20. *Financial Times,* December 17, 1995.

21. Ibid.

22. The name "euro" was not affixed to the single currency until December 1995. In this section I use it synonymously with the single currency for the sake of consistency.

23. *Financial Times,* November 15, 1995.

24. *Financial Times,* November 14, 1995.

25. At the Madrid summit, the heads of state allowed an exception to the government debt rule in deference to Germany. During the transition, nontradable debt will be allowed to be denominated in national currencies. See *Financial Times,* December 15–16, 1995.

26. *Financial Times,* September 21, 1995.

27. *New York Times,* November 29, 1995.

28. *Financial Times,* September 25, 1995.

29. *Focus Magazine,* September 16, 1995.

30. *Financial Times,* November 11, 1995.

31. *Financial Times,* March 28, 1996.

32. *New York Times,* September 11, 1996.

33. *Financial Times,* December 14, 1996.

34. A drop in GDP of 2.0 percent or more per year would automatically be classified as exceptional circumstances and the sanctions would not apply. A fall of between 0.75 percent and 2.0 percent of GDP would enable that member state to petition the Council of Ministers for special status. The Council would vote by qualified majority on whether or not to apply the sanctions.

35. *Financial Times,* December 17, 1996.

36. As a result of the decision to use actual 1997 data rather than projections, the decisive European Council summit was pushed to the weekend of May 1–3, 1998. Not wanting to make EMU an electoral issue in the French parliamentary elections, Chirac called the elections nine months earlier, on May 25 and June 1, 1997. His decision probably cost him his parliamentary majority; in any case, a socialist-communist coalition was returned to power.

37. *Financial Times,* February 8, 1997.

38. *Financial Times,* February 6, 1997.

39. *Financial Times,* March 1, 1997.

40. *Financial Times,* March 10, 1997.

41. *Financial Times,* May 19, 1997.

42. *Der Spiegel,* October 13, 1997.

43. *Financial Times,* February 9, 1998.

44. The Bundesbank had 95.2 million ounces of gold, France 81.9 million ounces, and Italy 66.7 million ounces. However, Germany's reserves were valued at only 25 percent of market price, compared to France's 100.2 percent and Italy's 102.8 percent of market price, making the German revaluation required by the Maastricht Treaty more significant than any other EU state's. See *Der Spiegel,* June 2, 1997.

45. *New York Times,* June 4, 1997. Half of this profit could have been transferred to the federal government to reduce its 1997 deficit.

46. Ibid., p. 32.

47. Ibid., p. 30.

48. Deutsche Bundesbank, *Monthly Report,* June 1997.

49. *New York Times,* June 4, 1997.

50. Kohl had commissioned a separate Bundesbank report at a particularly divisive party conference in September 1997. In order to appease significant euroskeptics in his own party, he determined that his party's recommendations about joining the euro in the April 23 Bundestag vote would be contingent on the opinions of the Bundesbank.

51. Deutsche Bundesbank (1998).

52. *Financial Times,* March 28–29, 1998.

53. Much of this section is taken from the *Financial Times,* May 5, 1998.

54. *Financial Times,* May 4, 1998.

55. *Financial Times,* May 5, 1998.

56. Ibid.

57. Survey Research Consultants International (1985), p. 576. A net negative response means that a greater percentage of people responded "against" than "for," that is, in this survey, 27 percent responded "for" and 67 percent responded "against."

58. *Eurobarometer 30,* November 1988.

59. *Eurobarometer 34,* fall 1990.

60. *Eurobarometer 36,* fall 1991.

61. *Süddeutsche Zeitung,* July 25, 1996.

62. "Political establishment" includes the other parties, the press and media, and former government officials.

63. *Financial Times,* March 17, 1992.

64. Ibid.

65. *Süddeutsche Zeitung,* November 2, 1993.

66. Ibid.

67. Author interview, November 22, 1993.

68. *Financial Times,* November 12, 1993.

69. *Financial Times,* November 3, 1993.

70. *Financial Times,* January 24, 1994.

71. *Focus Magazine,* May 30, 1994.

72. *Financial Times,* June 14, 1994. After the party's dismal showing in the European elections, Brunner decided not to contest the national elections.

73. *Financial Times,* January 29–30, 1994.

74. *Financial Times,* September 2, 1994.

75. Ibid.

76. United Press International, September 10, 1994.

77. *Süddeutsche Zeitung,* October 7, 1994.

78. The CDU/CSU received 41.5 percent of the vote, compared to the SPD's 36.4 percent and the FDP's 6.9 percent.

79. *Financial Times,* October 31, 1995.

80. *Der Spiegel* November 6, 1995.

81. Ibid.

82. *Süddeutsche Zeitung,* November 16, 1995.

84. *Süddeutsche Zeitung,* November 9, 1995.

85. Reinhardt (1997), p. 79.

86. Heisenberg (1998).

87. Ibid.

88. Ibid.

89. Ibid.

8

Conclusion

When the fifteen European Union leaders met in Brussels the weekend of May 1–3, 1998, they unanimously approved the launching of the euro with eleven members on January 1, 1999. Only Greece, Britain, Sweden, and Denmark remained outside the single currency, and even those countries will probably join at a later date. The EU had pulled off a major feat—the most important act of European integration since the Treaty of Rome in 1957—despite years of doubts about the feasibility and advisability of the project. This book has focused on Germany's role in making monetary cooperation possible and defining the parameters of that cooperation.

Germany, the largest export economy in Europe, had much to gain from exchange-rate cooperation in general. In fact, all chancellors in the post–Bretton Woods era sought to stabilize exchange rates with Germany's trading partners, a fact that illustrates the priority given to exchange-rate cooperation by all political parties. As such, explaining German cooperation would seem to be a simple matter of material interest dominating policy preferences. Certainly, the "Snake" and the EMS regimes can be explained by Germany's interest in maintaining stable exchange rates with its trading partners. The EMS, in particular, was especially advantageous to German material interests because it stabilized exchange rates without forcing Germany to bear much of the cost of policy adjustments or to relinquish monetary policy independence. In fact, one might rightly ask why the other member states were willing to participate in a regime that was so favorable to Germany's interests.

As Chapter 3 illustrated, weaker-currency countries like France and Italy were drawn to the German model of economic management. Indeed, as many other studies have suggested, the desire to reduce French inflation was an important element of Giscard d'Estaing's interest in negotiating a new system between France and Germany. However, the outcome of the regime negotiations, that is, the rules incorporated in the system, was not what Giscard d'Estaing had envisioned as being more accommodating to weaker-currency countries. On the contrary, the input of the Bundesbank in the latter stages of the EMS negotiations changed the system considerably and made it inimical to weaker-currency countries. Since Giscard d'Estaing had cosponsored the initiative, however, it was not politically feasible for him to abandon the project, and thus the EMS was launched. Because the French continued to try to modify the EMS for the next ten years, however, it is clear that the system was not what they had wanted. Most likely it was *too much* like the German model. Although Giscard d'Estaing and Barre wanted to harness the German credibility to reduce inflation somewhat, they did *not* want to converge on German levels of inflation. Thus, the French continued to press for a new monetary regime in Europe since changing the workings of the EMS to make the economies converge at a higher inflation rate was impossible within the existing rules of the EMS.

From Germany's point of view, the benefits of the EMS were substantial. For the government, the EMS locked in (albeit not permanently) exchange rates with Germany's trading partners that were often overvalued, resulting in enormous trade surpluses with these partners and a booming German economy. For the Bundesbank, the EMS did not require the foreign exchange interventions it had feared at its creation (against which it had an opt-out anyway). Moreover, the EMS had the felicitous effect of elevating the position of the Bundesbank from a domestic ratifier to an international institution of significant importance. In short, there was nothing in the EMS that would have given Germany reason to change the system in a meaningful way.

Yet this is exactly what the Kohl government allowed in 1988. By putting France's monetary union initiative on the European Council agenda in Hannover, Germany set in motion a process that resulted in Germany giving up its one symbol of postwar success, the DM, and forfeiting all of the benefits of the EMS. Why would Germany have taken this course of action?

Three of the most prevalent explanations are that (1) Germany benefited from EMU as much or more than the other member states, and thus it did not represent a concession; (2) EMU was not in Germany's interest, but Kohl traded it for German unification in 1989; and (3) Kohl traded off a material interest for a foreign policy interest. These explanations need to be examined in light of the empirical evidence presented in Chapters 5–7 in order to judge their validity.

The first explanation, that EMU was in Germany's economic interests or at least not in conflict with those interests, is the least compelling because in 1988, Germany already had most of the benefits of monetary union and none of the risks. There were no interest groups pushing monetary union (with the possible exception of the Association for Monetary Union in Europe, which was founded by Giscard d'Estaing and Schmidt in 1987 for the sole purpose of achieving monetary union). Employer, trade, and labor groups were agnostic about EMU, and the earliest position taking by these groups came after the Treaty had been signed.[1] There is no trace of any interest group pressure to justify claims that Kohl acted to promote certain economic interests when he put EMU on the agenda.

The claims that EMU was in Germany's economic interest rest on the untested assumption that, as Europe's largest export economy, Germany preferred stable (and, even better, overvalued) exchange rates with its primary trading partners. Of course, in 1988 Germany *had* stable and overvalued exchange rates with its primary trading partners through the EMS. Thus, the relevant environment for judging Germany's economic interests should be the status quo in January 1988, when Genscher made the decision to put monetary union on the EU agenda. Advocates of the "EMU was in Germany's economic interest" explanation contend that the EMS was unstable, that German policymakers knew this, and therefore that they had to find another system to stabilize exchange rates.

What empirical evidence is there that the EMS was fundamentally unstable and that policymakers knew this in 1988? The bulk of the evidence does not support either aspect of the explanation. In the late 1980s, the scholarship by both economists and political scientists extolled the stability of the EMS. Indeed, the editors of a volume titled *A European Central Bank: Perspectives on Monetary Unification After 10 Years of the EMS* begin their book with a telling synopsis of the status quo in June 1988:

> The initiatives to discuss the establishment of a centralized monetary authority in Europe, coming from government officials, have caught observers by surprise. The European Monetary System (EMS) has proved to the whole world to be a viable arrangement, and has been able to withstand the sizeable international shocks of the early 1980s: an immediate threat to the EMS is thus not evident.[2]

Moreover, the EU central bankers (who ought to have known exactly how stable the EMS was by virtue of dealing with it on a daily basis) thought it so stable as to make participation in the EMS for two years one of the Maastricht Treaty's convergence requirements. Until the 1992 crisis, the previous stresses on the system had been successfully overcome by means of politically orchestrated realignments. The system hinged critically on a *political* understanding—the norms of the regime—but there was good reason to believe that the system could survive indefinitely on that basis.[3]

The argument that the EMS was fundamentally unstable is usually made with the benefit of hindsight after the 1992–1993 EMS crises. The primary work on the instability of the EMS was done in 1993 by economists

Barry Eichengreen and Charles Wyplosz.[4] These authors argued that not only would real economic divergences cause attacks on the currency pegs, but speculative attacks without an underlying economic disequilibrium would also be self-fulfilling.

For those who would use this article as justification that the EMS was unstable and that policymakers (in Germany) needed a new system that would be more stable, the problem is that Eichengreen and Wyplosz's argument rested on the fact that the Maastricht Treaty's provisions *caused* the EMS to be unstable. As the authors explained:

> Until the summer of 1992, anticipations of a smooth transition to monetary union had stabilized expectations and hence the operation of the EMS. At that point, *the protracted process of negotiation and ratification allowed doubts to surface about whether the treaty would ever come into effect.* This altered the costs and benefits of the policies of austerity required of countries seeking to qualify for European monetary union, leading the markets to anticipate that those policies would ultimately be abandoned.[5]

Moreover, all of the significant conditions that undermined the EMS, including the politicians' unwillingness to realign, can be traced directly to the EMU plan. Eichengreen and Wyplosz highlighted the fact that the leading culprits of the 1992 crisis—a declining dollar and self-fulfilling speculative expectations—were precisely the same as in 1987, when the system did not fail.[6] The economic (and asymmetrical shock) of German unification was not in itself a cause for the crisis, since, as the authors pointed out, "[spreading the unification shock across different countries] can be achieved within the EMS so long as the deutsche mark is revalued at the time of unification."[7] Moreover, the markets did not begin to attack the currencies until after the 1992 failed Danish referendum. The turning point before Black Wednesday was August 25, when, for the first time, a public opinion poll predicted a slim rejection of the Treaty in France. The inability to reach consensus on a general realignment at the Bath summit was strongly influenced by the Maastricht convergence criterion requiring membership in the narrow bands of the EMS without devaluation for two years. Thus, all of the factors that caused the EMS crises were directly related to the Maastricht Treaty.[8] Had there been no EMU, the real economic divergences that afflicted the EMS in 1992 would have been settled in the way they had always been resolved: a general realignment. To argue that the EMS was rejected as unstable by policymakers in 1988 and that this was the reason for EMU is simply not supported by fact.

The second explanation for Kohl's willingness to consider EMU acknowledges that EMU was not in Germany's economic interest and contends that Kohl traded German unification for EMU.[9] This theory, which was highlighted by *Der Spiegel* in the week leading up to the May 1998 Brussels summit, is more difficult to reject because there are some elements of the explanation that fit. However, the explanation leaves some rather large gaps and inconsistencies and, on the whole, cannot be said to adequately explain Germany's motivation.

In its April 27, 1998, issue, *Der Spiegel* explained to Germans that the chancellor's own documents showed that EMU was a trade for German unification.[10] The documents show "the massive pressure from French President François Mitterrand: for Mitterrand, the binding of the German currency to Europe [was] a deciding factor to agreeing to reunification."[11] The case the magazine presented, however, was far from conclusive.

The documents from the chancellery cast real doubt on the central premise of the theory, that a deliberate quid pro quo was offered: "The unification Chancellor gave up the Mark in favor of the Euro—much earlier and under different conditions than he had ever planned—and not even for reunification but for the at-that-time vague prospect of a German-German confederation."[12] This quote precisely demonstrates two central problems with the quid pro quo theory: the timing and the actors.

The timing problem is that the impetus for monetary union came much earlier (in January 1988) than even the most farsighted analyst could have predicted that German unity was in the offing (November 1989). Moreover, momentum toward EMU continued after the April 1990 EU summit in which EU leaders gave Germany their blessing to unify. Plans for EMU were already highly evolved by April 1989. With the Delors Report as a blueprint for monetary union, many of the critical decisions having to do with EMU involved not *whether* to go ahead with EMU, but rather how the timetable should be constructed. Kohl's preferences, described at length in Chapter 5, were to link political union with monetary union as a package deal. He preferred to put off the beginning of the IGC on monetary union until as much progress had been made in planning the political IGC, and he wanted to defer the beginning of stage 2 to a later date than Mitterrand did.

What the possibility of German unity seems to have changed in Kohl's preferences was not EMU per se, but EMU being not contingent on political union. To the extent that Kohl's interest in political union was genuine, EMU had been the leverage to achieve greater EU political union. Thus, if anything was traded for German unity, it was Germany's requirement of significant EU political union. Indeed, the political union that emerged from the Maastricht Treaty (and even its successor, the Amsterdam Treaty) was anemic at best. With the timetable for EMU being hurried along by Mitterrand, the casualty was political union. Kohl, by putting EMU on the Hannover summit agenda, had always expected EMU at some point, but he had hoped to further his federalist ambitions with EMU as the sweetener to make political union palatable to recalcitrant states.

The second problem with the quid pro quo theory is that there were actually *three* significant actors who opposed German unification: Gorbachev, Thatcher, and Mitterrand. Of the four powers that still controlled

Germany's ultimate sovereignty, only the United States was an unambiguous supporter of Kohl's reunification ambitions. With two of Germany's large EU partners (and several smaller EU states) openly hostile to the idea of German unity, it is unclear why EMU would have been the grease to make German unification possible. Moreover, there are few payoffs that Margaret Thatcher would have wanted less. Thus, the logic of the quid pro quo argument is difficult to follow. It is not apparent why Kohl would have to bribe his friend Mitterrand with EMU to get France's agreement for unification but would not have to compensate Thatcher (and indeed, would choose deliberately to alienate her by agreeing to EMU plans).[13]

The final explanation of Kohl's motivation for EMU is a personal belief that Germany's long-term foreign policy interests (EU integration) were more important than Germany's short-term economic interests. Kohl's well-known bias in favor of EU federalism, his belief that good Franco-German relations were paramount in German foreign policy, and his personal friendship with Mitterrand made his willingness to consider EMU reasonably rare in German political circles. Of the other cabinet members, only Foreign Minister Genscher was more pro-European than Kohl. This explanation requires an assessment both of Kohl's "real" motives and of the policymaking environment that Kohl faced in the ten years from January 1988 to May 1998.

The pivotal role of Kohl is apparent in a number of significant decisions that made EMU possible.[14] When Genscher set the plan for monetary union into motion by reacting positively to French proposals, Kohl's assent was necessary to make that agenda item viable. Kohl often appeared to straddle the divide between the Finance Ministry/Bundesbank and Foreign Ministry positions, but when talks at the international level stalled, it was usually Kohl who found a compromise that allowed the negotiations to continue. With complex negotiations occurring from April 1989 to December 1991, there were many opportunities for the talks to break down in a serious way. The fact that they didn't demonstrates Kohl's real commitment to the project.

A key consideration in measuring Kohl's genuine preference for EMU was his decision to make EMU inevitable. With the benefit of hindsight, the Maastricht Treaty's language that allowed EMU in 1999 among only the member states that met the convergence criteria proved essential to launching the euro. Had that date not been in the Treaty, it is unlikely that EMU would have proceeded after 1997 because the member states' economic convergence was so limited.

How was the Treaty language that made EMU irreversible adopted? The issue remained unresolved until the EU leaders met in Maastricht. Here, the French and Italian leaders met privately with Kohl and proposed the new treaty language to him. As Wayne Sandholtz summarized:

Perhaps the most surprising aspect of the proposal [to make EMU in 1999 automatic] was that the Germans accepted it. Two German officials involved in the negotiations told me that Kohl's support for the final deadline was "very surprising to all of us." The same officials stressed that it was a personal decision by Kohl, and that nobody knew why he took it. They surmised that the chancellor wanted EMU to be irreversible, and the deadline would accomplish that. A British official shared that interpretation.[15]

Thus, in a late-night meeting, Kohl guaranteed that EMU would become a reality. Six years later, one can reasonably conclude that this Treaty provision was the impetus for the member states to change their economic behavior in a radical way. Had they not had a realistic fear of exclusion from the 1999 launching of the single currency, the economic convergence of 1996 and 1997 would surely not have taken place.

Finally, if one is to judge Kohl's genuine commitment to the project, one must also take note of his post-Maastricht behavior. In the face of undeniable German opposition to EMU, Kohl continued to support the timely launching of the single currency. Were there alternatives to this rhetoric? Chapter 7 detailed numerous occasions when the single currency could have been delayed. Moreover, there were interpretations (in the German finance ministry, no less) of the Maastricht Treaty's mandate that would have permitted a delay of any number of years. As we have seen, many different constituencies—both foreign and domestic—advocated that course, and yet Kohl consistently advocated a timely beginning. Thus, Kohl did not change or delay the treaty when another politician, using EMU as a political issue, might have. It is therefore unambiguous that Kohl had a real preference for EMU, based not on narrow German material interests but on Germany's foreign policy imperatives.

Critics of the theory that Kohl's personal motivations and preferences were the decisive factor in Germany's participation pointed to the undemocratic nature of such a premise:

Common interpretations of EMU include the assertion that, in some countries at least, the commitment to monetary union has been taken by independent executives in the face of broad popular skepticism. One problem with this approach is that it often seems to allow independent institutional actors to do just about anything. This is incompatible with the equilibrium selection story, in which political institutions restrict the range of feasible policies. If political institutions effectively shelter policy from social pressures, it is hard to know what sources of policy might be other than policymakers' particularistic biases.[16]

This criticism is typical of analysts who want to be able to generalize and abstract from political events. As worthy an enterprise as that may be, in this particular case, that approach fails. "Policymakers' particularistic biases" (one might even call them *preferences*) are the very nature of politics, and there is merit to exploring them in detail. The approach of historical institutionalism takes these preferences seriously and does not assume them away. The burden on the user of this approach, however, is to show when and how individual preferences matter. In this study on Germany, the preferences of Kohl are shown to matter because (1) the legal mandate of the Bundesbank precluded it from opposing the EMU plan outright, allowing it only to tinker with the structure; and (2) the historical legacy of Germany immobilized a political party opposition to EMU that might have derailed Kohl's ambitions. Both of these factors are unique to Germany and thus do not lend themselves to cross-country generalization. However, they offer the most accurate explanation of why Germany cooperated in EMU.

This book has highlighted the importance of the Bundesbank in European monetary cooperation decisions and shown that the Bundesbank was a legitimate actor that "restricted the range of feasible policies." The impact of the Bundesbank on Kohl's EMU policies was considerable. In fact, one cannot look at the ECB without seeing the indelible mark of the Bundesbank. Thus, Kohl's preferences were in fact modified significantly by other institutional actors, but on the crucial decision of "EMU: yes or no," the Bundesbank was legally precluded from having a voice. Given the hand the Bundesbank was originally dealt, however, the bank played its cards extremely well.

The Bundesbank has become an institutionalized opposition to force European-level initiatives proposed by the government. Because of the German historical legacy, political parties were unable to criticize European integration, especially after German unification, for fear that they would be labeled anti-Europe. The defense of German interests thus fell to the Bundesbank, which is normally outside the political process. Originally a small, domestic institution, the bank became an international actor and more of a defender of narrowly German economic interests than any political party. Its perceived technocratic and apolitical nature served to make this role possible and palatable. Without the fear that its positions be translated to a new German anti-Europeanism, the Bundesbank was able to speak more freely than the political establishment. Essentially, the political parties' hands were tied by a traditional pro-Europe stance, but the Bundesbank suffered no such restraint.

Internationally, its role became important as a result of the EMS and the bank's ability to veto German government decisions. The empirical chapters of this book have traced the evolution of the Bundesbank and demonstrated that the EMS actually benefited the Bundesbank institutionally. Whereas initially, the Bundesbank opposed the creation of the EMS, by 1990 the Bundesbank had a genuine *preference* for the EMS (especially in contrast to EMU). Before the EMS's existence, the Bundesbank was a small, German domestic institution, largely absent from the international press or foreign policy negotiations. This is not to imply that the stature or legitimacy of the Bundesbank was questionable before the EMS. It is, however, the case that the bank's stature and importance increased dramatically because of the EMS and that the opportunities for the Bundesbank to act autonomously of the government at an international level grew significantly over the EMS years. By 1989, the Bundesbank was an important international institution in its own right.

Functionally, how did the EMS change the Bundesbank's stature? The disinflationary character of the EMS had the effect of reinforcing the Bundesbank's policies. Its role as the anchor of the system caused the press and policymakers to focus much more attention on its behavior. Moreover, the increased tasks of monitoring the EMS and providing reports for the Commission and the Council strengthened the transgovernmental groups like the Monetary Committee and the Committee of Central Bank Governors. In these committees, the Bundesbank could make its imprint on policies with less resistance. The fact that central bankers have similar educational backgrounds and share conceptions of causal links (and are generally more conservative than the population at large) meant that the Bundesbank's voice was mainstream.[17] The EMS thus served to legitimize the Bundesbank's conservative policies and thereby raised the stature of the institution.[18]

This international recognition of the Bundesbank also filtered back into Germany. Although the Bundesbank had always enjoyed a good institutional reputation, the fact that all the other EU states were trying to emulate the policies of the Bundesbank raised the bank's standing among Germans even further. Thus the EMS came to be instrumental in reinforcing the stature of the Bundesbank as an actor on par with the chancellor in international monetary matters. This explains why the EMS, which it had opposed in the negotiations, was championed by the Bundesbank in the late 1980s and early 1990s.

A heuristic method of confirming this hypothesis is to search for the word "Bundesbank" in *The Economist* and the *Financial Times*. The results show a similar trend, but *The Economist* figures start at 1975 and give a better sense about how generally newsworthy the Bundesbank has become.

Table 8.1 shows that the number of articles mentioning the Bundesbank rose from 16 in 1975 to 33 in 1978 to a high of 121 in 1992, before dropping back to 32 in 1997. By contrast, the French central bank was mentioned in only one article in 1975, and one cannot discern a significant upward trend in the number of articles over the next twenty years.[19]

Table 8.1 Number of Articles in *The Economist* and *Financial Times* Mentioning "Bundesbank"

Year	The Economist		Financial Times
1975	16	(1)[a]	n/a
1976	15	(3)	n/a
1977	16	(0)	n/a
1978	33	(2)	n/a
1979	31	(3)	n/a
1980	39	(3)	n/a
1981	38	(5)	n/a
1982	25	(0)	560
1983	30	(0)	477
1984	22	(4)	603
1985	26	(1)	676
1986	36	(1)	355
1987	49	(1)	356
1988	39	(1)	375
1989	57	(1)	566
1990	83	(3)	609
1991	66	(3)	725
1992	121	(1)	1,000+[b]
1993	101	(9)	1,000+
1994	38	(1)	1,000+
1995	43	(1)	941
1996	50	(0)	825
1997	32	(2)	819

Notes: a. Numbers in parentheses represent the number of articles in which "Banque de France" or "French Central Bank" was mentioned.

b. This search was done on Nexis/Lexis. Nexis aborts the search when more than 1,000 articles are found, and so an exact number is unavailable.

For the Bundesbank, its new international importance had the paradoxical effect of making the Central Bank Council *less* amenable to incorporating the concerns of its partner states into German domestic monetary policy. Whereas the government preferred German cooperation in times of currency stresses like the 1992–1993 period, the Bundesbank asserted its role in the EMS as a stable anchor. This role would potentially have been undermined if the Bundesbank had allowed German inflation to rise because of international considerations, and thus the bank was willing to chance the breakup of the EMS regime.

Two factors should be considered in explaining the Bundesbank's intransigence during the 1992–1993 currency crises. First, the crises came on the heels of the bank's conflict with the federal government over German monetary unification. Still smarting from Kohl's treatment of the bank in that case, the Bundesbank resolved to thwart any impression it would do the gvernment's bidding. By driving the EMS to the brink of collapse, the bank made its point that neither the German government nor the other member states could dictate the Bundesbank's monetary policy.

Second, and more important, there was perhaps a hope within the Bundesbank that the crises or collapse of the EMS would force the governments to postpone or cancel their EMU plans. Although the EMS had been a useful tool to establishing the international role of the Bundesbank, the bank was willing to sacrifice the EMS if it would ensure the long-term survival of the independent central bank. Following this logic, the EMS had to break down radically, not just continue without Germany for a while. The bank refused to temporarily leave the regime in August 1993, which, although it might have stabilized the regime, would have mitigated the bank's importance in the EMS. Instead, the EMS bands were widened to such an extent that for many months most analysts questioned whether the EMS was still a real force in the monetary relations of European states. Ultimately, the governments of the member states decided to continue the progress toward monetary union, but the Bundesbank had sent a strong signal that its preferences were not to be discounted.

It is essential to make one final point about the Bundesbank's prominence. The status of the DM as an international reserve currency has occasionally been assumed to be the cause of the Bundesbank's importance. However, research shows the reverse is actually true: to a large extent, the EMS *caused* the DM to become a reserve currency.

> [Data] show that the expanding international role of the deutsche mark has stemmed in substantial measure from its importance as a key currency in Europe. . . . Furthermore, there has been a striking increase in the use of the deutsche mark for intervention within the EMS. . . . There has also been an increase in European use of the deutsche mark as a reserve asset.[20]

Thus the reserve currency status of the DM cannot account for the growing prominence of the Bundesbank. Only the EMS and the bank's role as anchor in it can explain the evolution of the Bundesbank.

To return to the question of why Kohl did not face as much institutional pressure on his pro-European and EMU position as theories of democracy would expect, one must remember the German exceptionalism in the issue area of Europe. Kohl's European vision was allowed to go unchallenged by other political actors or institutions for ten years. Chapter 7 showed that although some political entrepreneurs did attempt to use the issue, they failed to mobilize even their own party, not to mention the electorate. The "permissive consensus" that traditionally imbued Germany's European politics was not challenged in any serious way by the mainstream political parties.

In contrast to the quiescence of the mainstream political parties, however, the actions of the Bundesbank and the Constitutional Court took on a new political significance. Both of these institutions replaced a legitimate political opposition to EMU, and it is unclear that this is a positive political development in Germany. With mainstream parties unwilling to challenge Kohl's EMU plans, the Bundesbank and Court's role in making decisions and constraining the government was essential. Yet their involvement in an ultimately political enterprise thrust them into the political arena and ran the risk of undermining their institutional credibility as apolitical actors.

The recourse by Germans to nonpolitical actors like the Court to prevent a policy on which the political parties have agreed is not a new phenomenon.[21] However, the biggest cost to this type of policymaking is to the notion of democracy, which includes legitimate opposition. The fact that no voice was given to a legitimate position on the political spectrum by mainstream parties may have the consequence of delegitimizing these parties or the process. The EMU episode reinforced the notion of opposition being led not by *parties* of the opposition but by institutions like the Bundesbank, the Constitutional Court, and even academics. In the political parties' attempts to "do the right thing," they may unwittingly have hurt German democracy far more than they have helped a European Germany. And, if one were to poll Germany's neighbors, most would probably prefer a completely legitimate and functioning German *democracy* that embraces dissent than some dutiful chorus of pro-European beliefs by the elites.

In summary, in this book I have tried to explain Germany's role in monetary cooperation by highlighting the dynamics between the Bundesbank and the government. The Bundesbank's imprint on the new European institutions is unmistakable. The growing international role of the Bundesbank and its new domestic role as the voice of opposition to a politically driven monetary union made the Bundesbank an essential part of the EMU story.

In the final analysis, then, this book remains a work-in-progress, in a manner of speaking. Although EMU has been agreed upon, at the time of this writing, there is a great deal of uncertainty about what the true effects of the euro will be. We know the institutional outlines of the system, but we do not know whether they will function as planned. This book explains those institutional outlines and how they came to look so German. However, it is too early to tell if they will "act" German as well, since a whole new set of institutional dynamics will need to be established.

And what of the Bundesbank, which ultimately did not prevail against Kohl's plans? It is now just one of many central banks in the European System of Central Banks. Is there any reason to believe the Bundesbank itself will remain an important international actor? Or will it colonize the ECB in significant numbers and make that its new power locus?[22] With these and many other new questions to be explored, this would seem to be as good a point as any to finish analyzing the "old" European monetary cooperation. Now that the European Union has left charted territory, it should be a time to hope that the political will and optimism that launched EMU will continue to guide it through the challenges ahead.

NOTES

1. By and large, during the 1990–1991 EMU negotiations, interest groups like the chamber of commerce, the Employers Federation, and labor were preoccupied with the effects of assimilating the economies of the new East German *Länder* into the German economy. Their impact on EMU while it was being negotiated was negligible.

2. De Cecco and Giovannini (1989).

3. Harmon and Heisenberg (1993).

4. Eichengreen and Wyplosz (1993).

5. Ibid., p. 52, emphasis added.

6. Ibid., p. 57.

7. Ibid., p. 77.

8. Often, the dismantling of capital controls as mandated by the SEA is cited as another factor that caused the EMS to be unstable. There are two counters to this idea, however. First, real dismantling of the capital controls did not begin until German finance minister Stoltenberg made them a precondition to beginning EMU negotiations (and thus even capital control dismantling is related to EMU), and second, even without capital controls, the EMS—albeit with realignments—was economically viable, as Robert Mundell's "holy trinity" made clear. For more on the holy trinity, see Chapter 3.

9. Kaltenthaler (1998).

10. *Der Spiegel,* April 27, 1998, pp. 108–112. The article was based on a newly released set of chancellery documents.

11. Ibid., p. 108.

12. Ibid.

13. The large financial payoffs for Gorbachev were designed to allow a unified Germany to remain in NATO, and thus there was an additional element of favor that Kohl needed from Gorbachev. For more on the German unity question, see Pond (1993) and Zelikow and Rice (1997).

14. Genscher's role is also important because of his decision to put EMU on the agenda, and because of the pressure the Foreign Ministry put on the government to be more accommodating to the preferences of Germany's partners during the IGC. However, Genscher's influence was tempered by his retirement in 1992.

15. Sandholtz (1993b), p. 137.

16. Eichengreen and Frieden (1998), p. 4.

17. For more on the epistemic community of central bankers, see Kapstein, (1992), pp. 265–288.

18. It is generally true that all of the central banks became more important in the 1980s as the economic paradigm shifted. The Bundesbank is, however, an extreme case. For more on the importance of central banks, see Pauly (1997) and Solomon (1995).

19. The significant outlier is 1993, when there were nine articles dealing with the franc crisis.

20. Leahy (1994), p. 34.

21. Landfried (1994).

22. An interesting factoid is that a surprisingly *small* proportion of the Bundesbank staff has decided to move to the EMI. Contrary to what one might expect, given that the move requires nothing more than a slightly longer commute for most Bundesbankers, and given that most observers say the institutional culture of the Bundesbank can only be replicated by large-scale colonization of the ECB by

Bundesbankers, the Bundesbank's vice president seems doubtful that any department heads will want to move. One possible explanation for this is that the cushy job and working hours of the Bundesbank are not matched by the ECB. Another explanation is that, for the time being, more bank employees believe the Bundesbank will remain influential past January 1, 1999, than most observers believe. For more on the move to the EMI from the Bundesbank, see "Not Quite Dead," *Euromoney*, August 1997.

ACRONYMS

BDI	Confederation of German Industry (Bund Deutscher Industrie)
BfB	Bund freier Bürger
CAP	Common Agricultural Policy
CDU	Christian Democratic Union (Christlich Demokratische Union)
CSU	Christian Social Union (Christlich Soziale Union)
ECOFIN	Economic and Financial Affairs Council
DIHT	German Chamber of Commerce (Deutscher Industrie- und Handelstag)
DIW	German Institute for Economic Research (Deutsches Institut für Wirtschaftsforschung)
DM	deutsche mark
ECB	European Central Bank
ECU	European currency unit
EMA	European Monetary Agreement
EMCF	European Monetary Cooperation Fund
EMF	European Monetary Fund
EMI	European Monetary Institute
EMS	European Monetary System
EMU	European Monetary Union
EP	European Parliament, the Parliament
EPU	European Payments Union
ERM	exchange-rate mechanism
ESCB	European System of Central Banks
EU	European Union, the Union
EUA	European Unit of Account
FDP	Free Democratic Party (Freie Demokratische Partei)
GDP	gross domestic product

IGC	intergovernmental conference
IMF	International Monetary Fund
OECD	Organization for Economic Cooperation and Development
OEEC	Organization for European Economic Cooperation
PDS	Party of Democratic Socialism (Partei des Demokratischen Sozialismus)
PS	Partie Socialist
RPR	Rally for the Republic (Rassemblement pour la République)
SEA	Single European Act
SDRs	special drawing rights
SPD	Social Democratic Party (Sozialdemokratische Partei Deutschlands)
TEU	Treaty on European Union, the Treaty

BIBLIOGRAPHY

Ahern, Bertie (1993). "An Irish Perspective," in Paul Temperton, ed., *The European Currency Crisis*. Cambridge: Probus Publishing Company.

Alesina, Alberto, and Lawrence Summers (1993). "Central Bank Independence and Macroeconomic Performance: Some Comparative Evidence." *Journal of Money Credit and Banking* 25: 151–162.

Amouroux, Henri (1986). *Monsieur Barre*. Paris: Éditions Robert Laffont.

Anderson, Jeffrey, and John B. Goodman (1993). "Mars or Minerva? A United Germany in a Post–Cold War Europe," in Robert Keohane, Joseph Nye, and Stanley Hoffmann, eds., *After the Cold War: International Institutions and State Strategies in Europe, 1989–1991*. Cambridge: Harvard University Press.

Andrews, David M. (1993). "The Global Origins of the Maastricht Treaty on EMU: Closing the Window of Opportunity," in Alan W. Cafruny and Glenda G. Rosenthal, *The State of the European Community: The Maastricht Debates and Beyond*. Boulder, Colo.: Lynne Rienner.

Balkhausen, Dieter (1992). *Gutes Geld and Schlechte Politik*. Düsseldorf: ECON Verlag.

Balladur, Edouard (1989). *Passion et Longueur de Temps*. Paris: Fayard.

Bank for International Settlements (1982). *Fifty-Second Annual Report*. Basel: BIS.

Baring, Arnulf (1991). *Deutschland, Was Nun?* Frankfurt: Siedler Verlag.

Baring, Arnulf, ed. (1994). *Germany's New Position in Europe: Problems and Perspectives*. Oxford: Berg Publishers.

Baring, Arnulf, and Rupert Scholz, eds. (1994). *Eine Neue Deutsche Interessenlage? Koordinaten Deutscher Politik Jenseits von Nationalismus und Moralismus*. Köln: J.P. Bachem Verlag.

Barre, Raymond (1988). *Questions de Confiance*. Paris: Flammarion.

Barrell, Ray (1990). "Has the EMS Changed Wage and Price Behavior in Europe?" *National Institute Economic Review* 134: 64–72.

Barrell, Ray, ed. (1992). *Economic Convergence and Monetary Union in Europe*. London: SAGE Publications.

Baun, Michael J. (1996). *An Imperfect Union: The Maastricht Treaty and the New Politics of European Integration*. Boulder, Colo.: Westview Press.

Bleek, Wilhelm, and Hanns Maull, eds. (1989). *Ein Ganz Normaler Staat?* München: Piper Verlag.

Bofinger, Peter, Stephan Collignon, and Ernst-Moritz Lipp, eds. (1993). *Währungsunion oder Währungschaos? Was Kommt Nach der D-Mark*. Wiesbaden: Gabler Verlag.

197

Bordo, Michael D. (1993). "The Bretton Woods International Monetary System: A Historical Overview," in Michael D. Bordo and Barry Eichengreen, *A Retrospective on the Bretton Woods System*. Chicago: University of Chicago Press.

Bulmer, Simon J. (1986). *The Domestic Structure of European Policy-Making in Germany*. New York: Garland Publishing.

———— (1993). "Germany and European Integration: Toward Economic and Political Dominance?" in Carl F. Lankowski, *Germany and the European Community: Beyond Hegemony and Containment?* New York: St. Martin's Press.

———— (1994). "The Governance of the European Union: A New Institutionalist Approach." *Journal of Public Policy* 13, no. 4: 351–380.

Bulmer, Simon, and William Paterson (1987). *The Federal Republic of Germany and the European Community*. London: Allen and Unwin.

Bulmer, Simon, and William E. Paterson (1996). "Germany in the European Union: Gentle Giant or Emergent Leader?" *International Affairs* 72, no. 1: 9–32.

Bulmer, Simon, and Wolfgang Wesels (1987). *The European Council: Decision-Making in European Politics*. London: Macmillan.

Burda, Michael C. (1990). *The Consequences of German Economic and Monetary Union*, Working Paper 53. Fountainbleau: INSEAD.

Cameron, David R. (1992). "The 1992 Initiative: Causes and Consequences," in Alberta M. Sbragia, ed., *Euro-Politics, Institutions, and Policymaking in the "New" European Community*. Washington, D.C.: Brookings Institution, pp. 23–74.

———— (1993). "British Exit, German Voice, French Loyalty: Defection, Domination, and Cooperation in the 1992–93 ERM Crisis." Paper presented at the American Political Science Association Meeting, Washington, D.C., August.

———— (1995a). "Exchange Rate Politics in France, 1981–1983: The Regime-Defining Choices of the Mitterrand Presidency," in Anthony Daley, ed., *The Mitterrand Presidency*. New York: New York University Press.

———— (1995b). "From Barre to Balladur: Economic Policy in the Era of the EMS," in Gregory Flynn, ed., *Remaking the Hexagon: The New France in the New Europe*. Boulder, Colo.: Westview Press.

———— (1995c). "Transnational Relations and the Development of European Economic and Monetary Union," in T. Risse-Kappen, ed., *Bringing Transnational Relations Back In: Non-State Actors, Domestic Structures, and International Institutions*. Cambridge: Cambridge University Press.

Checkel, Jeffrey T. (1997). *Ideas and International Political Change: Soviet/Russian Behavior and the End of the Cold War*. New Haven: Yale University Press.

Coffey, Peter (1987). *The European Monetary System—Past, Present, and Future*. 2nd ed. Dordrecht: Kluwer Academic Publishers.

Collignon, Stefan, with Peter Bofinger, Christopher Johnson, and Bertrand de Maigret (1994). *Europe's Monetary Future* (a study prepared at the request of the European Parliament). London: Pinter Publishers.

Commission of the European Communities. *Eurostat*. Various years. Luxembourg: Office for Official Publications of the European Communities.

———— (1969). "Commission Memorandum to the Council on the Co-ordination of Economic Policies and Monetary Co-operation within the Community" ("First Barre Plan"). *Bulletin of the European Communities* (March). Luxembourg: Office for Official Publications of the European Communities.

———— (1970a). "Final Communique of the Conference." *Bulletin of the European Communities* (January). Luxembourg: Office for Official Publications of the European Communities.

———— (1970b). *Bulletin of the European Communities* (February). Luxembourg: Office for Official Publications of the European Communities.

———— (1970c). "Commission Memorandum to the Council on the Preparation of a Plan for the Phased Establishment of an Economic and Monetary Union" ("Second Barre Plan"). *Bulletin of the European Communities* (March). Luxembourg: Office for Official Publications of the European Communities.

———— (1970d). "Report to the Council and the Commission on the Realization by Stages of Economic and Monetary Union in the Community" ("Werner Report"). *Supplement to Bulletin 11–1970 of the European Communities* (November). Luxembourg: Office for Official Publications of the European Communities.

———— (1982). *European Economy.* Luxembourg: Office for Official Publications of the European Communities, no. 12.

———— (1988). *Bulletin of the European Communities,* 1–88. Luxembourg: Office for Official Publications of the European Communities.

———— (1995). *Green Paper on the Practical Arrangements for the Introduction of the Single Currency.* Luxembourg: Office for Official Publications of the European Communities, May 31.

———— (1998). *Convergence Report for EMU.* Luxembourg: Office for Official Publications of the European Communities, March 25.

Committee for the Study of Economic and Monetary Union (1989). *Report on Economic and Monetary Union in the European Community.* Luxembourg: Office for Official Publications of the European Communities.

Connolly, Bernard (1995). *The Rotten Heart of Europe: The Dirty War for Europe's Money.* London: Faber and Faber.

Conradt, David P. (1993). *The German Polity.* 5th ed. New York: Longman Publishing Group.

Council of the European Communities/Commission of the European Communities (1992). *Treaty on European Union.* Luxembourg: Office for Official Publications of the European Communities.

Crawford, Beverly (1996). "Explaining Defection from International Cooperation: Germany's Unilateral Recognition of Croatia." *World Politics* 48 (July): 482– 521.

Cukierman, Alex (1992). *Central Bank Strategy, Credibility, and Independence: Theory and Evidence.* Cambridge, Mass.: MIT Press.

De Cecco, Marcello, and Alberto Giovannini, eds. (1989). *A European Central Bank: Perspectives on Monetary Unification After 10 Years of the EMS.* Cambridge: Cambridge University Press.

De Grauwe, Paul (1992). *The Economics of Monetary Integration.* Oxford: Oxford University Press.

De Grauwe, Paul, and Lucas Papademos, eds. (1990). *The European Monetary System in the 1990's.* London: Longman Group UK.

Dell, Edmund (1994). "Britain and the Origins of the European Monetary System." *Contemporary European History* 3, no. 1: 1–60.

Destler, I. M., and C. Randall Henning (1989). *Dollar Politics: Exchange Rate Policymaking in the United States.* Washington, D.C.: Institute for International Economics.

Deutsche Bundesbank (various years). *Annual Report of the Bundesbank.* Frankfurt: Bundesbank.

———— (various years). *Monthly Report of the Bundesbank.* Frankfurt: Bundesbank.

———— (various years). *Statistische Beihefte zu den Mondtsberichten der Deutschen Bundesbank, Reihe 3, Zahlvngsbilanz.* [Balance of Payments Statistics]. Frankfurt: Bundesbank.

————— (1990b). "Statement on the Establishment of an Economic and Monetary Union in Europe." *Monthly Report of the Deutsche Bundesbank* 42, no. 10 (Frankfurt).

————— (1992). *Entschliessung des Deutschen Bundestages zum Vertrag vom 7. Februar 1992 über die Europäische Union.* Bonn: December 2.

————— (1998). *Stellungnahme des Zentralbankrates zur Konvergenzlage in der Europäischen Union im Hinblick auf die Dritte Stufe der Wirtschafts- und Währungsunion.* March 26. Frankfurt: Bundesbank.

Deutscher Bundestag (1990). *Jahreswirtschafsbericht 1990 der Bundesregierung.* Bonn.: Drucksache 11/6278.

Deutscher Bundestag (1992). *Entschliessung des Deutschen Bundestages zum Vertag vom 7. Februar 1992 über die Europäische Union.* Bonn: December 2.

Directorate-General for Economic and Financial Affairs (1989). *The EMS: Ten Years of Progress in European Monetary Cooperation.* Luxembourg: Office for Official Publications of the European Communities.

Duwendag, Dieter, ed. (1973). *Macht und Ohnmacht der Bundesbank.* Tronberg: Athenäum Verlag.

Dyson, Kenneth (1994). *Elusive Union: The Process of Economic and Monetary Union in Europe.* London: Longman.

Ehrenberg, Herbert (1991). *Abstieg vom Währungsolymp: Zur Zukunft der Deutschen Bundesbank.* Frankfurt: Fischer Taschenbuch Verlag.

Eichenberg, Richard C., and Russell Dalton (1993). "Europeans and the European Community: The Dynamics of Public Support for European Integration." *International Organization* 47, no. 4 (autumn): 507–534.

Eichengreen, Barry (1989). "Hegemonic Stability Theories of the International Monetary System," in Richard Cooper, Barry Eichengreen, C. Randall Henning, Gerald Holtham, and Robert Putnam, *Can Nations Agree?* Washington, D.C.: Brookings Institution.

Eichengreen, Barry, and Jeffry Frieden, eds. (1994). *The Political Economy of European Monetary Unification.* Boulder, Colo.: Westview Press.

————— (1998). "Introduction," in Barry Eichengreen and Jeffry Frieden, eds., *Forging an Integrated Europe.* Ann Arbor: University of Michigan Press.

Eichengreen, Barry, and Charles Wyplosz (1993). "The Unstable EMS." *Brookings Papers on Economic Activity* 1. Washington, D.C.: Brookings Institution.

Emerson, Michael, Daniel Gross, Alexander Italianer, Jean Pisaniz Frey, and Horst Reichenbach (1992). *One Market, One Money.* Oxford: Oxford University Press.

Emminger, Otmar (1986). *D-Mark, Dollar, Währungskrisen.* Stuttgart: Deutsche Verlags-Anstalt.

Evans, Peter, Harold K. Jacobsen, and Robert D. Putnam, eds. (1993). *Double-Edged Diplomacy: International Bargaining and Domestic Politics.* Berkeley: University of California Press.

Favier, Pierre, and Michel Martin-Roland (1990). *La Décennie Mitterrand.* Paris: Editions du Seuil.

Fearon, James D. (1991). "Counterfactuals and Hypothesis Testing in Political Science." *World Politics* 43 (January): 169–196.

Feldman, Lily Gardner (1991). "The EC and German Unification," in Leon Hurwitz and Christian Lequesne, eds., *The State of the European Community: Policies, Institutions, and Debates in the Transition Years.* Boulder: Lynne Rienner.

Fonteneau, Alain, and Pierre Alain Muet (1985). *La Gauche Face à la Crise.* Paris: Fondation Nationale des Sciences Politiques.

Franz, Otmar, ed. (1990). *Die Europäische Zentralbank.* Frankfurt: Europa Union.

Fratianni, Michele, and Jurgen von Hagen (1992). *The European Monetary System and European Monetary Union.* Boulder, Colo.: Westview Press.

Frieden, Jeffry (1994). "Making Commitments: France and Italy in the European Monetary Sysetm, 1979–1985," in Barry Eichengreen and Jeffrey Frieden, eds., *The Political Economy of European Monetary Unification.* Boulder: Westview Press.

——— (forthcoming). "Economic Liberalization and the Politics of European Monetary Integration," in Miles Kahler, ed., *Liberalization and Foreign Policy.* New York: Columbia University Press.

Garrett, Geoffrey (1995). "Capital Mobility, Trade and the Domestic Politics of Economic Power." *International Organization* 49, no. 4 (autumn): 657–688.

Garrett, Geoffrey, and Peter Lange (1995). "Internationalization, Institutions and Political Change." *International Organization* 49, no. 4 (autumn): 627–656.

Genscher, Hans-Dietrich (1995). *Erinnerungen.* Berlin: Siedler Verlag.

Giavazzi, Francesco, and Marco Pagano (1988). "The Advantage of Tying One's Hands: EMS Discipline and Central Bank Credibility." *European Economic Review* 32: 1055–1082.

Giscard d'Estaing, Valéry (1988). *Le Pouvoir et La Vie.* Paris: Compagnie Douze.

Goldstein, Judith, and Robert Keohane, eds. (1993). *Ideas and Foreign Policy: Beliefs, Institutions, and Political Change.* Ithaca: Cornell University Press.

Goodman, John B. (1992). *Monetary Sovereignty: The Politics of Central Banking in Western Europe.* Ithaca: Cornell University Press.

Gros, Daniel, and Niels Thygesen (1992). *European Monetary Integration.* New York: St. Martin's Press.

Guerrieri, Paolo, and Pier Carlo Padoan (1989). *The Political Economy of European Integration: States, Markets and Institutions.* Hertfordshire, U.K.: Harvester Wheatsheaf.

Haas, Ernst (1958). *The Uniting of Europe: Political, Social, and Economic Forces, 1950–1957.* Stanford: Stanford University Press.

——— (1964). *Beyond the Nation State: Functionalism and International Organization.* Stanford: Stanford University Press.

Haggard, Stephen, Marc A. Levy, Andrew Moravcsik, and Kalypso Nicolaïdis (1993). "Integrating the Two Halves of Europe: Theories of Interests, Bargaining and Institutions," in Robert Keohane, Joseph Nye, and Stanley Hoffmann, eds., *After the Cold War: International Institutions and State Strategies in Europe, 1989–1991.* Cambridge: Harvard University Press.

Hall, Peter A. (1986). *Governing the Economy: The Politics of State Intervention in Britain and France.* Oxford: Oxford University Press.

——— (1987). "The Evolution of Economic Policy Under Mitterrand," in George Ross, Stanley Hoffmann, and Sylvia Malzacher, eds., *The Mitterrand Experiment.* New York: Oxford University Press.

———, ed. (1989). *The Political Power of Economic Ideas: Keynesianism Across Nations.* Princeton: Princeton University Press.

——— (1992). "The Movement from Keynesianism to Monetarism: Institutional Analysis and British Economic Policy in the 1970s," in Sven Steinmo, Kathleen Thelen, and Frank Longstreth, eds., *Structuring Politics.* Cambridge: Cambridge University Press.

——— (1994). "Central Bank Independence and Coordinated Wage Bargaining: Their Interaction in Germany and Europe." *German Politics and Society* 31: 1–23.

Hamalainen, Pekka Kelevi (1994). *Uniting Germany: Actions and Reactions.* Boulder, Colo.: Westview Press.

Handschuch, Konrad (1994). *D-Mark Ade: Das Maastrichter Experiment.* Frankfurt: Fischer Taschenbuch Verlag.

Harmon, Mark (1995/1996). "British Unilateralism in a Multilateral Europe: Sterling In and Out of Exchange Rate Mechanism." *New Political Science* 33/34 (fall/winter): 51–104.

Harmon, Mark, and Dorothee Heisenberg (1993). "Explaining the European Currency Crisis of September 1992." *German Politics and Society* 5: 19–51.

Hefeker, Carsten (1997). *Interest Groups and Monetary Integration: The Political Economy of Exchange Regime Choice.* Boulder, Colo.: Westview Press.

Heisenberg, Dorothee (1998). "A Survey of Bundestag Members' Opinions About EMU." Centre for European Policy Studies Working Paper.

Henning, C. Randall (1994). *Currencies and Politics in the United States, Germany, and Japan.* Washington, D.C.: Institute for International Economics.

Holtham, Gerald (1989). "German Macroeconomic Policy and the 1978 Bonn Economic Summit," in Richard Cooper, Barry Eichengreen, C. Randall Henning, Gerald Holtham, and Robert Putnam, *Can Nations Agree?* Washington, D.C.: Brookings Institution.

Hrbek, Rudolf, ed. (1992). *Der Vertrag von Maastricht in der Wissenschaftlichen Kontroverse.* Baden-Baden: Nomos Verlagsgesellschaft.

Huelshoff, Michael (1993). "German and European Integration: Understanding the Relationship," in Michael G. Huelshoff, Andrei Markovits, and Simon Reich, *From Bundesrepublik to Deutschland: German Politics After Unification.* Ann Arbor: University of Michigan Press.

Iida, K. (1993). "When and How do Domestic Constraints Matter? Two-Level Games with Uncertainty." *Journal of Conflict Resolution* 37, no. 3 (September): 403–424.

International Monetary Fund. (various years). *Direction of Trade Statistics Yearbook.* Washington, D.C.: International Monetary Fund.

——— (various years). *International Financial Statistics Yearbook.* Washington, D.C.: International Monetary Fund.

James, Harold, and Marla Stone, eds. (1992). *When the Wall Came Down: Reactions to German Unification.* New York: Routledge.

Jenkins, Roy (1978). "European Monetary Union." *Lloyds Bank Review* 127 (January): 1–14.

Jochimsen, Reimut (1994). *Perspektiven der Europäischen Wirtschafts- und Währungsunion.* Köln: Bund-Verlag.

Johnson, Christopher, and Stefan Collignon, eds. (1994). *The Monetary Economics of Europe: Causes of the EMS Crisis* (a study prepared at the request of the European Parliament). London: Pinter Publishers.

Kaelberer, Matthias (1995). *Money and Power in Europe: The Political Economy of European Monetary Cooperation.* Ph.D. diss., Princeton University.

Kaiser, Karl, and Hanns W. Maull, eds. (1993). *Die Zukunft der Deutschen Aussenpolitik: Eine Diskussion.* Bonn: Europa Union Verlag.

——— (1994). *Deutschlands Neue Aussenpolitik: Band 1 Grundlagen.* München: R. Oldenbourg Verlag.

Kaltenthaler, Karl (1998). *Germany and EMU.* Chapel Hill: Duke University Press.

Kaplan Jacob J., and Gunther Schleiminger (1989). *The European Payments Union: Financial Diplomacy in the 1950s.* Oxford: Clarendon Press.

Kapstein, Ethan (1992). "Between Power and Purpose: Central Bankers and the Politics of Regulatory Convergence." *International Organization* 46, no. 1 (winter), pp. 265–288.

Katzenstein, Peter J. (1987). *Policy and Politics in West Germany: The Growth of a Semisovereign State.* Philadelphia: Temple University Press.

Kaufmann, Hugo M. (1985). *Germany's International Monetary Policy and the European Monetary System.* New York: Columbia University Press.

Kenen, Peter B. (1992). *EMU After Maastricht.* Washington, D.C.: Group of Thirty.

——— (1995). *Economic and Monetary Union in Europe: Moving Beyond Maastricht.* Cambridge: Cambridge University Press.

Kennedy, Ellen (1991). *The Bundesbank: Germany's Central Bank in the International Monetary System.* London: Pinter Publishers.

Keohane, Robert (1980). "The Theory of Hegemonic Stability and Changes in International Regimes, 1967–1977," in Ole Holsti, Randolph Siverson, and Alexander George, eds., *Change in the International System.* Boulder, Colo.: Westview Press.

——— (1984). *After Hegemony.* Princeton: Princeton University Press.

——— (1988) "International Institutions: Two Approaches." *International Studies Quarterly* 32: 379–396.

Keohane, Robert, and Joseph Nye (1977). *Power and Interdependence: World Politics in Transition.* Boston: Little, Brown.

Keohane, Robert, and Stanley Hoffman (1990). "Institutional Change in Europe in the 1980s," in William Wallace, ed., *The Dynamics of European Integration* London: Pinter Publishers.

——— eds. (1991). *The New European Community: Decisionmaking and Institutional Change.* Boulder, Colo.: Westview Press.

Kindleberger, C. P. (1986). *The World in Depression, 1929–1939.* Rev. ed. Berkeley: University of California Press.

King, Gary, Robert Keohane, and Sidney Verba (1994). *Designing Social Inquiry.* Princeton: Princeton University Press.

Kirshner, Jonathan (1995). *Currency and Coercion: The Political Economy of International Monetary Power.* Princeton: Princeton University Press.

Klotz, Audie (1995). "Norms Reconstituting Interests: Global Racial Equality and U.S. Sanctions Against South Africa." *International Organization* 49, no. 3: 451–478.

Kohl, Helmut (1990). *Deutschlands Zukunft in Europa: Reden und Beiträge des Bundeskanzlers.* Heinrich Seewald, ed. Herford: Busse Seewald.

Krägenau, Henry, and Wolfgang Wetter (1993). *Europäische Wirtschafts- und Währungsunion: Vom Werner-Plan zum Vertrag von Maastricht.* Baden-Baden: Nomos Verlagsgesellschaft.

Krasner, Stephen D. (1983). *International Regimes.* Ithaca: Cornell University Press.

——— (1991). "Global Communications and National Power: Life on the Pareto Frontier." *World Politics* 43: 336–367.

Kruse, D. C. (1980). *Monetary Integration in Western Europe.* London: Butterworth and Company.

Kühnhardt, Ludger, and Hans-Peter Schwartz, eds. *Zwölf Nachbarn—ein Europa: Deutschland und die Europäische Zukunft aus Sicht der Diplomaten Umliegender Länder.* Bonn: Bouvier Verlag, 1991.

Kurzer, Paulette (1993). *Business and Banking.* Ithaca: Cornell University Press.

Kurzer, Paulette, and Christopher S. Allen (1993). "United Europe and Social Democracy: The EC, West Germany, and Its Three Small Neighbors," in Carl F. Lankowski, *Germany and the European Community: Beyond Hegemony and Containment?* New York: St. Martin's Press.

Lamfalussy, Alexandre (1994). "Central Banking in Transition." 1994 Per Jacobsson Lecture. Washington, D.C.: International Monetary Fund.

Landfried, Christine (1994). "The Judicialization of Politics in Germany." *International Political Science Review* 15: 113–124.

Lankowski, Carl F. (1993). *Germany and the European Community: Beyond Hegemony and Containment?* New York: St. Martin's Press.

Lawson, Nigel (1993). *The View from No. 11.* New York: Doubleday.

Leahy, Michael (1994). "The Dollar as an Official Reserve Currency Under EMU." Board of Governors of the Federal Reserve System, International Finance Discussion Papers no. 474.

Leibfried, Stephan, and Paul Pierson, eds. (1995). *European Social Policy: Between Fragmentation and Integration.* Washington, D.C.: Brookings Institution.

Lindberg, Leon, and Stuart Scheingold (1970). *Europe's Would-Be Polity: Patterns of Change in the European Community.* Englewood Cliffs, N.J.: Prentice-Hall.

Lindblom, Charles (1977). *Politics and Markets.* New York: Basic Books.

Lohmann, Susanne (1993). "Designing a Central Bank in a Federal System: The Deutsche Bundesbank, 1957–92." Graduate School of Business Research Paper no. 1249, Stanford University, March.

Loriaux, Michael (1991). *France After Hegemony.* Ithaca: Cornell University Press.

Ludlow, Peter (1982). *The Making of the European Monetary System.* London: Butterworth and Company.

March, James G., and Johan P. Olsen (1984). "The New Institutionalism: Organizational Factors in Political Life." *American Political Science Review* 78.

——— (1989). *Rediscovering Institutions: The Organizational Basis of Politics.* New York: Free Press.

Markovits, Andrei S., and Simon Reich (1993). "Should Europe Fear the Germans?" in Michael G. Huelshoff, Andrei S. Markovits, and Simon Reich, eds., *From Bundesrepublik to Deutschland: German Politics After Unification.* Ann Arbor: University of Michigan Press.

——— (1997). *The Predicament of German Power.* Ithaca: Cornell University Press.

Marsh, David (1992). *The Bundesbank: The Bank That Rules Europe.* London: William Heinemann.

Maxfield, Sylvia (1994). "Financial Incentives and Central Bank Authority in Industrializing Nations." *World Politics* 46 (July).

McCarthy, Patrick, ed. (1993). *France-Germany, 1983–1993: The Struggle to Cooperate.* New York: St. Martin's Press.

McNamara, Kathleen (1993). "Common Markets, Uncommon Currencies: Systems Effects and the European Community," in Jack Snyder and Robert Jervis, eds. *Coping with Complexity in the International System.* Boulder, Colo.: Westview Press.

——— (1998). *The Currency of Ideas.* Ithaca: Cornell University Press.

Merkl, Peter (1993). *German Unification in the European Context.* University Park: Pennsylvania State University Press.

Milward, Alan S. (1984). *The Reconstruction of Western Europe, 1945–51.* Berkeley: University of California Press.

——— (1992). *The European Rescue of the Nation State.* London: Routledge.

Monetary Committee of the European Communities (1988). *Twenty-Ninth Activity Report.* Luxembourg: Office for Official Publications of the European Communities.

Moravcsik, Andrew (1991). "Negotiating the Single European Act: National Interests and Conventional Statecraft in the European Community." *International Organization* 45, no. 1: 651–688.

——— (1993a). "Introduction: Integrating International and Domestic Theories of International Bargaining," in Peter Evans, Harold K. Jacobsen, and Robert D. Putnam, eds., *Double-Edged Diplomacy: International Bargaining and Domestic Politics.* Berkeley: University of California Press, pp. 3–42.

———— (1993b). "Preferences and Power in the European Community: A Liberal Intergovernmentalist Approach." *Journal of Common Market Studies* 31, no. 4 (December): 473–521.

———— (1998). *The Choice for Europe.* Ithaca: Cornell University Press.

Moutot, P. P. (1994). "What Might Explain the September 1992 Speculative Attacks on the French Franc?" in H. M. Scobie, ed., *The European Single Market Monetary and Fiscal Policy Harmonization.* London: Chapman and Hall.

Mundell, Robert (1960). "The Monetary Dynamics of International Adjustment Under Fixed and Flexible Exchange Rates." *Quarterly Journal of Economics* 74: 227–257.

Newhouse, John (1997). *Europe Adrift.* New York: Random House.

Nölling, Wilhelm (1993). *Unser Geld.* Berlin: Verlag Ullstein.

North, Douglass C. (1990). *Institutions, Institutional Change and Economic Performance.* Cambridge: Cambridge University Press.

"Oral Statement of the Chairman of the Monetary Committee on the Development of the EMS to the Informal Meeting of Economic and Finance Ministers," May 17, 1982 (1982). *European Economy* 12 (July).

Oye, Kenneth (1986). "Sterling-Dollar-Franc Triangle: Monetary Diplomacy 1929–1937," in Kenneth Oye, ed., *Cooperation Under Anarchy.* Princeton: Princeton University Press.

Pauly, Louis (1997). *Who Elected the Bankers? Surveillance and Control in the World Economy.* Ithaca: Cornell University Press.

Pierson, Paul (1996). "The Path to European Integration: A Historical Institutionalist Analysis." *Comparative Political Studies* 29: 123–163.

———— (1997). "Path Dependence, Increasing Returns, and the Study of Politics." Center for European Studies, Harvard University, October 3.

Pohl, Gerhard (1991). *Economic Consequences of German Reunification: 12 Months After the Big Bang.* Washington D.C.: World Bank Working Paper no. 816.

Pöhl, Karl Otto (1992). "A New Monetary Order for Europe." 1992 Per Jacobsson Lecture. Washington, D.C.: International Monetary Fund.

Pond, Elizabeth (1993). *Beyond the Wall: Germany's Road to Unification.* Washington, D.C.: Brookings Institution.

Putnam, Robert D. (1988). "Diplomacy and Domestic Politics: The Logic of Two-Level Games." *International Organization* 42, no. 3: 427–460.

Putnam, Robert D., and Nicholas Bayne (1984). *Hanging Together: Cooperation and Conflict in the Seven Power Summits.* Cambridge: Harvard University Press.

Reinhardt, Nickolas (1997). "A Turning Point in the German EMU Debate: The Baden-Württemberg Regional Election of March 1996," *German Politics* 6, no. 1: 77–99.

Risse-Kappen, Thomas (1994). "Ideas Do Not Float Freely: Transnational Coalitions, Domestic Structures and the End of the Cold War." *International Organization* 48 no. 2: 185–215.

———— (1996). "Exploring the Nature of the Beast: International Relations Theory and Comparative Policy Analysis Meet the European Union." *Journal of Common Market Studies* 34, no. 1: 53–80.

Rittberger, Volker (1993a). "Nach der Vereinigung—Deutschlands Stellung in der Welt," in Hans-Hermann Hartwich and Göttrik Wewer, eds., *Regieren in der Bundesrepublik 5: Souveränität, Integration, Interdependenz—Staatliches Handeln in der Aussen- und Europapolitik.* Opladen: Leske and Budrich.

Rittberger, Volker, ed. (1993b). *Regime Theory and International Relations.* Oxford: Clarendon Press.

206

Bibliography

Robert, Rüdiger (1978). *Die Unabhängigkeit der Bundesbank.* Tronberg: Athenäum Verlag.

Rogowski, Ronald (1989). *Commerce and Coalitions.* Princeton: Princeton University Press.

Ross, George (1995). *Jacques Delors and European Integration.* New York: Oxford University Press.

Rossi, S. (1981). "Alternative Methods of Adjusting the EMS Divergence Indicator for the Effects of the Lira and Pound Special Regime," in Banca d'Italia Research Department, *Discussion Papers on International Economics and Finance.* Seminar on the Indicator of Divergence in the EMS, July 3.

Russell, Robert W. (1973). "Transgovernmental Interaction in the International Monetary System, 1960–1972." *International Organization* 27, no. 4 (autumn): 431–464.

Sachs, Jeffrey, and Charles Wyplosz (1986). "The Economic Consequences of President Mitterrand." *Economic Policy* 2 (April): 262–322.

Sandholtz, Wayne (1993a). "Choosing Union: Monetary Politics and Maastricht." *World Politics* 47, no. 1: 95–128.

——— (1993b). "Monetary Bargains: The Treaty on EMU," in Alan W. Cafruny and Glenda G. Rosenthal, *The State of the European Community: The Maastricht Debates and Beyond.* Boulder, Colo.: Lynne Rienner.

Sandholtz, Wayne, and John Zysman (1989). "1992: Recasting the European Bargain." *World Politics* 41, no. 1: 95–128.

Sbragia, Alberta M., ed. (1992). *Euro-politics: Institutions and Policymaking in the "New" European Community.* Washington, D.C.: Brookings Institution.

Schäuble, Wolfgang (1994). *Und der Zukunft Zugewand.* Berlin: Siedler.

Schaling, Eric (1995). *Institutions and Monetary Policy: Credibility, Flexibility, and Central Bank Independence.* Brookfield, Vt.: Edward Elgar.

Scharrer, Hans-Eckart, and Wolfgang Wessels, eds. (1987). *Stabilität Durch das EWS?* Bonn: Europa Union Verlag.

Schmidt, Helmut (1990). *Die Deutschen und Ihre Nachbarn.* Frankfurt: Goldmann.

Schneider, Gerald, and Lars-Erik Cederman (1994). "The Change of Tide in Political Cooperation: A Limited Information Model of European Integration." *International Organization* 48, no. 4 (autumn): 633–662.

Schönfelder, Wilhelm, and Elke Thiel (1994). *Ein Markt—Eine Währung: Die Verhandlungen zur Europäischen Wirtschafts- und Währungsunion.* Baden-Baden: Nomos Verlagsgesellschaft.

Schwarz, Hans-Peter (1994). *Die Zentralmacht Europas: Deutschlands Rückkehr auf die Weltbühne.* Frankfurt: Siedler Verlag.

——— (1995). "United Germany and European Integration." *SAIS Review* 15 (fall): 83–101.

Shepsle, Kenneth, and Barry Weingast (1987). "The Institutional Foundations of Committee Power." *American Political Science Review* 81, no. 1 (March): 85–104.

Sherman, Heidemarie C., and Fred R. Kaen (1994). "The Behavior and Thinking of the Bundesbank," in David Cobham, ed., *European Monetary Upheavals.* Manchester: Manchester University Press.

Sikkink, Kathryn (1991). *Ideas and Institutions: Developmentalism in Brazil and Argentina.* Ithaca: Cornell University Press.

Simmons, Beth A. (1993). "Why Innovate? Founding the Bank for International Settlements." *World Politics* 45 no. 3: 361–405.

——— (1994). *Who Adjusts? Domestic Sources of Foreign Economic Policy During the Interwar Years.* Princeton: Princeton University Press.

Simonian, Haig (1985). *The Privileged Partnership: Franco-German Relations in the European Community 1969–1984*. Oxford: Clarendon Press.

Slater, Martin (1982). "Political Elites, Popular Indifference and Community Building." *Journal of Common Market Studies* 21 nos. 1–2: 69–87.

Smeetz, H. (1990). "Does Germany Dominate the EMS?" *Journal of Common Market Studies* 29 (September): 37–52.

Snidal, Duncan (1985). "The Limits of Hegemonic Stability Theory." *International Organization* 39, no. 4 (autumn): 579–614.

Solomon, Steven (1995). *The Confidence Game*. New York: Simon and Schuster.

Spaventa, Luigi (1980). "Italy Joins the EMS—A Political History." Johns Hopkins University Bologna Center, Occasional Paper, no. 32 (June).

Sperling, James (1994). "German Foreign Policy After Unification: The End of Cheque Book Diplomacy." *West European Politics* 17, no. 1 (January): 73–97.

Statler, Jocelyn (1981). "EMS: Cul-de-Sac or Signpost on the Road to EMU?" in Michael Hodges and William Wallace, eds., *Economic Divergence in the European Community*. London: George Allen and Unwin.

Steinmo, Sven, Kathleen Thelen, and Frank Longstreth, eds. (1992). *Structuring Politics*. Cambridge: Cambridge University Press.

Stephens, Philip (1996). *Politics and the Pound: The Conservatives' Struggle with Sterling*. London: Macmillan.

Story, Jonathan (1981). "Convergence at the Core? The Franco-German Relationship and Its Implications for the Community," in Michael Hodges and William Wallace, eds., *Economic Divergence in the European Community*. London: George Allen and Unwin.

Story, Jonathan, ed. (1993). *The New Europe: Politics, Government and Economy Since 1945*. Oxford: Blackwell Publishers.

Strange, Susan (1980). "Germany and the World Monetary System," in Wilfrid Kohl and Giorgio Basevi, eds., *West Germany: A European and Global Power*. Lexington: DC Heath.

Sturm, Roland (1989). "The Role of the Bundesbank in German Politics." *West European Politics* 12 no. 2.

Sumner, M. T., and George Zis, eds. (1982). *European Monetary Union: Progress and Prospects*. London: Macmillan.

Survey Consultants International (1985). Index to International Public Opinion, 1985–1986. Westport, Conn.: Greenwood.

Taylor, Christopher (1995). *EMU 2000? Prospects for European Monetary Union*. London: Pinter.

Temperton, Paul, ed. (1993). *The European Currency Crisis: What Chance Now for a Single European Currency?* Cambridge: Probus Europe.

Tetlock, Philip, and Aaron Belkin, eds. (1996). *Counterfactual Thought Experiments in World Politics: Logical, Methodological, and Psychological Perspectives*. Princeton: Princeton University Press.

Thatcher, Margaret (1993). *The Downing Street Years*. New York: HarperCollins.

Thygesen, Niels (1995). "The Prospects for EMU by 1999—and Reflections on Arrangments for Outsiders." European Union Policy Papers I. Edinburgh: Royal Bank of Scotland (November 2).

Tietmeyer, Hans, and Wilfried Guth (1990). *Two Views of German Unification*. Washington D.C.: Group of Thirty.

Trezise, Philip H., ed. (1979). *The European Monetary System: Its Promise and Prospects*. Washington, D.C.: Brookings Institution.

Tsoukalis, Loukas (1977). *The Politics and Economics of European Monetary Integration*. London: George Allen and Unwin.

——— (1989). "The Political Economy of the European Monetary System," in Paolo Guerrieri and Pier Carlo Padoan, *The Political Economy of European Integration: States, Markets and Institutions*. Hertfordshire: Harvester Wheatsheaf.

Ungerer, Horst, Owen Evans, Thomas Mayer, and Philip Young (1986). *The European Monetary System: Recent Developments*. Washington, D.C.: International Monetary Fund.

Ungerer, Horst, Jouko J. Hauvonen, Augusto Lopez-Claros, and Thomas Mayer (1990). *The European Monetary System: Developments and Perspectives*. Washington, D.C.: International Monetary Fund.

Urwin, Derek (1995). *The Community of Europe: A History of European Integration Since 1945*. 2nd ed. London: Longman Group.

Usher, J. A. (1994). *Law of Monetary and Financial Services in the European Community*. Oxford: Clarendon Press.

Van Ypersele, Jacques, and Jean-Claude Koeune (1985). *The European Monetary System: Origins, Operations and Outlook*. Luxembourg: Office for Official Publications of the European Communities.

Van den Bempt, Paul, ed. (1987). *The European Monetary System: Towards More Convergence and Closer Integration*. Leuven, Belgium: Acco.

Vesperini, Jean-Pierre (1989). *Le Franc Dans le Système Monétaire International*. Paris: Economica.

Wallace, William, ed. (1990). *The Dynamics of European Integration*. London: Pinter Publishers.

Walsh, James I. "Rules Rule: Stabilization Policy in France and Britain, 1979–1988." Unpublished manuscript.

——— (1994). "International Constraints and Domestic Choices: Economic Convergence and Exchange Rate Policy in France and Italy." *Political Studies* 42, no. 2 (June).

——— (1997). *Global Finance, Domestic Politics: International Monetary Politics in Britain, France and Italy*. Ph.D. diss., American University.

Weber, Axel (1991). "Reputation and Credibility in the European Monetary System." *Economic Policy* 12 (April): 588–602.

Weiler, J. H. H. (1995). "The State ' Über alles': Demos, Telos and the German Maastricht Decision." European University Institute Working Paper 95/19. Florence: European University Institute.

Welfens, Paul J. J., ed. (1996). *European Monetary Integration: EMS Developments and International Post-Maastricht Perspectives*. 3rd ed. Berlin: Springer Verlag.

Wendt, Alexander (1987). "The Agent-Structure Problem in International Relations Theory." *International Organization* 41, no. 3 (summer).

——— (1992). "Anarchy Is What States Make of It: The Social Construction of Power Politics." *International Organization* 46, no. 2 (spring).

Wessels, Berhard (1996). "Evaluations of the EC: Elite or Mass-Driven?" in Oskar Niedermayer and Richard Sinnott, eds., *Public Opinion and Internationalized Governance*. Oxford: Oxford University Press.

Woolley, John T. (1984). *Monetary Politics: The Federal Reserve and the Politics of Monetary Policy*. New York: Cambridge University Press.

——— (1992). "Policy Credibility and Political Institutions," in Alberta Sbragia, ed., *Euro-politics: Institutions and Policymaking in the "New" European Community*. Washington, D.C.: Brookings Institution.

——— (1994). "The Politics of Monetary Policy: A Critical Review." *Journal of Public Policy* 14, no. 1: 57–85.

Zelikow, Philip, and Condoleezza Rice (1997). *Germany Unified and Europe Transformed: A Study in Statecraft*. Cambridge: Harvard University Press.

INDEX

ABOUT THE BOOK

With the Bundesbank now a dominant German actor in international monetary cooperation, Germany's partner states have begun to consider the requirements of the bank—rather than the government—as paramount. Dorothee Heisenberg maintains that the evolution of the Bundesbank is key to understanding how and why Europeans chose to achieve monetary union.

Heisenberg demonstrates that the domestic relationship between the Bundesbank and the German government is a significant determinant of cooperation at the European level. Drawing on historical evidence from 1968 to the present, she reveals that the bank has at times been willing to change its domestic monetary policies solely on the basis of the international situation. Similarly, it has become increasingly likely to challenge the government's monetary policy and was the primary force in negotiating EMU.

Dorothee Heisenberg is a lecturer in the department of political science at Yale University.